PIONEERS
IN BLOOMERS

PIONEERS IN BLOOMERS

THE INTREPID PEDESTRIENNES–
BRITISH SPORT'S FIRST FEMALE CELEBRITIES

ROB HADGRAFT

The Book Guild Ltd

First published in Great Britain in 2022 by
The Book Guild Ltd
Unit E2 Airfield Business Park,
Harrison Road, Market Harborough,
Leicestershire. LE16 7UL
Tel: 0116 2792299
www.bookguild.co.uk
Email: info@bookguild.co.uk
Twitter: @bookguild

Typeset in 11pt Minion Pro

Printed and bound by CPI Group (UK) Ltd, Croydon, CR0 4YY

ISBN 978 1915352 323

British Library Cataloguing in Publication Data.
A catalogue record for this book is available from the British Library.

Walk! Walk! Walk!
Till the brain begins to cake
Walk! Walk! Walk!
Till the sole begins to bake;
Lap, and double and turn,
Turn and double and lap,
Till over the rail in vain to leap
In search of a quarter-nap.

19th century pedestrienne walking song (unknown origin)

No preacher can draw so large a congregation as a walking woman. She appears to have a greater hold over the popular mind than a talking man.

LEICESTER DAILY POST, May 1875.

CONTENTS

CONTENTS

AUTHOR'S NOTE

Researching and writing this book allowed me to delve back into a forgotten and fascinating world. Professional female pedestrianism in Great Britain was a pursuit largely confined to the second half of the 19th century. The women who took part often found themselves derided, denounced, even assaulted – but a couple of dozen of them stuck at it and emerged as strong, courageous and talented characters. They walked mile after mile, day after day – often completely alone – to entertain the public and earn money to feed their families. With the benefit of hindsight it is clear these women deserve credit for their pioneering efforts, for they laid the foundations for modern women to participate in competitive sport.

It is unclear exactly when, but there came a point when these women started being referred to as 'pedestriennes' to distinguish them from their male counterparts. The term was rarely used in British newspapers of the day however, probably due to it being seen as a cheap Americanism. The sobriquet 'equestrienne' had been coined in the USA around 1860 for female horsewomen, and 'pedestrienne' duly followed when pedestrianism took off stateside a few years later.

This book tells the stories of the British women who, despite everything, achieved prominence during the pedestrianism era. Within the narrative are the specific stories of 21 women – a 'Pedestrienne Pantheon' if you like – which pins down the main characters who made a name for themselves on British soil. To the best of my knowledge all 21 were British-born, apart from the influential Kate Irvine, an American who I felt warranted inclusion for her two lengthy visits to the UK in the early 1850s, during which she made an important mark on the sport. Later on a good number of other American pedestriennes came to prominence on the other side of the Atlantic, but this book concentrates on those who led the way on the tracks and fields of Britain, the spiritual home of modern athletics.

To track down the facts and figures behind the women's stories I had to rely heavily on newspapers and journals of the time. But of course the 19th century can be a tricky period to research as news and sports reporting back then was a very different animal from today. The basic facts – names, ages, locations, dates, timings – were often missing from published accounts of pedestrianism, which was of course a largely unregulated sport anyway. However, I've made every effort to tell the story of the GB pedestriennes with as much accuracy and detail as possible, and on the few occasions I was forced to estimate, assume or use educated guesswork, I endeavoured to make that clear in the text. Therefore, I can say that to the best of my knowledge, the weird and wonderful happenings documented in this book really did take place!

FOREWORD

BY SANDRA BROWN
(ULTRA-DISTANCE WORLD RECORD BREAKER)

By researching and recounting the stories of the pioneers of women's long-distance running and walking, with a unique focus on the British pedestriennes, author Rob Hadgraft has performed a great service for ultra-distance athletics and athletes. As we read about and admire their groundbreaking feats of courage and endurance, we recall that such women ran and walked without the advantages of modern equipment, shoes and clothing, and perhaps of nutrition (though that is more debateable) that we enjoy today.

Present-day ultra-walkers and runners relate closely and with empathy to the demands and pressures the pedestriennes would have faced, because this is the personal journey of self-discovery we too chose to travel, and these are the challenges we also seek out and set ourselves, again and again. These wonderful stories will inspire us all – women and men alike – to seek new challenges and set ourselves new goals.

Women from past centuries through to recent decades have shown what they can do, asserting by their performances their right to be on the tracks and trails, equally valued and recognised. Among them are Ann Sayer, the first lady member of the UK Centurions, who broke through that glass ceiling in the late 1970s, and excelled, as a race walker and in ultra-running events like the 48 hours, later becoming the first lady Chairman of the LDWA and President of the Centurions.

In the USA, athletes such as Ann Trason, with her remarkable catalogue of 100-mile wins, and in the UK Jasmin Paris, outright winner and record-holder of the gruelling mid-winter, multi-day 'Spine Race' along the Pennine Way backbone of England, have rewritten the record books and fundamentally changed perceptions of what women athletes can do. The pedestriennes of the past would have been fascinated by the stories of their successors!

Perhaps my own contribution, besides setting records at various distances and events in race walking and running, is that of the 'serial offender'... without knowing it at the time, I was the first person to complete 100 events and then over 200 events of 100 miles or more. These include many races of 100 miles on track, road and trail, and many 24-hour events, as well as multi-days, 1,000 miles and journeys like the LEJOG. They also include all seven of the Centurions race walking qualifications worldwide, and over 50 completions of such Centurions events. I have often completed ten or more events a year of 100 miles or more, interwoven with my work and voluntary commitments and the happy life of my family (my husband and daughter fortunately also fascinated by, and active in, the ultra-world).

As this compelling book illustrates, the sport of running and walking at ultra-distances is perhaps, along with other extreme efforts like single-handed round-the-world sailing, distinguished by the importance of psychology. The athletes' motivation and mindset can trump the more obvious metrics of physique and experience and produce races which are fascinating – not least in their variety, uncertainty and unpredictability. Ultra-distance athletics attracts all ages, shapes and sizes, among men and women. While some athletes have great natural gifts, an apparently perfect physique is no guarantee of success. In a sport in which lasting the course – survival, perhaps in very difficult conditions – can itself be the supreme challenge, the athlete's psychology, self-management and motivation are of paramount importance. Little and large, young and old, men and women, can achieve success.

Men's and women's physical attributes tend to differ in obvious ways, leading to long-standing generalised assumptions that women are the 'weaker' sex and, on average, can go less far and less fast than men. However, interesting studies have shed light on the physical differences between the sexes as they relate to ultra-distance athletics. Findings, for example, relating to endurance or the immune system (some of these studies by researchers who are themselves female long-distance athletes), suggest that evolution may have conferred some advantages on women.

And what of the mind? Psychology, including mental endurance and perceptions of competition and mutuality: might these differ between men and women? Generalisations are hazardous, and both men and women can astonish us with their courage, determination and resourcefulness, and their acts of great kindness to others. There is, however, a growing body of evidence – and promising scope for further study – about the ability of women to tolerate discomfort and pain, even for hours and days on end and for hundreds and thousands of miles, in order to achieve some goal, perhaps a record or personal best, perhaps 'just' finishing a gruelling course.

This book shows how women from the 19ᵗʰ century showed enterprise, ambition and prowess in ultra-distance sport, and thrived, sometimes against great odds. In recent decades, women have re-emerged from the shadows of long-distance athletics to break through the barriers placed on their participation. Author Rob Hadgraft vividly reminds us of the pioneers in bloomers who blazed the trail all those years ago.

SANDRA BROWN

*   *Born in 1949, Sandra Brown from Dorset was hailed "the top ultra-distance walker of all-time" by* UltraRunning *magazine. In 2019 she completed her 200th event of 100 miles or more, a unique achievement by man or woman. Her Land's End to John O' Groats record of 1995 (830 miles in 13 days, 10 hours) stood for almost a decade. In Australia in 1996 she set world records for 1,000 kilometres (8 days 12 hours 16 mins 20 secs) and 1,000 miles (14 days 10 hours 27 mins 20 secs). She also set world walking records on tracks in France (100km and 12 hours), New Zealand (100 miles) and Hertfordshire (24 hours).*

INTRODUCTION

THE RISE OF THE 'PEDESTRIENNES'

The very earliest images of a female runner or walker date back 2,500 years or so. They show women of Ancient Greece with their hair hanging loose, wearing a short dress above the knees, their right shoulder uncovered and right breast revealed.

Depictions of early female foot racing in the UK don't date back that far, but do have vaguely similar erotic overtones, for they show the bawdy scenes at the popular 'smock races' staged across rural Britain during the Georgian and Regency eras.

By the time Victoria was on the throne things had become a little more respectable. A small number of ordinary, working-class women began emerging from nowhere to perform incredible athletic challenges for money, walking for days on end without sleep, often in highly unfavourable surroundings. These women became known as 'pedestriennes'.

These daring newcomers accomplished feats of endurance that made them Britain's first famous female athletes and therefore pioneers in the history of women's sport. They were the prophets who paved the way for women of all backgrounds and ability levels to participate in sport without fear of condemnation or humiliation.

So where did these pedestriennes spring from, and what prompted their highly unlikely change of lifestyle? Their main motivation was clearly to win money and prizes, indicating the roots of their sporting endeavours sprang from the 'smock racing' phenomenon of the pre-Victorian era. Smock racing was often a bawdy and highly popular feature of country fairs and suchlike. A typical event of the time was 'The Hungerford Revels' where the main race had young maidens chasing the prize of a linen smock, while further down the bill came the older women, racing to win a pound of tea.

According to historian and Olympian Peter Radford, women and girls were prominent stars of this old rural culture – hundreds of them running every year for an embroidered smock or a guinea in gold. Smock racing was seen as a good way for a humble rural maiden to catch the eye of a potential husband as well as win a nice chemise. *The Sporting Magazine* of 1797 made no bones about this: "Maids who wish to be wives cannot do better than run for the smock, as it will afford ample opportunity to demonstrate their strength and pliability when called into action".

But this early form of women's athletics was roundly condemned by puritans. One prominent clergyman described smock races as "dunghills and filth" which attracted crowds of "loytering idle persons, ruffians, blasphemers, swingebucklers and tossepottes". He was presumably referring to the fact that many of the female competitors routinely suffered serious 'wardrobe malfunctions' during these chaotic races; having arrived at the start line barefoot, wearing a flimsy smock and little else, by the later stages any restraint had usually been abandoned and much flesh was on show.

Some races could be more ribald than others – one on Manchester's Kersal Moor, for example, reportedly featured "young women running stark naked, only their privitys covered with a rag". The diarist Oliver Heywood called this "a horrid shameless spectacle", but it attracted a crowd of thousands including, reportedly, a group of 40 clergymen who needed several firkins of ale to calm themselves after witnessing such shocking scenes!

Bare breasts on the village green was never a tradition likely to survive the 19th century, and the smock race had just about died out by around 1825. But women's opportunities to race for gain didn't quite vanish with it.

The celebrated Captain Robert Barclay Allardice and his famous 1,000-miles-in-1,000-hours feat of 1809 had by then given birth to a new long-distance culture that would flourish for decades, although initially dominated by men of course.

The Captain's extraordinary stunt on Newmarket Heath was unprecedented and captured the public imagination, pulling in vast crowds and setting the scene for pedestrianism to become a major sporting pursuit of the 19th century. Rather like the four-minute mile and the two-hour marathon of much later eras, the Captain's 1,000-mile target had been thought an impossible dream. Huge sums were bet on the outcome. But not only did he triumph, he became very rich, and British sport – not just pedestrianism – was never quite the same again.

The fortune Captain Barclay is said to have won amounted to something like 16,000 guineas, equivalent to millions in modern terms. No wonder others would want a crack at this 1,000-miles-in-1,000-hours game. After all, to receive just a fraction of the Captain's winnings would be life-changing for the majority. The problem with such thinking was that Captain Barclay was no ordinary citizen – he was a sporting toff with the freedom, resources and contacts to devote himself full-time to preparing for such an ordeal. In the late 18th century long-distance, multi-day events had become popular with self-described 'gentlemen amateurs' walking for large cash wagers. They had the time and money for such pursuits. Nevertheless, in the wake of the Newmarket Heath extravaganza the lower classes wanted a taste of the action too.

Pedestrian hopefuls emerged all over Britain, many tackling shorter distances, but others bewitched by the holy grail of 1,000 miles – the ultimate challenge. Working-class male pedestrians gradually replaced the gentry as the sport's main practitioners and began to attract mass audiences. They walked purely for money, not sporting idealism – some were subsidised by publicans, some solicited donations on the day, while the more experienced and organised would be backed by individuals or syndicates and walked for wagers. 'Pedestrian mania' became unstoppable as the newcomers learned to cope with vast distances, entrepreneurs learned to organise and control multi-day events, and the authorities generally refrained from interfering. By the end of 1816 (seven years after Barclay) there had been around a dozen 1,000-milers performed in Britain – all by men. The challenge had become known as 'The Barclay Match' or 'The Barclay Feat'.

One option might be attempting 1,000 miles in three weeks, a pace of 50 miles per day, but the 1,000-hour format that Barclay pioneered (i.e. walking one mile each hour for 41 days and 18 hours) remained the most popular for years.

Unsurprisingly, it would be some years post-Barclay before women got involved. There existed a school of thought that in the civilised world frequent exercise, especially in public, increased a man's masculinity but was highly unladylike and inappropriate for women. Occasionally women would defy this assumption, notably Ellen Weeton, a Lancashire schoolmistress, author and divorcee, who made it her business to walk 30 miles a day over a number of years, evidently for leisure and health reasons rather than sporting ones. She routinely went on these rambles "alone and decently clad", often in hilly areas, and found the women she encountered were civil to her but the men were often rude. She reflected: "Women are something better than potatoes… although they are often treated little better".

Ellen's jaunts were private, solo affairs, but one or two brave female souls did put their head above the parapet in the first half of the 19th century to take on 'public' long-distance challenges. But these were few and far between. It would take until the 1850s before a slowly increasing number of feisty, determined working-class women were able to elbow their way into the male-dominated Victorian pedestrianism scene. These became known as the pedestriennes. They caused quite a stir by demonstrating that stamina and endurance were certainly not exclusively male attributes, but faced all sorts of social barriers and occupational hazards in attempting to make a living from their efforts. It was not until the mid-1860s that any degree of acceptance and fair treatment

The world's first fun runs? These bawdy 'smock races' were popular among country folk and a precursor to pedestrianism.

came the way of a woman tackling a multi-day, long-distance challenge. This 'heyday' would last barely 20 years and by the start of the 20th century the pedestriennes had faded back into obscurity.

A woman who put herself on public display by walking or running for money, often in less than salubrious surroundings, never quite gained society's approval in Victorian Britain, however determined, athletic and courageous they might appear. It was considered by many to be vulgar, dangerous and simply inappropriate for women to behave in this way, especially those married with children. Although the world was changing and thousands of working-class folk found these walks highly entertaining to watch, the cloud of disapproval never quite went away. With hindsight it is clear the pedestriennes were intrepid characters who braved the puritanical disdain of the high-minded in society and the lascivious gaze of the low.

The early professional pedestriennes managed between ten and 15 'Barclay feats' between 1852 and 1854 alone. They found the novelty aspect of a woman walker aroused great public attention – usually supportive at street level but scorned by the middle and upper classes. These women were not participating in any Corinthian spirit of course. Their walks were blatant money-making affairs, promoted by proprietors of pubs, hotels and pleasure gardens. It was a new and ambitious way for women to try and earn a living – with a number of them believing they were well suited to it, having already spent their working lives plodding through town and country as door-to-door hawkers. Others, who toiled in mills or factories, might also be well conditioned by long-distance daily treks to their workplaces.

Pedestrianism was the first spectator sport to identify and exploit the rising market for commercially based play in the industrial areas, and the first to spot the opportunity that early factory closing was giving for Saturday afternoon events. The sport became reliant on pubs as local HQs, alongside pursuits like quoits, fives, pigeon racing and prize-fighting. These pubs also served as betting shops. The contribution of the publican, many of whom didn't trade strictly within the rule of law, was huge.

After women became involved in pedestrianism, public interest was boosted – from both a spectator and participatory point of view – when Mrs Amelia Bloomer and her American acolytes began advocating a new form of emancipated dress for women in the early 1850s.

This was the 'Bloomer Costume' of ankle-length pantaloons and a loose, knee-length tunic. This new fashion was seen as perfect for distance walking, comfortable and practical compared to the voluminous garments traditionally worn by women. The costume was initially regarded as daring and unfeminine and inevitably led to leering and jeering from the men on the sidelines. Unlike their smock-chasing predecessors, the pedestriennes were women who generally didn't welcome being sized up or lusted after.

Eye-catching bloomers or not, the walks were often fraught with frauds, con artists and unprofessional behaviour. Hardly surprising really, given the ale-house settings, and the unlicensed gambling going on. Events were sometimes staged for a wager, betting stakes based on the walker either achieving or failing the challenge. In the early part of the 19th century foot racing attracted respectable middle-class audiences, but by the time of the pedestriennes, more and more unsavoury characters were involved.

Nevertheless, despite all the dubious activity going on, the women themselves were generally impressive individuals who displayed unseen levels of stamina and determination as they trekked day and night in pursuit of reward. The vast majority were ordinary working women, many with young families to support; they were not doing this to feather an already comfortable nest but toiling often to the point of collapse to put food on their family's table. In some cases, a pedestrienne might be a somewhat reluctant participant, perhaps forced into the sport by a bullying or feckless husband.

The occupational hazards they faced were manifold. The local authorities would constantly get on their case for stirring up disturbances and encouraging unwanted gatherings of drinkers and gamblers, as well as causing offence by performing on a Sunday and generally behaving in an unladylike manner as wives and mothers. The more genteel members of society would regard their public perambulations as making them little better than street-corner prostitutes. To make matters worse, the women would sometimes be subjected to verbal and physical assault as they walked, by gamblers and associates who wanted to block their progress in order to protect a bet. Tripwires, spiked drinks and the scattering of tacks were not unheard of.

As a sport, pedestrianism grew and developed in strange ways through the Victorian age. There was a constant search for new novelty challenges that would pull in crowds. In Margate, for example, an athlete was challenged to pick up and move a long line of 100 stones within 40 minutes. And the *Belfast Telegraph* told the story of a woman who lost a race on foot against a horse called Reindeer. There were also tales of disreputable venues staging bizarre 'walk the plank' endurance trials, where a female participant would walk back and forth on a three-foot wide plank that could be anything from 15 to 40 feet long: "The prettiest walker I have ever seen", commented a well-refreshed male observer of a certain Mrs Bentley's performance on the plank, but much sympathy would be expressed when it was later revealed Mrs B was in the advanced stages of consumption and had resorted to this activity purely to support her three children.

These sideshows proved the exception rather than the rule. The pedestrianism challenges that really caught the public imagination were the long-distance walking feats at which the main novelty was the mere fact a woman was involved. At best, the newspapers of the day treated women's multi-day walks as dubious, and at worst as beneath contempt. Many of them would ignore events altogether even though thousands of spectators might have turned out to watch. Some coverage was remarkably vindictive: for example, the right-leaning journal the *St James's Gazette* announced: "Most of these performances are exceedingly silly, and of no sort of service to the great national love of athletic prowess which has had so large a share in making England what she is. Properly speaking, they are not athletic feats at all, but sensational attempts to fly in the face of nature… 1,000 miles in 1,000 hours [is] not a feat of walking so much as of insomnia".

However, times and attitudes change, and with the benefit of hindsight, 21st-century social and sporting historians tend to agree that the participation of women was the most positive and important development to come out of the whole Victorian distance-walking vogue.

By the late 1860s the initial obsession (of both men and women) to emulate the 1,000-miles Barclay feat began to fade. It was replaced by new challenges throughout the 1870s during which a small cohort of increasingly professional pedestriennes emerged. Their walks were generally of shorter duration than the six-week 1,000-milers but were given a time constraint to make them just as tough. This made the events far more spectator-friendly. Between 1870 and 1884 more than 50 ultra-distance walks took place involving roughly 12–15 identifiable female performers. The best of this generation proved to be Londoner Ada Anderson, whose achievements included a trouncing of Barclay's effort, covering 1,500 miles in 1,000 hours at Leeds in 1878. The articulate and multi-talented Ada soon headed west to seek fame and fortune in the USA where female pedestrianism thrived for a spell and offered bigger paydays.

The 1880's pedestrianism scene that Ada left behind in Britain lost its place in public esteem to the newly regulated and codified world of amateur athletics. The ethos of the Amateur Athletic Association (AAA) – founded in April 1880 by three men from Oxford University – was ideologically opposed to both professionalism and unfeasibly long events in the tradition of Captain Barclay, and there was no place for women. This meant the remarkable story of the British pedestriennes was quietly and quickly forgotten. Their heyday had lasted barely 20 years.

Nevertheless it is clear the pioneers-in-bloomers had made great early strides for British women's involvement in sport. They paved the way for participation in cycling, for example, with the emerging suffragist movement embracing the bicycle and the wearing of bloomers as a means of promoting equality in wider society.

Around this time women began taking up tennis, bowling and rowing too, although usually found they had no platform to compete officially. Archery and croquet were also socially acceptable among the upper echelons. The satirical journal *Punch* mocked the way female sport progressed at such a snail's pace over the course of the 19th century, going "from croquet to golf via a rather sedate form of lawn tennis". It was a fair point, but it was also true that many girls' schools did begin introducing gymnastics, hockey and cricket – another little push for the very gradual advancement of women in sport.

In her book *How to be a Victorian* (Penguin, 2013), Ruth Goodman explains that part of the overall problem was the widespread belief a young woman's body would be easily upset and at risk of permanent damage through even the lightest of energetic pursuits – she could be left unable to fulfil her primary function in life, the bearing of children. This was fuelled by the Ancient Greek theory that the womb was mobile within the torso and would be bashed about if a young woman threw herself into sport and exercise.

It was not only bouncing wombs that made women unsuitable for sport – they were prone to hysteria too! Or so said the influential journal *Bell's Life in London* in 1872: "We say most emphatically that public contests of strength and wind are not likely to find favour in the eyes of gentle English girls. We have no wish to see our wives and sisters rival those Roman matrons who fought in the arena... Public races, whether in the water or on land, are, to our English modes of thinking, only fit for hoydenish [i.e. high-spirited] lasses at a country fair. It is enough that we have barmaid shows. Moreover woman is physically unfit for contests of the kind we have mentioned. There is a hysterical something [sic] about girls and a tendency to undue excitement".

Fortunately a voice of good sense responded from the English Midlands when prominent surgeon Pye Chevasse advocated daily walks for women of all ages; saying that walking, and lots of it, would hugely aid general health and wouldn't place undue strain on the reproductive system.

All these years later it is clear some important stories concerning women in sport have long lay buried, the emergence of the British pedestriennes a prime example. Twentieth-century marathon pioneers like Violet Piercy, Dale Greig and Kathrine Switzer have gained due recognition in relatively recent times as important female sporting icons and they have been followed by the likes of Paula Ratcliffe, Jasmin Paris and many more. But it is those British pedestriennes of around 150 years ago who should take the credit for actually setting women's long-distance foot racing on its way.

This is their story.

ONE

MARY AND ESTHER COME A CROPPER

In the autumn of 1817 sporting history was made when a woman stepped forward for the first time to make a serious attempt at walking 1,000 miles, or 'the Barclay Feat', as it had become known. A little-known Londoner called Esther Crozier was the pioneer in question. Esther was among the first 'pedestriennes' to emerge in this male-dominated world, intending to make good money from her efforts and ready to face all the difficulties this might involve as a woman.

With a few notable exceptions, there wouldn't be too many women prepared to follow her example for at least three decades. However, shortly before Esther was ready to toe her 1,000-mile start line, another Kentish woman also bravely announced she was planning a trek in early 1816 that was slightly shorter in distance but still extraordinarily tough for a 'mere' woman: her name was Mary Frith, and her bold plans were partly inspired by a sensational male pedestrian event that had occurred near her home just a few weeks earlier.

George Wilson, a 50-year-old itinerant Geordie pedlar with a flair for showmanship, had attempted in September 1815 to walk 1,000 miles by doing 50 miles a day while based at the Hare and Billet pub on Blackheath. His efforts provoked such scenes of uncontrolled rowdiness among the crowds that the only way police could restore normality was to halt the walk and nick him for causing a breach of the peace. Poor Wilson had reached 751 miles at this point and looked certain to win his challenge; he complained bitterly that he'd done nothing wrong and had been preparing for this event for months as it was the only way he could properly feed and clothe his huge family. The decision by magistrates to issue a warrant for his arrest was later ruled incorrect, but by then it was too late.

Although Wilson's arrest highlighted a major occupational hazard that could trip up any pedestrian, it is clear the attendant fuss, publicity and talk of big money at Blackheath influenced others to try and grab a slice of the action for themselves. As well as Wilson's aborted effort, men like Josiah Eaton, John Baker and William Tuffee had already taken up challenges of 1,000 miles or more around now. And by 1815 even the interest of women had been piqued.

Examples of women who soiled their hands (or feet) for filthy lucre prior to the emergence of Mary Frith and Esther Crozier are hard to come by. They tended to involve fairly short distances covered – one example from 1761 states that four Welsh women walked from Westminster Bridge to the Boot and Crown inn at Deptford Bridge and back again in 105 minutes. This won them a wager of £20, easily beating the 150-minute target they had been given. On another occasion, the Duchess of Charteris beat her husband in a footrace of 200 yards to win herself 200 guineas in 1776: "The duchess was allowed to secure her petticoats above the knees of her drawers", according to the *Morning Post*.

STORY 1: MARY FRITH – A TRUE ORIGINAL

And so it came to pass that Saturday 9th December 1815 became a significant day in women's sporting history. On this cold evening in Kent arrangements were announced for a local mother of six to walk hundreds of miles against the clock, a stunt that was part of a programme of public entertainment. There was big money at stake, meaning this was effectively the very first example of professional multi-day walking involving a woman.

"This match is likely to cause considerable interest in Maidstone," reported a number of newspapers in understated fashion. The star of the show was to be 36-year-old Mrs Mary Frith, attempting to walk 'heel and toe' fashion a distance of 600 miles, by way of 30 miles on 20 successive days, starting on New Year's Day 1816, a Monday. Three unnamed local gentlemen were said to have backed her to the tune of 30 guineas to achieve the feat. Mary and her helpers seemed undeterred by the severe wintry weather SE England had been suffering at this time, some of the worst in living memory.

Being a relative unknown, Mary was to start her ordeal a few days after the male pedestrian William Tuffee and his son finished their own relay challenge at the same venue, the field beside the Roebuck Inn, Harrietsham, a few miles east of Maidstone. Mary may have been lower down the bill than the famous Tuffee, but plenty of interest was anticipated. The pre-publicity painted her as an impressive, hard-working woman who was taking her challenge very seriously and had a good chance of success. Despite having to bring up a large family, Mary had spent years as a travelling pedlar, clocking up 20–25 miles a day, which seemed like perfect preparation for this new challenge.

The Morning Chronicle noted: "Her friends, who are many, are most sanguine in her completing it, and are offering any odds. It appears that for many years, for the support of her family, this industrious woman has frequently gone traversing the country with different articles for sale, and returned home to her family at night 20 and 25 miles a day". A woman attempting such a huge multi-day challenge had real novelty value and was the talk of Maidstone, but Mary had to take a back seat and suffer a nervous wait while 35-year-old labourer Tuffee and 12-year-old Tuffee Junior took the spotlight and finished their performance first.

It had bothered the elder Tuffee greatly that he'd failed a recent challenge to cover 1,000 miles in 20 days in nearby Rochester. To regain pride and form, he had created this new stunt – a 1,200-mile relay with his boy that would take 20 days to complete. With Tuffee covering around two-thirds of the mileage, the pair reached halfway after 11 days, speeding up a little to hit 1,200 on the morning of the last day. Good-sized crowds attended and it was clear Kent was becoming a pedestrianism hotbed with many events springing up in the rural areas beyond Blackheath.

According to several sources, Mary Frith's 600-mile trek duly got underway at the appointed time but the full story of what happened remains a mystery. This author and other researchers have been unable to find confirmation she was able to finish, the absence of published information suggesting she probably encountered problems and quietly retired early. It is certain the bad weather played a big part in proceedings, for this was a cold, wet and relentlessly miserable winter. Indeed, atmospheric conditions had been unusual for several months, ever since the eruption of Mount Tambora on an island in the Indian Ocean. It had been the most violent volcanic event in recorded history and temperatures were seen to drop all around the globe as a result. Mary had the ill-fortune of having to start her ordeal on the very first day of what would become Britain's coldest ever instrumentally recorded year.

With Mary's chances of becoming the first woman to win fame and fortune from ultra-walking apparently disappearing into the mud of the Roebuck Inn's field, for the time being pedestrianism would remain a man's world. It would take another 18 months or so before another female thrust her head above the parapet to tackle a high-profile sporting challenge. Step forward Esther Crozier.

STORY 2: ESTHER CROZIER – AN OBSTINATE WOMAN

Despite rainfall well above average for the time of year, pedestrianism captured the imagination of the good people of Essex in a big way during the summer and autumn of 1817.

First, they were enthralled by a heroic three-week performance from well-known exponent Josiah Eaton, which *The National Register* reckoned had more money resting upon its outcome than any pedestrian feat before it. Naturally the smell of big money piqued many a nostril, and Eaton's performance paved the way a week or two later for a previously unknown walker called Crozier to attempt a shorter but no less heroic journey. What caught everybody by surprise was the fact that Crozier was female.

Josiah Eaton had pursued his "Herculanean task" of walking for 20 successive days up and down the 52-mile route between Colchester and London, nowadays the hectic A12 trunk road. This affable fellow was a baker from Northamptonshire who had taken up the sport a year or two earlier aged 45. His epic Essex escapade began at Colchester at dawn on a Monday morning in late August 1817 and saw him stroll into Witham nearly five hours later for breakfast. On he marched to Chelmsford where he stopped for brief refreshment, reaching Ingatestone at 3pm where he took lunch. After another refreshment stop at Romford he reached his lodgings at the Nags Head, opposite Whitechapel Church by 10.20 that night. At the crack of dawn the next day he headed back to Colchester along the same route and repeated this without a break until he'd passed the 1,000-mile mark. It proved a colourful and hugely popular event, with Eaton cheerfully powering along with a stick in each hand, availing himself of every opportunity for a quick chat with locals. According to *The National Register*: "The ladies and gentlemen of Romford and Brentwood have entered into a subscription for his benefit; he has also received presents from several ladies of Chelmsford, and a gentleman at Boreham presented Eaton with a glass of port every time he passed his door".

Within weeks Esther Crozier, thought to be aged around 40, embarked on her own Essex challenge. Although some newspapers would later refer to her efforts as highly impressive, very little detail about distance and location was published, as had been the case with Mary Frith 18 months earlier. This lack of coverage suggests the press were not quite ready to take seriously the efforts of women pedestrians. Esther Crozier's walk was perhaps seen as an attempt to cash in on the surge of interest created locally by Josiah Eaton and not a credible sporting endeavour. Nevertheless, the walk impressed those who witnessed it and, undeterred by the lack of widespread acclaim, Esther had by mid-October made it known she now wanted to emulate Eaton by walking 1,000 miles in 20 successive days herself – not in bucolic Essex but in grimy London. The 1,000-mile target had become quite the thing to strive for among male pedestrians ever since Captain Barclay's efforts of 1809, but Esther appears to have been the very first woman to take on such a task. It was a formidable job, requiring 50 miles per day over a period of just under three weeks.

Again publicity wasn't particularly widespread, but Esther's intentions did spark a little interest from Fleet Street: "Pedestrianism extraordinary!" exclaimed *The Public Ledger*, adding: "We understand, desirous of emulating the light-heeled heroes of the day, a female has undertaken to walk 1,000 miles in 20 successive days. The scene of action is to be in the vicinity of the metropolis; but we believe neither the time nor the exact spot is yet fixed on".

Sending a woman out on to London's streets alone was a hazardous step to take in 1817. The Lord Mayor of London and other eminent figures would meet this very month, October, to address what was called the "extravagant advance of prostitution" on the city streets. The situation had spiralled out of control, and it was reported that in just three London parishes alone there were now 360 houses of ill-repute and more than 3,000 "wretched women" plying their trade. A day or two before these shocking statistics were announced, the full story of Esther Crozier's plans emerged.

She and her helpers intended her to set off on Wednesday 29th October 1817 from a milepost positioned close to her base in South London – thought to have been the Old White Horse inn (a building in modern times occupied by Jamm night club) – on the stretch of main road known as The Washway, between Brixton and Croydon. In contrast with Eaton's daily point-to-point journeys through ever-changing scenery in Essex, Esther's plan was to process up and down a single, short stretch of road. It would surely become mind-numbingly monotonous, but had the advantage of ensuring that if she came to any harm her accommodation and friends would always be close at hand.

Esther was performing at Brixton less than a year after Eaton had used the same road to achieve what some called the greatest pedestrian feat ever seen, even though he didn't quite complete the task as originally intended. He had walked an incredible 1,998 half miles in 1,998 successive half hours by Thursday 5 December 1816 – at which point he deliberately stopped in order to make a protest. He explained: "I have been deceived by the gentleman who should have supported me". Stopping just short of 2,000 miles in 2,000 half hours meant Eaton could ensure all bets would become null and void and the men who had upset him would not be rewarded. Eaton went on to assure the public the episode had left him seriously out of pocket too. As we shall see, Esther's walk would come to a similar, rancorous end.

The novelty of a woman signing up for something normally the exclusive territory of men meant Esther inevitably became the subject of close scrutiny in terms of her appearance and clothing. She was described in one syndicated report as "an amazon" and in another as "prepossessing and effeminate". What seems certain is that she was a feisty, no-nonsense character, so these sort of comments probably concerned her much less than the vital matter of how much she could earn from her walking.

Like thousands of others in Georgian London, her daily life was often a struggle to make ends meet and pedestrianism provided a possible means of escape from the drudgery. Along with her backers, she was confident of her stamina and resilience for the task ahead – and the *Morning Post* described her associates as "sanguine" about her completing the job, particularly given her extraordinary recent performance in Essex. *Saunders's Newsletter* even made the bold prediction that Esther's 1,000-mile undertaking could excite as much interest as that of Wilson on Blackheath, where vast and rowdy crowds had congregated. Esther normally made a living by selling pocketbooks in the counties surrounding London – Middlesex, Kent, Surrey and Essex – which meant she was well used to covering mile after mile on foot hawking her wares. Surely perfect conditioning for ultra-distance pedestrianism?

Early on the misty morning of Thursday 29 October she commenced her bid to complete 20 days of walking to and fro along a busy stretch of Brixton Causeway (later renamed Brixton Hill) better known in 1817 as The Washway. According to the *Salisbury & Winchester Journal*: "Thursday morning, at seven o'clock, this amazon commenced performing her arduous task of walking 1,000 miles in 20 successive days [from] near the two-mile stone on the Croydon Road, going three quarters of a mile out and in".

There were plenty of people around to observe and encourage Esther as she passed by, for Brixton was changing fast from a district of market gardens to a busy urban area, particularly since the recent opening of the Vauxhall Bridge nearby. The main thoroughfare known as The Washway followed the route of a tributary of the River Effra, and was now flanked by newly built, handsome terraces and ornamental villas. There was even a new windmill. Plenty of sights, then, to keep Esther's mind occupied as she worked her way up and down. Some of the pervading smells were not so welcome however, for the nearby Effra was effectively an open sewer, polluted with all the newly arrived domestic waste and often subject to flooding.

Some nine hours after starting Esther had completed a steady 34 miles and "was going on quite fresh" said *The Public Ledger*. She reached her target of 50 miles that evening at 9.35. Many onlookers were fascinated by the spectacle, while others glanced across as she passed but carried on with their daily business. For those not able to get a look, *Saunders's Newsletter* studied her appearance: "This heroine is rather of prepossessing appearance, about the middle size, and very effeminate. She wore a brown stuff gown, coloured shawl, white stockings, and stout shoes".

Day two's walking started with discouraging wet and cold weather at 6.45am and by 8am. Esther had stopped for a 15-minute breakfast with just 4.25 miles done. The awful conditions didn't relent but she resumed until 12.40 when she took a lunch stop around the 23-mile mark. Despite the difficulties, she was keen to get going again after only 15 minutes. The applause and shouts to help her on her way were sympathetic as well as encouraging. By 4.15 she had recorded 32.75 miles, similar to day one, and was still proceeding in spirited fashion.

The final day of October, a Friday, saw her complete another steady 50 miles despite more miserable heavy rain. At several points it was clear she was drenched through, and her friends called on her to stop and change her clothes but she refused and pressed on. Another 7am start on the fourth day led to a 10.30pm finish with 200 of the 1,000 miles safely under her belt. Day five was a Sunday and Esther opted to get away to an early start at 4am progressing through the day with slightly longer meal stops and another mid-evening finish. Her pace remained roughly 4mph while on the move, and although the effort must have been starting to take a toll, she rarely, if ever, showed any real discomfort or distress.

Monday 3rd November saw her reach the 300-mile mark in the evening and the seventh day followed with a 6am start and some very welcome fine weather. Her presence on The Washway was no longer a novelty, meaning very few locals stopped to watch for any length of time. Nevertheless, it was reported that some of the better-off "ladies and gents of the neighbourhood" had donated to a collection for her, so as long as she kept going it looked like the rewards would come. News of the collection must have been comforting as the monotonous miles slowly became harder. The good weather on this Tuesday morning meant she was "visited by a number of genteel persons" during the course of her journey which must have also boosted her spirits.

However, despite all these encouraging signs as the halfway point approached, the whole project suddenly began to unravel. All was clearly not well with Esther. The trouble was not physical, it seems, for she had reached 38 miles by 4pm on the Tuesday, similar or faster to previous days' efforts. After retiring to the nearby inn that night along with her helpers, harsh words were exchanged and some serious differences aired. The following morning, which should have been the start of day eight of the walk, saw Esther call the whole thing off. Her specific reasons for doing so went unreported, and are lost in the mists of time.

There were distinct echoes of 10 months earliar when Josiah Eaton also finished his walk early on this very same road after a dispute. The reasons for Esther's abandonment after 350 miles in seven days mystified *The National Register*, which reported: "Esther was obstinate and no entreaty or persuasion could prevail on her to resume it. She was quite fresh and there is no doubt had she continued she would have accomplished the task".

The newspapers happy to report on her progress over the previous week showed little interest in probing the reasons for this disastrous *denouement*. It seems likely that matters of a pecuniary nature were to blame, particularly as she was described as remaining in good shape physically.

Little more would be heard henceforth of Esther Crozier. A week later a furious letter to *The Times* castigated her and others for disrespecting the sanctity of Sundays by performing on that day for money. The writer called for public houses who help stage pedestrianism to have their licenses revoked and claimed his were widely held views:

"The Lark Hall public house, at which a pedestrian was lately lodged while he thus offended against all morality and decency has recently obtained a renewal of its license, in spite of the remonstrances [sic] and petition of a whole neighbourhood against it; and another public house in the Brixton Road, emboldened no doubt by such magisterial remissness, has, since the licenses were renewed, invited a woman [Esther Crozier] to profane the day in the same manner, and maintained her during her progress".

Esther was clearly a woman of principle. Despite being on schedule (averaging 50 miles per day) and in good condition, she'd thrown away the chance of becoming the first woman to complete a 1,000-miler, and all because of a behind-the-scenes dispute rather than being forced out by physical collapse or rioting spectators. Perhaps she thought other opportunities would follow in due course, but that was not to happen. In fact, the evidence suggests her life after this brief brush with fame would take a downhill path: records show the only Esther Crozier of that era living in London ended up in the workhouse in Little Grays Inn Lane [now Mount Pleasant]. She died here in May 1850 aged 73, and was buried in the nearby graveyard at Trinity Church.

TWO

CHILDREN AND ELDERLY JOIN THE FRAY

By the early 1820s pedestrianism had emerged as a new and colourful way for working-class people to potentially make money, so it was only a matter of time before somebody, somewhere, would decide to pitch their children into this unregulated pursuit. After all, children have boundless energy, they don't like sitting still, they run around a lot. And wouldn't the moneyed, genteel sectors of society find them cute and worthy of a donation or two? What could possibly go wrong?

Three days after Christmas 1822 a race was staged in freezing weather in Scotland between a boy and a girl who were challenged to cover 15 miles in two hours. The girl hailed from Queensferry and ran a commendable eight miles in 60 minutes at which point she collapsed exhausted beside the Edinburgh-Glasgow road at West Craigs. Her male opponent went on to complete the 15 miles in 1 hour 53 minutes. Onlookers with no financial stake in proceedings must have felt sympathy for the poor girl – too much had clearly been expected of her. But worse exploitation was to follow south of the border when a much younger girl called Emma Freeman was sent out on her own to complete even tougher tests on fields in the London area.

STORY 3: EMMA FREEMAN – AN EXTRAORDINARY INFANT

Emma Matilda Freeman from Strood in Kent was a few days short of her eighth birthday when she was thrust into the spotlight by her eager parents. They seized on her aptitude for walking and set up a series of solo long-distance events for her in the summer and early autumn of 1823.

The Freemans were jumping on a pedestrianism bandwagon that was gathering pace, but had become regarded as something of a rather vulgar pursuit now that it was tainted by money and driven by the working classes instead of the wealthy gents of high society. Arranging such physically demanding tasks for such a young girl as Emma will have prompted a wide spectrum of responses. There would have been enthusiastic interest because of its sheer novelty value, but also firm condemnation. This was an age of extremes, and the story gets even worse: on another occasion a tiny girl aged just 18 months was apparently instructed to 'run' in public for a wager. The toddler is said to have progressed half a mile down the Mall in London, taking about 23 minutes as thousands cheered her on. Compared to this, Emma Freeman and the girl from Queensferry were positively long in the tooth!

Little Emma Freeman's first outing came in heavy rain on Monday 7 July 1823, when she found herself spending the day walking 30 miles around a quarter-mile circle marked out on Penenden Heath, just north of the centre of Maidstone. She beat the eight-hour target by finishing in 7 hours 57 minutes and 33 seconds and didn't seem particularly concerned by the persistent rain. She averaged around 15 minutes per mile, a good pace for a small child over such a long period, particularly given the tedium of having to complete 120 laps of the same path.

No doubt encouraged by this performance, her parents firmed up details of a second and bigger event, this time at the Wellington Cricket Ground in Chelsea. The track was even smaller this time, needing six circuits to complete a single mile. A good crowd gathered on Monday 11th August to see how the little girl would cope, having been engaged for a wager of 100 sovereigns to walk or run 30 miles within eight hours. She had recently passed her eighth birthday. *Bell's Weekly Messenger* noted that she made good progress, occasionally stopping for refreshment and given small amounts of wine and water, and appeared in excellent spirits throughout. She was backed to the tune of 25 sovereigns to do the final mile in less than 12 and a half minutes, and achieved this, making it the quickest mile of the entire journey. She was timed in at 7 hours, 49 minutes.

Making hay while the sun shone, Emma's parents agreed to another 30-mile challenge in London just a fortnight later, this time in the gardens of the Green Dragon pub in Stepney. By now word had spread of Emma's impressive performances and "an immense concourse of people" assembled on Monday 25 August to watch her walk the outer edge of the gardens. This time 150 laps would be needed to cover 30 miles, with eight hours again her target. At exactly midday she appeared alongside her father ready for the off. Seven hours and 52 minutes later she completed the task, onlookers amazed at the absence of obvious fatigue. A collection was taken and many in the crowd willingly rewarded Emma for another remarkable feat.

Another wager, this involving two gentlemen and 100 guineas, was put up for Emma's fourth appearance during this mild and rather cloudy summer of 1823, this time involving 30 miles to be completed in seven hours and 50 minutes. It would be staged in the popular New Bagnigge Wells Tea Gardens in Bayswater, an attractive spot that was by now used by an interesting mix of middle- and working-class people seeking to escape the sights, sounds and smells of grubby 1820's London. Outdoor pleasure gardens and tea gardens had proliferated in London in recent times, but their character was by now undergoing radical change, with tea, formerly the chief article of consumption, supplanted in many cases by beverages of a stronger nature. The peace and elegant tranquility that attracted genteel middle-class folk had been threatened by various entertainments such as concerts and pedestrianism, which tended to pull in a lower class of visitor. It is safe to say the eight-hour performance of little Emma Freeman wouldn't have gained universal approval.

One guidebook of the day described the issues facing Emma's Bayswater venue and other tea gardens: "It is not that the gardens are themselves a nuisance – what can be more innocent or calculated for health and recreation, than the assemblage of decent people in a tea garden? [But in many cases] this recreation has been denied to the people because prostitutes resorted to these places; insulted public morals, promoted lewdness and debauchery, and banished modest and decent families".

At the Bayswater tea rooms' six-laps-per-mile track, Emma was backed to do the final mile of the 30 in 12 minutes as an extra incentive to win 12 guineas. The proprietor Mr Davis announced beforehand that the prospect of "her wonderful undertaking" had given rise to many bets with considerable sums at stake. He promised the police would be in attendance to prevent trouble from pickpockets and suchlike, and there was the added attraction of a "professional gentleman presiding at the organ" to perform vocal and instrumental music.

However, for unspecified reasons, possibly bad weather, Emma's Bayswater show was apparently cancelled. It was stated she would now appear at the Old Bagnigge Wells Tea Gardens at Spa Fields, Clerkenwell on Monday 22nd September, to walk 30 miles in seven hours and 50 minutes for 75 sovereigns a side. Twenty-three guineas was agreed for a final lap of 11 mins 30 seconds, and the whole thing would be done on a tiny circle of less than 60 yards, meaning 310 laps would be needed. No results can be found for this, or for a further promotion billed for early October in which Emma was to go up against another eight-year-old girl in a contest in the tea gardens at the Green Man pub on the Old Kent Road in Walworth, SE London. The two girls were to meet on a "pay or play" basis, it was announced by landlord Henry England. Emma would attempt 30 miles while her less experienced opponent would attempt 25 miles in the same time (seven hours, 45 minutes) for ten sovereigns a side. They would use a small track, Emma required to cover 300 laps. The complete absence of published results afterwards suggests these too were probably called off.

Evidently Emma and her parents' extraordinary summer of sporting fame and fortune was over. The Freemans, and any other cases of 'junior' pedestrianism would rarely be heard of again. Instead, from the other end of the age scale, a grandmother from the north of England strode into the limelight a year or two later.

STORY 4: MARY MCMULLEN – THE BAREFOOT GRANNY

Being in her sixties was no handicap as far as Mary McMullen was concerned when she became one of the first women to appear regularly as a professional pedestrienne. Mary had a good idea of what was involved, for she had four sons who were already high achievers in the pursuit of money for mileage. Mary was almost 61 when she took the plunge herself, going on to gain fame during these latter years of her life with remarkable feats of pedestrianism. Just to add to her uniqueness, Mary liked to perform whenever possible in bare feet.

Irish-born in the 1760s, she was mostly based in Yorkshire, but spent long spells of her sixties travelling from town to town, mostly accompanied by one or more of her pedestrian sons. Raising money from walking became a real family affair. Mary chalked up at least half a dozen solo performances in the mid-to-late 1820s that revealed her penchant for accepting a challenge. During 1826 and 1827 she is said to have made good sums of money in events ranging from 20 to 92 miles.

But although male pedestrianism was by now commonplace, these were still early days for female involvement – and she often encountered trouble. The majority of spectators would admire her pluck and determination, but the danger of verbal and physical abuse from others was never far away. Some onlookers would make it clear they found it unbecoming for women to perform for money, others would act threateningly as they needed her to fail in order to win private bets.

Women walkers willing to risk the dangers of taking to the roads on their own were few and far between over the first few decades of the 19th century. But Mary McMullen was driven by the knowledge that her gender, advanced age and penchant for going barefoot would make her the centre of attention and thus increase potential earning power. Even with her sons often around to help protect her, she was a brave woman and a true sporting pioneer.

Britain was changing fast in the 1820s thanks to the industrial revolution, but life would remain a struggle for the millions of working poor for many more decades, most forced to toil for long hours in mills, mines, factories and docks. The dreadful working and living conditions persisted in many areas until the end of the Victorian age and the dark shadow of the workhouse loomed over the unemployed and destitute.

Nevertheless, at an age when many women were no longer physically able to work or flourish, Mary McMullen decided it was time to stretch her legs and expand her horizons. The exploits of sons William, James, Peter and Barney provided clear evidence that stamina, resilience and showmanship ran in the McMullen family. One of the lads even liked to spice things up by walking backwards during parts of his events!

Mother Mary was described as a tall, thin woman who did her walks in a long dark dress, coloured scarf and white muslin cap. She always preferred to go barefoot if the terrain allowed – an aspect that always helped pull in good crowds, on one occasion an estimated 6,000 looking on. Her most prolific year was 1826, when during one eight-week spell she completed six events – three of 92 miles, one of 40 miles and two of 20. She demonstrated in dazzling fashion that age was no barrier, covering 20 miles inside four hours, 40 miles inside nine hours, and 92 miles in around 24 hours. Spectators cheered her on, amazed and amused by her resilience and chutzpah. But there were plenty who heartily disapproved, seeing it as inappropriate behaviour from any woman, let alone an older one.

Shortly before Mrs McMullen began turning heads, a 27-year-old called Mary Morgan dipped her toe into pedestrianism, appearing at two events in East Devon in the early part of 1826. She walked ten miles in under two hours at Exmouth, netting herself a modest reward, and followed this up with a more daring challenge of 50 miles in ten and a half hours. She completed the latter task as part of the St Thomas Fair in Exeter – walking up and down a 400-yard path from the Lamb & Lion pub towards the Dunsford turnpike gate – and finished it with a massive two hours in hand. She benefitted from an on-the-spot collection among highly impressed onlookers. Presumably any betting on the outcome would have been done very discreetly that day, as the walk and the rest of the day's festivities were supervised by St Thomas Church, right next door to the pub at 54 Cowick Street.

Meanwhile, several hundred miles to the north, the much older Mary McMullen prepared herself for bigger and longer challenges. To get herself into the swing of things, one of her first high-profile walks came on Wednesday 27th September 1826 when she agreed to complete 40 miles in 10 hours, over a half-mile piece of ground from the Micklegate Bar gateway in York. The bellman (town crier) had proclaimed her intentions the previous day and a good early morning crowd had gathered by the time she appeared at the starting point. Here a collection box had been affixed to a chair, bearing a label urging spectators to donate cash to "the pedestrianess". From this chair, half a mile had been measured along the main road heading south, and her task was to walk out and back 40 times in the allotted ten hours.

She was a taller-than-average woman attired in a white muslin cap, a white cotton 'waist' [blouse], over which was pinned a coloured neckerchief, a dark skirt and black stockings – but no shoes. She set off briskly at 8.30am, looking confident and strong; onlookers made mention that her impressive gait closely resembled that of the stylish Foster Powell (1734–1793) the first notable exponent of pedestrianism in Britain, who had famously walked from London to York and back.

Over the course of her day's work, inevitably some cheeky onlookers couldn't resist the urge to accompany Mary for a stretch, but nobody could match her walking pace without breaking into "a shuffling trot". Mary rested briefly after completing 18 miles in just under four hours, and then went on to complete the task without visibly tiring at all, her pace remarkably even, in a time reported as two minutes under nine hours, well within the limit. She declared afterwards she could have continued for much longer and revealed she wasn't a complete novice, having walked similar distances elsewhere. One report stated: "On these occasions she depends entirely on the generosity of the spectators for remuneration. In the present instance, we understand, the spectators were not parsimonious in rewarding her labours".

"Taking into account her age, this was one of the greatest feats we know on record", wrote the *Bell's Life in London* correspondent. Mary was heartily congratulated by many in the crowd milling around Mickelgate Bar, and there was clearly no danger she would suffer the same fate as rebels and traitors of the past, whose severed heads had been displayed above this well-known gateway, including that of Richard, Duke of York!

Encouraged by the day's proceedings, Mary arranged another performance in York less than a week later, this time aiming to cover 90 miles in 24 hours on Monday 2nd October. It took place from another of the city's four gateways, Bootham Bar. This one featured a large door-knocker that had been installed back in the days when people from Scotland were required to knock first and seek permission from the Lord Mayor to enter the city. No such trifle was required of Irishwoman Mary, who again attracted a big crowd to the area to watch her efforts.

She started at 4pm from the Asylum gates, heading northwards to Clifton on another out-and-back course of half a mile each way. For the first three hours she walked at a brisk 5mph. She continued just short of that pace for the next few hours until the crowd increased to a point where she found herself constantly impeded. It appears most of the attention was generally well-intentioned, including many offers of sips of wine and spirits to help her on her way. She was said to have mostly turned these down "with great cheerfulness".

Interestingly, the *Belfast Commercial Chronicle* reckoned that these offers of drink had come from parties intent on slowing her down because they had bets on her failing to make 24 hours: "Some individuals attempted to prevent the old lady completing her object by giving her proper liquids to drink, but they were very properly prevented from accomplishing their object".

Walking through the night with just one reported break, where she sat for a while on a chair at the starting point, Mary had clocked up 71 miles by 9am Tuesday morning, still averaging well over four miles per hour. It was a very decent pace considering she was being impeded and annoyed by what one paper referred to as "droves of beasts" along the route.

She pressed relentlessly onward, but was looking very tired by noon, finally accomplishing the task at seven minutes past three, some 53 minutes inside the target. The final mile turned into a real spectacle, scenes presumably unprecedented as far as female pedestrians were concerned in Britain: a sovereign, a blue ribbon, a white apron and a new cap were all presented to her on the move by the mistress of a house at Clifton who said they were "on behalf of some gentlemen". Wearing these items and a big smile, Mary came home in triumphant fashion, preceded by a fiddler and tambourine player, and was greeted by hearty cheers from the estimated gathering of 6,000.

The *Tyne Mercury* called it "a truly animated scene, the concourse every moment increasing, among which we noticed several elegantly dressed ladies many of whom were liberal in their *'douceurs'* [niceties] to the poor old woman". It had been good entertainment for the crowd, who demonstrated their admiration for this locally based woman's efforts by donating generously at the finish. The sight of the cash rewards encouraged Mary and made her forget the problems she'd encountered earlier. Newspaper reports added to the evidence that she had been deliberately hampered, particularly by young men who had bet against her: "[They] attempted by every means to induce her to relinquish her undertaking and to render her incapable of preserving it", said one. Although they failed to thwart her in York, it was pointed out they had been successful earlier in Lincolnshire, for in that city she failed by just eight minutes to hit 92 miles in 24 hours, thanks to the unwanted attentions of a party of "boys of loose character".

The money and plaudits earned at York encouraged Mary to press on, and one of her next ports of call was the market town of Newark in Nottinghamshire. By now it was mid-November, meaning the weather was less amenable, but her challenge here was to cover 93 miles in 24 hours, starting in the late afternoon. A course was measured from the George & Dragon Inn (nowadays called the Royal Oak) opposite Newark Castle in Castlegate. She set off in very brisk fashion at 4pm on Tuesday 14th November, crossing the bridge over the River Trent and heading north on the main road out of the town, turning back after half a mile – a route to be repeated 92 more times!

Mary's first mile was timed at 10 mins 52 secs, and she managed five miles in 62 minutes, putting her well ahead of schedule. From then on it seems to have been plain sailing, and she even accelerated slightly in the final five miles, completing them in 65 minutes with the final mile a smooth and undistressed 12 mins 02 secs. She arrived triumphantly back opposite Newark Castle for the 93rd and final time with the clocks showing it was 3.43pm on the Wednesday afternoon. This was a healthy 17 minutes inside target time, although *Bell's Life in London* mistakenly stated she'd got home 17 seconds inside 24 hours. (Ironically, after making this mistake, the paper's guilty athletics correspondent then made fun of another newspaper which had recently stated that a farmer from Bath had run a mile in 3 mins 45 secs!)

Mary McMullen was by now on a roll and her next appearance was soon fixed up for January 1827 in Leicester. Billed this time as being 65 years old, Mary took on the challenge of walking 92 miles in 22 successive hours on Wednesday 10th January. The event would take place over the usual half-mile distance, up and down New Walk, a popular and fashionable promenade laid out by the Corporation of Leicester to connect Welford Place with the racecourse (now Victoria Park). It was a pleasant leafy walk at the heart of the busy city, and regarded as "the most respectable street" in Leicester, but Mary's presence no doubt attracted a crowd from all strata of local life, including a few unwelcome rogues.

She set off with a flourish in the afternoon at the bottom of New Walk and headed for the seat near trees at the upper end, where she turned to complete her first mile back at the start. Despite the pleasant surroundings it was a monotonous task which she maintained with great determination till 3 the next afternoon, completing 92 miles with an hour to spare. A good crowd gathered to witness this novel sight and happily handed over a few shillings when she finished. The *Leicester Chronicle* said this was "the only reward she received for her fatigue" for no wagers had been struck.

Less than a fortnight later she returned to the East Midlands for a somewhat shorter task, a walk of 20 miles to be completed in four and a half hours – again with a collection purse the only reward. On Tuesday 23rd January she set off at 10am from the Blue Bell public house just outside the centre of the market town of Mansfield. The out-and-back one mile method was used to make sure she was seen by people in the busiest area, and although the ground was very slippery after recent bad weather, she completed the undertaking in an impressive 4 hrs 10 secs. Those who lined the streets to watch her pass might have been reminded of the occasion less than five years earlier (September 1822) when another elderly woman amazed locals with a remarkable walking feat. On that day 78-year-old Mrs Wilson arrived in Mansfield after a 180-mile trek from her home in Westmorland. Her journey took five days and was to visit her son rather than make money.

Mary McMullen managed several more long walks during 1827, heading to the Cumbrian coast in May to perform at the coal-trade port of Whitehaven. On Thursday 20th May the town crier whipped up considerable interest by announcing her intention to set off the following day on another task of 92 miles in 24 hours over a half-mile stretch of road. At two minutes past 4 o'clock on the Friday afternoon she headed out of town on the road to Carlisle, starting not far from the busy harbour, between the upper end of Lonsdale Place and Bransty Turnpike. Figures calculated at the end showed her combined rest periods amounted to 4h 40m and her walking time to 18h 45m, a brisk pace of 12 and a quarter minutes per mile. She finished looking in good shape mid-afternoon on the Saturday. It was another tremendous effort for a woman her age and her finish was no doubt arranged to coincide with the maximum amount of people being in the area, to help swell her coffers.

Several newspapers announced on Monday 29th October 1827 that Barney McMullen, one of Mary's sons, had undertaken to walk 100 miles in 24 successive hours at Aylesbury in Buckinghamshire. He would start at 2pm on a half-mile stretch of road from near the Kings Head inn and Mr Rickford's bank, just outside Aylesbury towards Bierton village. He maintained a speed of 5mph well into the night, took an extended rest of 75 minutes, and resumed reinvigorated to finish with a swift eight-minute mile to achieve his goal. Reports described him as a "slender young man apparently of the sister kingdom [Ireland]". The applause was loud and generous but the crowd was mostly working folk with little cash to spare, and McMullen's rather meagre reward was £2 collected near the finish line. His mother Mary was an interested onlooker, and a few days later it was her turn to be the centre of attention.

On the Thursday morning in Aylesbury, the town crier rang his bell vigorously: "Oyez, oyez, oyez!" announcing that "an old woman upwards of 60 – the mother of the previous walker" would traverse the same road for 20 miles in four hours, with 15 minutes allowed for rest and refreshments. As tradition dictated, the 'bellman' ended with "God save the Queen" and posted a notice on the door of the nearest inn.

Mary McMullen duly started at 2pm from the Cock Inn at The Kingsbury, which was a triangle of open space to the north of the busy Market Square in Aylesbury. Her first mile passed in ten minutes, the second in 11, and she went on to accomplish the whole task without distress in 3 hrs 49 mins to the surprise of the crowd. She was not escorted or protected during her journey and was consequently the victim of many interruptions on the road, much of which was very crowded. She'd been followed from the start by a large crowd of noisy local lads for the first mile, and made them work hard to keep pace – but very few could stay with her as she passed the second mile.

Less than three weeks later, on Monday 19th November 1827, Mary accepted the challenge of walking 15 miles in three hours from the Windsor Town Bridge – an impressive nine-year-old iron and granite arch bridge that crossed the Thames – into Eton and back. The *Morning Advertiser* said she performed the task with amazing alacrity and had 15 minutes to spare by the end, and as a result was handsomely rewarded by the collection among the many spectators.

The McMullen family bandwagon rolled on in 1828 and Mary proved she wasn't finished yet despite having reached her mid-sixties. Along with family members Peter and John, Mary was in action during the autumn months not far from their home in NE England. It became evident that the boys were struggling to make much money from their efforts, but Mary – being female and elderly – found it easier to gain sympathy and generosity from the public and appears to have earned reasonably good amounts. Strange times indeed in this particular Northumberland household with grandmother Mary apparently now the main breadwinner!

Peter and John tackled several challenges to complete 110 miles in 24 hours during the very rainy autumn of 1828. Peter walked in the Bishopwearmouth area of Sunderland, and also on Newcastle's Great North Road near the Barras Bridge, while John was in action in Durham. The *Durham County Advertiser* described Peter as "a slender consumptive-looking young man of about 18 [who] belongs to a family famous for their walking capabilities. His manner is stiff and shuffling, bearing much upon his heels and sawing the air with his arms like a windmill". Peter finished strongly in Newcastle and within his time limit, but looked in some distress by the end. A collection for him yielded very little, a fate that would also befall John in Durham. John recorded a time of 23 hours 42 minutes on Palace Green, an attractive grassy area flanked by the city's cathedral and castle. There was no 'match' arrangement or big-money gentlemanly wagers and Peter's only remuneration was the usual collection among spectators amounting to roughly £2. A week or two earlier Peter had walked 13 miles in just under two and a quarter hours in Chester-le-Street – and a collection described as "door to door" afterwards yielded a mere few pence. Instead of sympathy, another *Durham County Advertiser* report stated in no uncertain terms that the McMullen family ought to abandon all this walking-for-money nonsense: "It is high time this species of vagabondising was put down, and that the extraordinary powers of the family of the McMullens was applied to some more useful purpose".

Mary didn't worry what the local papers thought, and undertook to walk the lower part of Newcastle's Town Moor Racecourse for 92 miles in 24 hours. Her son Peter was simultaneously attempting 100 miles in 24 hours at the same venue. Not for the first time, Mary's choice of clothing attracted much interest. At the age of 64, she had few inhibitions about all this and stripped for action in full view of everyone. The *London Courier* recorded: "She peeled, threw off her upper garment, and shewed, not in her 'fainter lawn' but in a dimity vest and petticoat, with a silk handkerchief girt tight about her waist. Just before starting she took a pinch of snuff – clasped her hands – muttered a short prayer to the presiding god, and bolted".

Off she strode at 6.30pm on Monday 13 September 1828 to big cheers, and after darkness fell found no shortage of company, a number of people making a point of coming out to encourage her on her way during the early hours. The following day dawned with good weather, leading to another large crowd gathering ("immense" said the *Newcastle Courant*). Early on she moved along at roughly five miles per hour but this dropped during the night and she didn't appear comfortable for much of the trip, but encouragement from spectators seemed to act as a painkiller. She finished her 92 miles in 23 hours 33 minutes amid scenes of great excitement and, according to the *London Courier*, responded to the crowd by quoting from *Hamlet*: "Let the galled jade wince, my withers are unwrung!". Either the reporter was paraphrasing her actual words, or Mary's knowledge of Shakespeare belied her humble background!

If the man from the *London Courier* was joking, his mood quickly changed by the conclusion of his report. He became furious that Mary's sons should encourage their elderly mother to make a distressing exhibition of herself just for the sake of money: "Mary is a piece of good stuff unquestionably, but though tough, she is old – too old to war against nature by an effort so violent. Besides it is a painful sight, and reflects discredit on her sons, who thus urge on an old parent to such an indecent exhibition for the gain of a few shillings. Humanity revolts at it".

Subscriptions taken on the course saw her rewarded to the tune of around £20 (equivalent purchasing power of roughly £1,800 in 2021). Mary, no doubt feeling she was getting a little old for all this, appeared completely exhausted, unlike previous walks, and had to be helped into a hackney carriage. She was whisked back to her base, the Bay Horse pub at the top of Northumberland Street, where she again received a warm ovation from onlookers. It was in stark contrast to son Peter's reception for completing 110 miles in 24 hours. For him the crowd chose not to donate generously – the amount collected was described by the *Tyne Mercury* as "precarious".

Two months later, Mary set off in nearby Bishopwearmouth in an attempt to cover 96 miles in 24 hours, only to be stopped by police two hours into the walk. To her noisy dismay they ordered her to discontinue due to the alleged offence of begging.

The outbreak of distaste by press and police for Mary's involvement in pedestrianism was echoed in the case of other women, even when the perpetrator was much younger. A 17-year-old female walked 40 miles on six successive days a week or so earlier, also attempting to attract cash donations from racegoers, this time at Warwick. The disapproval was relayed by the *Leamington Courier*:

"Not content with her sex's undoubted superiority in the rapid movement of one member, [she] resolved to compete with the lords of the creation in the exercise of the feet, as well as the tongue... the venue was the Punch Bowl inn on the Butts, Warwick, going through Leamington, five miles out and back again, which she traversed four times a day. The self-imposed task was not for any wager but merely for such remuneration as a generous public might bestow... we believe she acquired little beyond the fame of her exploit – the public wisely discouraging an abandonment of useful labour for the vagabondising habits of a female pedestrian".

Evergreen Mary McMullen popped up again just over a year later in late 1829, reportedly having walked 96 miles in 24 successive hours in Hampshire in front of an appreciative crowd. This was mid-December and her perambulations were from a starting point on the corner of St Thomas Passage in Southgate Street, Winchester, heading a quarter of a mile out towards cottages positioned below Southgate House on the Southampton Road. She walked back and forth along this route, finishing the task some 20 minutes inside 24 hours, and was rewarded with a good-sized collection from spectators.

After this little was seen or heard of Mary for another four years. Then, in 1833, reports emerged of an unnamed woman – said to be approaching the age of 70 – attempting a walk of 96 miles in 24 hours in Scotland. Some newspapers carried quite detailed accounts of the event, but in the style of the day chose not to name the walker, probably a sign of disapproval. However the evidence suggests it was almost certainly Mary. The walk was to take place in Paisley, the same venue that had witnessed one of Mary's sons achieving 100 miles in 24 hours earlier that same year – 30 of those miles performed walking backwards!

Mary wouldn't be attempting any crowd-pleasing tricks like this, the fact she was female and almost 70 years old being more than enough to create huge public interest. She set off at 6pm on Wednesday 20th August on the main road from Paisley to Renfrew. Substantial crowds assembled along the route, eager for some entertainment, and by about 9pm the road half a mile beyond the toll bar was almost completely blocked. After 10 hours and 45 miles of largely difficult walking, Mary found herself at the centre of a serious disturbance among the crowd, with drinking, fighting, road blockages and people injured (one small boy was run over by a cart and badly hurt). The county sheriff felt he had no option but to call a halt to the walk and arrested Mary for causing a breach of the peace and carted her off to a prison cell at the Paisley tolbooth. The *Glasgow Courier* reported colourfully: "During the night several battles took place by some who had made free with John Barleycorn [intoxicating liquor] to defend themselves from the night air".

As these were effectively unlicensed events on public roads and paths, causing a 'breach of the peace' had become an occupational hazard for the pedestrians and pedestriennes. They were seen as directly responsible for any trouble that might occur in connection with their walks. By the 1820s Mary's alleged 'offence' was one of those regarded by the authorities as a less serious matter that could be dealt with summarily by local magistrates. It ranked alongside common assault, minor riot and affray, drunk and disorderly conduct, vagrancy and breaches of licensing laws. Nevertheless it was highly unwelcome. Being arrested while merely attempting to walk from A to B meant she suffered the same indignity as male counterpart George Wilson in the infamous Blackheath riot of 1815. Magistrates later threw out the case against Wilson, but whether Mary was shown leniency is unknown. However, her Scottish misadventure almost certainly signalled the end of her pedestrianism.

THREE

BEGINNING OF THE BOOM

Following the death of King William IV, his niece Victoria ascended the throne in the summer of 1837, the first female monarch for 123 years. But British pedestrianism at this point had no 'queen' of its own – Mary McMullen's walking days were done and the stage was again populated almost exclusively by men.

The sport itself was continuing to thrive, a view underlined by the fact that leading sporting publication *Bell's Life* gave it a section of its own and actively began promoting men's matches. It compiled a calendar of fixtures, acted as a stakeholder, provided a forum for issuing and answering challenges and regularly featured detailed and often favourable accounts of the matches. The 1840s saw pedestrianism undergo a boom period in England which would spill over to the USA. Cinder tracks, generally called 'paths', were created in the grounds of many pubs and races took place, often involving two runners for small stakes and occasionally huge crowds would be drawn in.

As the historian and Olympian Peter Radford would point out many years later: "Many pedestrian matches were [by now] squalid affairs, riddled with fraud and drugs, and no one could trust that the competitions were fair". Given this, it is hardly surprising that it was taking time for women to get any sort of foothold in the sport. However courageous and impressive their performance might be, the feeling that female pedestrians were cheap exhibitionists with little self-respect was firmly entrenched. And even though female walking exploits in the first half of the 19th century were few and far between (Mary

McMullen apart), some undoubtedly took place and went unreported because newspaper editors and publishers disapproved.

To help precipitate change, a female walker with star quality was badly needed. None would materialise until the tail end of 1843 when another working-class woman from Northern England suddenly emerged – the redoubtable Mrs Harrison.

STORY 5: MRS. HARRISON – ACHIEVING THE 'IMPOSSIBLE'

Since the mysterious dispute that caused Esther Crozier to quit her 1,000-mile attempt in 1817, a quarter of a century had passed before another woman would make a serious attempt at the landmark feat commonly referred to as 'the Barclay Match'.

During this fallow period the very first women's suffrage petition was presented to Parliament, and Queen Victoria's long reign commenced. But, as the lists published regularly in *Bell's Life* proved, although men's pedestrianism continued to thrive in the 1840s, participation of women remained scarce. It would take somebody special to take the stage in these circumstances – and in Leeds they had just the woman. Step forward a 39-year-old always referred to as simply 'Mrs. Harrison'.

The booming wool town of Leeds (population circa 225,000 and yet to achieve city status) was a hotbed of pedestrianism at the time, a recent highlight being James Searle's much heralded 1,000 miles in 1,000 hours, which finished in mid-November 1843. Searle, a small but sturdy fellow from a severely poverty-stricken background, had risen to the challenge that no man from Leeds could achieve the Barclay feat. He walked back and forth between the New Peacock and Shakespeare pubs (around a mile apart) over the required six-week period, one mile every hour, and finished in triumph on Monday 13 November to great local acclaim, exceeding the 1,000-mile mark by some distance.

It was one in the eye for the haughty London sporting press, who had earlier poured cold water on Searle's chances. Such was the surge of confidence in the Leeds area that within days other locals were planning to tackle the same 1,000-mile challenge. These included Benjamin Riding, John Worsnip, Thomas Gledhill and John Perry – but their efforts were deliberately ignored by local paper *Leeds Times*, who explained: "As we have no means of ascertaining their adherence to [terms and conditions], we shall not notice them further".

But this news blackout didn't apply to Mrs Harrison whose attempt to become the first female in the world to emulate Captain Barclay was apparently being taken seriously – with its start proposed for Tuesday 27th November 1843.

Looked after by landlord James Wilkinson, Mrs Harrison based herself at the Dragon Inn, just outside central Leeds in Wortley, on the Whitehall Road (now the A58). The weather was unseasonably mild as she set off early in the morning from outside the pub. She looked confident and composed, despite the six-week ordeal ahead. Achieving 1,000 miles in consecutive 1,000 hours would mean enduring all sorts of hardships, with of course the main hurdle being the lack of proper sleep. Once underway, the accepted best practice had become setting off around 15 minutes before the end of an hour and keeping going for 15 minutes into the next hour. This would allow the walker to tick off two miles in two hours, and then have around 90 minutes available for rest before the next stint. Mrs Harrison is likely to have used this tried and trusted format. It would feel fairly comfortable at first, but as the days and then weeks went by, serious fatigue would raise its ugly head. However, by all accounts, she was able to stay remarkably focussed, determined and in apparent control.

As might have been expected, the December weather wasn't helpful for long-distance walking, veering unpredictably between mildness and bitterly cold, but Mrs Harrison coped well with all the wind, rain and severely cold nights. After about two weeks of good progress the *Leeds Times* reported that she looked likely to finish, the only things causing her worry being "a dark moon and wet weather". Interestingly the paper also suggested that if she did succeed it would surely bring an end to the "walking mania" currently gripping the Leeds district. They were presumably suggesting that no self-respecting Leeds man would be prepared to risk an athletic challenge that a mere woman had already managed to achieve!

As Christmas approached it was clear Mrs Harrison was suffering from sore feet but had rallied and was determined to push on. Her backup team vehemently denied suggestions she had fallen behind the required pace and had contravened the conditions of her task. They claimed proudly that after passing 600 miles her progress had continued to be "indisputably perfect".

Early January brought some snow and ice to contend with, but even when she coped admirably with this there were still some notes of dissent to be heard; the *Banbury Guardian*, for example, gave a short description of her progress but couldn't resist adding a pompous ticking off: "It is a pity that the husband of this woman can't find her some employment more befitting her sex. Such exhibitions are a disgrace to society".

Disgrace or not, a number of people happily got stuck into a celebratory meal in Mrs Harrison's honour on the very chilly night of Wednesday January 3rd 1844, while the walker herself headed their way outside in the cold. It was her 40th birthday and the special meal was arranged by the Dragon Inn landlord, Wilkinson. Having hit 906 miles that evening, the heroine of the hour was eventually able to join the other diners in the pub, soak up their praise, and acknowledge the raising of a glass in her honour.

She maintained her progress with little fuss and duly finished the walk at 12 midnight on Sunday 7th January. She was in no obvious distress and, after 42 days her body was so used to the hourly routine that she decided to press on until noon the next day. It would ensure her total was well into four figures, and would mean a decent-sized crowd could be present to witness her finish in daylight. It was a wise move: the celebrations were long and loud, and would continue well into the Tuesday with Mrs Harrison able to put her feet up and be chaired triumphantly through Leeds.

Mrs Harrison was hailed throughout the region and further afield for taking women's athletic achievement to a new level. Many people had to eat their words as news spread that this 40-year-old married woman had emulated the so-called impossible feat of the great Captain Barclay some 35 years earlier. Other women might well go faster and further in the future, but nobody could take away Mrs Harrison's claim to have notched up a world first. She was a true pioneer.

FOUR

ENTER THE BLOOMERISTS!

The small number of British women brave or desperate enough to try pedestrianism in the first half of the 19th century – some of whom were probably pushed reluctantly into it – found out the hard way it was not a pursuit that welcomed female involvement with open arms.

Getting out and about was not viewed as an appropriate or healthy alternative to looking after family or working in a factory or mill. Apart from anything else, there had been a severe outbreak of cholera across England and Wales which lingered for years and killed many thousands. It led to the creation of the Public Health Act of 1848 which placed supply and treatment of water and waste in the hands of local authorities, a move that thankfully resulted in more favourable sanitary conditions in towns and cities.

It was clear that to gain some sort of proper acceptance, female pedestrianism was in need of a helping hand. This would duly arrive in a most unexpected way from America. It came thanks to a group of forward-thinking, strong-minded feminists who caused a sensation by brazenly parading in 'bloomers' outside the main pavilion of the 1851 Great Exhibition in London. Enter the Bloomerists!

The innovative costume took its name from Mrs Amelia Bloomer, a passionate advocate of women's rights from upstate New York who also happened to be editor of *The Lily*, the first newspaper exclusively by and for women. Amelia, born in 1818, had become a key figure in the popularisation of this new mode of dress aimed at women who desired a more active life than conventional bulky crinoline dresses would allow.

The controversial new outfit would permit a woman to move far more freely than ever before in public. In particular, it would be a boon for distance walkers, and a few years later, for those taking up cycling. This is how the new bloomer outfit was described at the time: a pair of Turkish pantaloons, wide and nearly meeting the shoe, of such material and texture as the season demanded, and of a hue adapted to the taste of the wearer; a neatly fitting outer garment (a bodice, or coatee) buttoned, or permanently closed on all sides, with skirt extending to just below the knee, of a material and texture that would ward off cold.

The costume was seen as dramatically daring for the times, titillating even, although in reality the bloomer pioneers were not exposing any hitherto hidden flesh. What made bloomerism really radical was the fact women were evidently seeking to 'wear the trousers', and thus challenging male dominance. With newspapers everywhere decrying the new style, bloomers became an overnight feminist firestorm. Although the costume looked like a godsend for female walkers, some might have been hesitant to jump on the bandwagon once it became central to a form of social protest in which everyday dress – in public and in the home – became a political act.

The new look provided a huge contrast to the prevailing fashion of the day, which was five or six layers of quilted, stiffly starched petticoats which held out women's voluminous overskirts and hid the tightly laced whalebone corset that held in their waists.

Because her name was used, Amelia Bloomer received the plaudits for 'inventing' bloomers, but in reality all she did was write about and promote them. Partly responsible for bloomers was the male editor of Amelia's local paper, who published a tongue-in-cheek cartoon of a woman wearing a short dress and pantaloons. He was known to be an opponent of promoting women's rights but had unwittingly come up with an illustration of exactly what was needed! Much of the real credit belongs to another New Yorker, Elizabeth 'Libby' Miller, who designed the bloomer costume after seeing or hearing about the style of trousers worn by the first Turkish envoy to visit America in 1850. Miller had reached her wits' end attempting to do gardening in long dresses, so she grabbed her sewing kit and whipped up an outfit of Turkish trousers to the ankle, underneath a skirt well above ground level, four inches below the knee. She showed it to fellow free-thinker and friend Elizabeth Cady Stanton, who put it through its paces. Libby was ecstatic at the results, and wrote:

"Like a captive set free from his ball and chain, I was always ready for a brisk walk through sleet and snow and rain, to climb a mountain, jump over a fence, work in the garden, and was fit for any necessary locomotion. What a sense of liberty I felt with no skirts to hold or brush, ready at any moment to climb a hilltop to see the sun go down or the moon rise, with no ruffles or trails impeded by the dew or soiled by the grass".

Once the costume and its liberating effect had come to the attention of Amelia Bloomer, she wrote about its convenience and practicality in her newspaper *The Lily*. It caused a sensation among American women. Importantly, it came hot on the heels of the first women's rights convention, staged in 1848 at Seneca Falls, New York, where an agenda was drawn up and a set of 12 resolutions adopted, calling for equal treatment under the law and voting rights. However, as much as these pioneering women loved the new fashion, the rest of America, and subsequently British society too, were slow to accept it, and the close circle of Bloomer advocates had to fight hard to keep the trend alive.

As with so much before and since, what happens in America eventually gets a foothold this side of the Atlantic too. Before long the first organised movement for English feminism was born in the shape of the Langham Place Circle, which campaigned for women's causes, including improved rights in employment and education. But before the LPC got established, bloomerism arrived in London at the Great Exhibition where its supporters set up unofficial displays outside the big Hyde Park event. Significantly, the women parading around wearing bloomers were identified in the newspapers as coming from respectable backgrounds, and were not lower-class 'trollopes' doing it for money.

The old and the new: The arrival of bloomers (left) liberated women from the restrictions of conventional dress (right).

The British press was fascinated and although much of decent society was horrified by this American fad, it was clear that among its most obvious advantages was the making of athletic endeavours for women far more feasible than before. The early British pedestriennes such as Mary McMullen and Esther Crozier, both no longer active, must have been green with envy.

The crusading women – labelled 'the bloomerists' – came across from the USA with the express intent of publicising their new costume and its benefits. On the second day of the Great Exhibition *The Times* reported that in Hyde Park five people wearing "the habiliments of the new sect" had appeared to be persons of some station in society as at least two of them were connected to a respectable family from Torrington Square. The quintet were clearly carrying out a pre-arranged advertising stunt, and they bore with considerable good humour the inevitable taunts that came their way from thousands of onlookers as they paraded around outside the main buildings of the exhibition. As well as showing off the new 'bloomers' they handed out printed bills announcing a public lecture about the new costume scheduled for North London the following Monday. They aroused huge interest and spent at least 90 minutes in the area before being spirited away in an open, four-wheeled horse-drawn carriage known as a phaeton.

They linked up with British supporters, notably feminist Caroline Dexter from Nottingham. They were able to secure publicity by organising public meetings in a large number of major towns and cities, events which often received very good press coverage, thus spreading the word about bloomers far and wide.

One of the bloomer tourists was a Mrs Smart, who spoke on Monday 6th October 1851 at the Royal Soho Theatre in London, the audience whipped up by the newly formed 'London Bloomer Committee' who had earnestly urged mothers and daughters of England to attend in order to "help take forward the welfare of present and future generations by adopting an improved method, instead of the present injurious and artificial mode of dress". The committee members all wore bloomer costumes themselves for the night, and the interest was phenomenal.

According to the *Evening Standard*, eight females aged between 7 and 50 appeared on the RST stage looking timid and uncomfortable in their bloomers. But Mrs Smart explained to an enthusiastic audience that the bloomer movement was not dictated by vanity or personal motives. Strong moral reasons had induced American women to favour this major fashion reform. They had found they had a despot in their way, one that refused to be questioned either by morality, religion, or law. That tyrant was known to the world by the name of 'fashion', she said. They wanted this tyrant to face three separate charges: (1) Nature had been violated by his rules, and life endangered; (2) In consequence of his requirements a vast amount of money had been expended which might have been devoted to higher and holier purposes; and (3) By encumbering women he prevented them rendering services to society worthy of their high destiny.

The prevailing dress arrangements in the USA and Britain caused women to be physically, spiritually, and morally injured, and rendered them less vigorous in body and mind and incapable of performing their duties to the human race. This had prompted the women of America to introduce bloomer costumes – "And we now look to Great Britain most earnestly for assistance in this our work of reformation. This is not merely a matter of fancy!".

The excited audience lapped it up and cried, "Three cheers for Mrs. Amelia Bloomer!" before launching into the national anthem. Gatherings throughout the country witnessed similar scenes, attendees entertained and fascinated by what they saw, although it remained to be seen how many British women were ready to ditch their dresses immediately in favour of bloomers.

Inevitably there was some opposition – the aristocrat Lady Chesterfield, for example, called the bloomer costume absurd and immodest, and believed it would provoke ribald comments from men about parts of a lady's dress of which they ought to remain ignorant.

In these early days, wearing the new costume was deemed by police and other authorities as likely to create a public nuisance. After a woman in bloomers was apprehended in Central London in September 1851 by a panic-stricken policeman ("a rosy-gilled, well-fed constable, puffing and blowing like a stranded grampus"), she reportedly cried out, "Who do you call a nuisance, you muffin-faced bluebottle?" Charged with public nuisance, the very vocal Sophia Edwards, wife of a cabinet maker living in Stingo Lane, told a court she had walked up and down Marylebone's New Road in the costume and had never felt so comfortable in her life. She sparked fits of laughter by adding: "Ah gentlemen, how cosy you must all feel in those dear, delicious tights!" She said without conventional women's clothing ("nasty" petticoats, and suchlike) she could now run like a deer. The case against her was dismissed and outside the court Mrs Edwards refused to take a cab home, setting off on foot amid great cheering.

Many of the critics seemed convinced women in bloomers were deliberately attempting to break down social distinctions by donning trouser-like garments.

"It should be discouraged", exclaimed *The Dundee Courier*. "Why should ladies quarrel with their petticoats?". The paper suggested a cunning plan was afoot to assert the rights of women by allowing them to "wear the breeches" in relationships and in society.

Sometimes the appearance of the costume on the streets could cause the atmosphere to turn nasty. In East London two women in bloomers, one aged around 17 and the other 40, had to seek refuge in a grocer's shop on Kingsland Green when a rowdy mob began following them and hurling abuse of a very personal nature. They eventually escaped from a rear entrance of the shop, but the chasing hordes, of both sexes, grew to around 500, and neighbouring shops had to close until the police were able to restore peace. Something similar occurred in Clare Market in Central London, where two women's frilly costumes were tugged vigorously and mocked by a gang of young boys and when the victims fled, unsympathetic onlookers began grabbing vegetables from the market stalls to fling at them.

Launched for women in the late 1840s, *The Lady's Own Paper* took a dim view of the new outfit, running an article that politely urged mature women to remember they were no longer slender girls of 14, and to steer clear of bloomers as they merely made them look ridiculous and undignified.

Typical of the early hysteria was a 'Bloomer Ball' organised in London's Hanover Square. No females were allowed inside unless wearing 'pantilettes' which meant a large crowd gathered outside the entrance to watch arrivals, plus a large body of police. By 10.30pm dancing was supposed to commence inside, but at this point only one 'bloomerist' had turned up and she was outnumbered by men to the tune of 50-1. Happily, there were many latecomers and at the midnight hour around 30 bloomerists had taken to the dance floor.

The Hereford Journal provided a quite rare show of press support for the costume – commenting that fresh air and exercise were essential to the well-being of females as well as males, yet women were expected to flounder and struggle with an umbrella in one hand and a huge dress gathered up in the other, merely to proceed a few yards. A party of ladies attempting a walk in a wet season was a mournful, melancholy spectacle that can now be banished thanks to bloomers coming along to offer respite.

Discussion of the pros and cons went on for months, but it was clear the bloomer costume had truly arrived with major impact and would not be going away. It would only be a week or two before the first serious evidence emerged that women pedestrians in Britain would benefit greatly in particular.

In late October 1851 a young, unnamed woman appeared unexpectedly at Kennington Oval in South London to accompany the celebrated pedestrian Richard Manks (known as 'The Warwickshire Antelope') for a small section of his 1,000-miles-in-1,000-hours attempt. It was a calm and overcast late afternoon on Thursday 23rd October when she appeared in her bloomers and strode out confidently alongside the great Manks, who had by now completed more than 600 miles and was suffering quite badly from the effects. His new friend fell in with him and kept pace with no sign of fatigue for around 16 miles. The stunt created enormous interest – of a largely positive nature – and was witnessed by a good number of women spectators, and on leaving the ground the 'bloomerist' promised to return a few days later to walk another 20 miles with 32-year-old Manks.

As author and athletics historian Peter Lovesey would later reflect: "The most positive and important development to come out of the distance-walking vogue was the participation of women. The anonymous young woman who walked with Manks at Kennington Oval demonstrated not only that long-distance walking was perfectly adapted to the staying powers of her sex, but also that the costume popularised by Mrs Amelia Bloomer enabled them to get out of their crinolines and become the pioneers of women's athletics. There was a rush to the tracks of America and Britain and soon scores of women were taking up the challenge. The newspapers treated all this at best as dubious activity and at worst beneath contempt, but sufficient accounts have survived to merit at least a chapter in any history of women's athletics".

FIVE

MORE FAMOUS THAN THE QUEEN!

When Cornish fishwife Mary Kelynack walked from Penzance to London at the age of 84, an astonished Prince Albert told her she was now the most famous woman in England – even ahead of his wife Queen Victoria!

Tough-as-teak Mary had become one of a small handful of elderly women to make headline news for their remarkable feats of long-distance walking, and in this way surely inspired some younger women to give competitive pedestrianism a try in the mid-19th century.

People marvelled at how veterans like Mrs Kelynack, Mary McMullen, Mary Wilkinson and Margaret Jones – ages ranging from 56 to 90 – covered many hundreds of miles on foot in single journeys and miraculously didn't kill themselves in the process!

The achievements of these elderly role models beggar belief considering the lifestyle, hardships and other factors relevant to their era. Even at their advanced age they showed what the so-called 'weaker sex' could achieve with a modicum of confidence, courage and bravado. If proof were necessary, they also underlined how stamina and determination were major assets of the female repertoire, even though men had the upper hand in speed and strength. Once their deeds had been reported in the newspapers it is fair to assume their exploits influenced younger would-be women walkers. Strictly speaking, Kelynack and Wilkinson never walked professionally nor competitively, but their stories still deserve telling as part of the pedestrienne narrative.

STORY 6: MARY KELYNACK – FISHWIFE'S FABULOUS FORAY

Average life expectancy in England across the 19th century ranged between 40 and 50, so when 84-year-old Mary Kelynack of Penzance set out on the 1851 walk that made her famous, she'd already doubled the lifespan of many women of her time. But that was never going to stop her.

In the spring of that year everyone had been talking about the forthcoming 'Great Exhibition' planned for London. The sheer scale of the event caused waves of unprecedented excitement throughout the land. All manner of folk wanted to visit the capital to see it, even rural types who'd barely set foot outside their home county till now.

Around 100,000 exhibits were being mounted inside a purpose-built temporary iron and glass edifice in London's Hyde Park, which would become known as the original Crystal Palace. It took 5,000 navvies to create it, and on display was almost every marvel of the Victorian age. Although aiming to be a World Fair (its full name: The Exhibition of the Works of Industry of All Nations), this was a showcase for British manufacturing. Many thousands of Queen Victoria's loyal subjects, however humble or far-flung, were evidently desperate to see it. Great-grandmother Mary Kelynack was one of them.

But how to get there? The obvious mode of transport was via the new expanding railway network, or by horse-driven coach – but only if you could afford a ticket. Mary Kelynack, who at 84 had for decades scraped a living selling fish in and around Penzance, was known to be something of a traditionalist – deeply attached to old customs, they said – but to the surprise of her acquaintances had now been gripped by an urgent desire to see the spectacular show in London everyone was talking about.

She'd been widowed five years earlier but remained a bright and confident woman, remarkably robust for her age. She craved excitement and adventure in these final years of her hard-working life. Like many others in her circle, she'd never ventured outside of Cornwall before and was determined to do so before it was too late.

Mary's meagre income from hawking fish meant there was little or no chance of scraping together a rail or coach fare to London. In any case, the railway linking Penzance and the far south-west to the network was still a few months from completion. Although the golden age of the stagecoach was coming to an end, this was still an option if the funds could be found, but even a coach would take around ten days, with stops for changes of horses. Though well known locally, Mary didn't mix in the sort of circles where a sponsor might easily be found. She was just one of many Cornish folk expressing a fancy for seeing the Great Exhibition, few of whom had a realistic chance of ever getting there – and most were far younger than Mary.

It didn't take long for Mary to conclude that her only chance of getting to London was to walk. Never mind the journey would be at least 350 miles long – and never mind that at 84 she was one of the oldest residents of the Mounts Bay and Fradgan district of Newlyn: "I've walked to Truro many times carrying a basket of fish, so London can't be much further than that," she declared, to a mixture of astonishment and hilarity from her friends and family.

It seems nobody was willing, or brave enough, to tell Mary the harsh truth. Her treks to Truro, highly commendable though they were, had been roughly 45 miles each – whereas London would be a round trip at least 15 times longer! It seemed a crazy idea, but Mary's mind was made up. And, what is more, she had a second reason for wanting to go to London: she'd been unable locally to secure any form of financial help in her old age, and believed if she could confront the right officials in London could use her gift of the gab to persuade them to sanction some sort of pension or annuity to make her final years a little more comfortable.

The daughter of Nicholas Tresize, Mary had been born in 1766 just outside Penzance, then a fishing port populated by around 2,000. She married into the huge local Kelynack family (commonly pronounced 'Kly-nack') and throughout the first half of the 19th century was a well-known, lively character whose boundless energy would remain undimmed, even by the cumulative effect of 60 years' hard and poorly paid labour and the loss of husband Will around 1846.

Life was tough, even though Mary and the other elderly fish-hawking females had, according to a travel guide of the time, become a "tourist sight" in West Cornwall by now. Their work was entirely conducted by women, originally distinguished by a jaunty beaver hat which was now being superseded by a bonnet. They took their fish to market with a cowl around their head and neck, a heavy shawl crossed over the chest and tied behind to protect their backs from the wet fish, with an apron and attached kerchief to wipe their hands. They were said to be part of "a class full of vigour and courage" with picturesque attire that also included gaily coloured calico jackets, coarse flannel skirts and buckled shoes. Reaching her eighties, Mary's life was a daily struggle to make ends meet, but she still had good health and wasn't willing to let her London dream die.

So, one damp day in August 1851, with a tiny amount of saved cash, several layers of the best clothing she could find and a minimum of baggage, she set off from Penzance on the greatest adventure of her life.

Little detail of the journey itself survives in print, apart from a small illustrated book published specifically for children. This book's narrative may have been embellished for the young readership's entertainment, but is largely based on what really happened. It relates how Mary set out wearing a bonnet, shawl and cloak, a pair of thick shoes with wooden soles, and aided by a sturdy walking stick. She had tearfully stroked her beloved cat farewell, shut up her cottage with great care and set off. After just five miles it began to rain hard, the clouds thick and heavy, the wind fierce and cold and the rain so violent that anyone else would have surely quit, but not Mary. She pushed onward and was rewarded when the sky cleared and rain ceased: "The sun came out and shone like gold, and the old woman smiled when she saw it and she walked quicker and quicker and, old as she was, sang like a little girl and thanked God for being so kind and making such a fine day".

It would ultimately take her five weeks but she made it to London, her arrival thought to be on the weekend of September 20/21, by which time the Great Exhibition at the Crystal Palace had been underway for around 20 weeks and had only another three to run. Mary claimed she did all 350 miles on foot, but it seems likely some kindly people will have offered lifts on horse-driven cars and wagons en route. The columnist 'Native' wrote in *The Cornishman* that she was "a great talker who well advertised herself" so it is certain extrovert Mary would have encountered dozens of folk during the trip. She would have been only too pleased to explain where she was headed and why, but nobody knows how many rides – if any at all – she might have accepted. Given the journey took her 35 days or so, we have no real reason to disbelieve her story that she walked every step of the way.

Embarking on such an adventure with very little cash would ultimately prove less of a problem than might have reasonably been expected. The interest shown in her from various important figures in London life, including offers of help, was significant. Cornishmen who were by now based in London were prominent among the many people enchanted by the story of this elderly woman walking the width of the country all alone, her smile as big as the bag on her bent back.

It is thought Mary's arrival in London came exactly five weeks after leaving home. She made her way to Hyde Park to join the massive crowds milling daily around the exhibition venue where she had never seen excitement or crowds like it. Total attendances would later be reported as 6.2 million over the 23-week period the show was open. It was a momentous event – a pioneering 'world fair' that would come to be viewed as Albert, the Prince Consort's crowning achievement. It promoted enterprise and art from across the globe and Queen Victoria was immensely proud of her husband for organising it. The event would even impact the English language itself, for the phrase 'spending a penny' originated here, arising from the need to pay one penny for the use of its public toilets!

Mary would spend three full days wandering around the show, enjoying what the papers called an unparalleled array of attractions, which included "an Amazon woman striking down the tiger that was trying to kill her horse, a Greek slave, stuffed birds and beasts, the Queen of Spain's jewels, a gold and silver chessboard, and Gulliver among all the little people". Mary made herself known, and received a mention in *The Times*: "It is not a small excitement which drags up humble provincials en masse from the country [including…] an old woman of 84 to travel on foot all the way from the Land's End…".

Mary's bizarre dream of reaching London on foot and seeing the exhibition had become an unlikely reality – and this news would soon be relayed back to her amazed family and acquaintances in Cornwall thanks to coverage in many newspapers. Mary Kelynack, unlikely as it seemed, was famous: not only had she made it to the Crystal Palace safely and in good health, she went on to be feted by the great and good of London society, and important people stepped forward to cover the costs of her accommodation and return journey to Cornwall. The working folk back in Penzance could not believe it.

The *Royal Cornwall Gazette* revealed to its awestruck readership that their humble kinswoman had spent much of Tuesday 23rd September living it up at The Mansion House with the Lord Mayor of London and his Lady Mayoress. The paper told how she was ushered into the building's Justice Room to meet his Lordship. Not overawed in the slightest, Mary seized the chance to press her claims for a handout: "God bless you! I never was in such a place as this. I have come up [to London] asking for a small sum of money. I am 84."

She then explained, for the umpteenth time no doubt, how she'd left Penzance five weeks earlier and ever since had been walking the 350 miles to the metropolis where she had "a little matter to attend to" as well as wanting to visit the Great Exhibition. She added that all her money had been spent during the journey bar fivepence ha'penny. The various officials and VIPs listening in were enchanted and highly amused by her boldness and charm, and the remarkable tales of her adventures. The Lord Mayor made her a gift of a gold one pound sovereign, telling her to take good care of it, as there were a good many thieves in London. Mary was overwhelmed and briefly lost for words, before bursting into tears and wailing: "Now I shall be able to get back!"

After this she spent time privately with the Lady Mayoress, chatting amiably and partaking of tea and hot buttered toast in the housekeeper's room. Marvelling at the delicacy of crockery and cutlery she'd never dreamed of encountering, Mary announced to great hilarity that this tea tasted "better than the choicest wine in the kingdom" although was quick to point out she hadn't touched any wine or alcohol in 60 years.

A report of her day at The Mansion House even made the columns of *The Times*, relating how she had made such a favourable impression it looked likely ample means would be provided by the charitable to enable her to return in comfort to Cornwall. She would be able to travel home in style and allow her overworked feet to recover.

Mary's pedestrian feat did not pass unnoticed in royal circles either. It was reported that a gentleman of Chelsea named Jago – a native of Cornwall – was so impressed with Mary that he got in touch with HRH Prince Albert about her, and as a result Queen Victoria was "graciously pleased to transmit, through Mr Jago's hands, a donation of £5". This was in addition to £2 already handed over by the Prince, who joked that the humble old lady had by now made herself "the most famous woman in all of England".

Mr Jago and his Cornish acquaintances based in London decided to use their influence to set up a Government annuity for the benefit of Mary – a payment of £20 "for our aged countrywoman" – but would need public subscriptions to keep it going. The *Royal Cornish Gazette* passed this news to its readers, agreeing to forward any sums sent in or left at their offices to the relevant people. Mary had done what her old acquaintances had thought a double impossibility – walking to London, and getting herself a pension.

Either side of her visit to The Mansion House, Mary spent time walking around the huge exhibition, apparently entranced and awestruck by what was on display and showing little sign of weariness. By now it had been open for almost five months, but daily attendance was still regularly exceeding 20,000. On September 29, the crowds numbered almost 70,000, including Mary herself, and *The Times* that day printed her temporary London address (12 Home Place, Crawford Street, Marylebone) in response to requests from well-wishers.

Given the publicity that attended Mary's astonishing walking feat, perhaps it was no coincidence that just hours after her second day at the Crystal Palace, three women and two men appeared in the open space to the west of the building and created a sensation by parading the new fashion craze from America – bloomerism.

Meanwhile, Mary's new friends in high places ensured accommodation for her in Crawford Street, Marylebone for the duration of her stay in London, and the gossip about her walk led to other unexpected encounters for the excited old woman. The accomplished sculptor Neville Northey Burnard heard about her, and asked her to sit for him. He was very taken with her "extraordinary character" and created a plaster bust as well as donating generously to the fund for her annuity and homeward journey. Burnard also hailed from Cornwall – the

Mary Kelynack walked from Penzance to London at the age of 84.

village of Altarnun on the edge of Bodmin Moor – and was by now a celebrated and award-winning society sculptor in London. He enjoyed telling the story of Mary's reaction to his request to create a bust of her: "She laughed heartily and said, 'yes, bless you my dear, for I'll always stick up for the Cornishmen as long as I have a drop of blood in my body,' thumping her table heartily." After she posed for Burnard at his Thames Street studio (having walked there) he insisted on returning her to Marylebone in a cab, but during the short journey this contraption was involved in a near-accident, coming within a whisker of overturning. Burnard said Mary reacted by promising never to travel this way again and to do every journey henceforth on foot!

Not long after his encounter with Mary, the artist Burnard's life would change dramatically. He is said to have turned to drink following the deaths of his daughter and wife, returning to Cornwall where he began sleeping rough before dying in Redruth Workhouse in 1878. In contrast, Mary's return home led to happier times. By the end of 1851 her unexpected celebrity status was well established in her home county. The printer and publisher Rowe & Son of Penzance began selling sheet music that included 'Mary Kelynack Polkas' and she went on to enjoy further adventures that included a trip to the Great

Industrial Exhibition of Dublin in summer 1853, where she again 'rubbed shoulders' with Queen Victoria and Prince Albert.

Her five-week walk to London had been a truly life-changing episode, and the columnist 'Native' would later reflect in *The Cornishman*: "She did little else for the rest of her life but wander about from place to place and relate her adventures in London. These relations brought her in small sums of money, but I never understood that she was ever tempted to give any of her money to the Blue Ribbon Army". The latter point about the BRA (the USA temperance movement) is presumably a thinly disguised reference to the fact Mary liked to take a drink or two during her final years. But after walking those 350 miles to London, who could begrudge her quenching what must have been an enormous thirst?

She died aged 88 in Dock Lane, Penzance on Wednesday 5th December 1855, and was buried in St. Mary's churchyard in the town. Her death came shortly after other members of the Kelynack family created their own headline news in the national press. There was clearly a strong spirit of adventure in the Kelynack DNA: her relative Job Kelynack, plus three Kelynack in-laws, went down in Cornish folklore as 'cockle-shell heroes' after they set off in a little 16-ton lugger called *Mystery* to join the Australian gold rush. Aiming for Melbourne 12,000 miles away, they beat the odds to arrive in just 116 days.

In the wake of Mary's journey to London, other tales of great walking feats by women occasionally emerged in the early 1850s. One concerned a married woman from Bourn in Cambridgeshire whose heroic and selfless lifestyle won her plaudits in the *Cambridge Chronicle* in summer 1854. To support her huge family of at least 11 children, the unnamed woman was said to have trekked 20 miles around local villages every single day for at least 30 years, trying to sell rush mats made by her husband. According to the *Chronicle*, she clocked up almost 200,000 miles on foot in this way before reaching the age of 60. The paper suggested any readers impressed with her efforts might like to send a small sum to her via the Bourn and Caxton Post Office, "so she can afford a pinch of snuff, one of her few remaining pleasures in life".

As a postscript to the Mary Kelynack story, it is only right and proper to pay tribute to another, lesser-celebrated veteran who also walked unfeasibly long distances well beyond her 80th birthday. Hardy northern lass Mary Wilkinson performed her own version of Dick Whittington's legendary walk from Yorkshire to London (minus the cat). She did it in a mere five days – at the grand old age of 90!

This astonishing feat cannot be accurately dated because it only received serious attention when local newspapers discussed the sketchily remembered details many years later. The maverick Mrs Wilkinson, said to be a prolific ale drinker, died in 1788, by which time she was apparently claiming to be 109 years old! Throughout her life she had been well known for her remarkable stamina and love of distance-walking. She would later warrant mention in several county history books as one of the longest-lived people to have come from the North Riding of Yorkshire.

Born in Lunedale in the Pennines, she settled in nearby Romaldkirk while still relatively young and from here was reported to have walked to London on several occasions as a young woman, covering the 260 miles or so in roughly four days each time. Average life expectancy across England around this time was barely 40 years, but when she reached the grand old age of 90 feisty Mary expressed a desire to see London one last time before she expired.

Defying the doubters in her local coaching inn, the Rose and Crown, she is said to have tied a keg of gin and a quantity of provisions on her back before setting off south, using the route that would later become widely known as the A1 and Great North Road. Her successful trek reportedly took her five days and three hours (an average of two marathons per day).

If the reports were accurate, Mary Wilkinson's long life spanned the reign of four different kings. Her many acquaintances put her longevity down to her long-distance walking and her love of beer. She was interred in 1788 in a stately tomb erected at the expense of fellow residents of Romaldkirk, who, it was said, absolutely revered her. Mary's final walk to London, at the start of her tenth decade, was later described by the *Northampton Mercury* as "an instance of vigorous age – not to be equalled by the boasting pedestrians of the present day". An excerpt from the epitaph inscribed on her monument reads as follows:

"Good God! Who lies here?
'Tis I, Mary Wilkinson, that lov'd good beer.
Look, gentle reader, as thou goest by,
109 years in this small compass doth lie:
Who, when alive, did many noble sights see,
And now in this small compass confin'd I must be.
I in my youthful days have gone through a vast [sic],
But alas! I poor foul am doom'd to my tomb at last,
To the great satisfaction of friends and relations,
Whose wish was that I'd departed before to their inclinations.

SIX

WITNESSING THE BLOOMER EFFECT

Female pedestrianism in both Britain and the USA began to show signs of taking off in the early 1850s. This was thanks in no small part to the advent of 'bloomers' which were not only proving a boon for the walkers themselves, but a major point of public interest and consequently a real crowd-puller.

The north of England showed the way again: early in the summer of 1852 the annual sports at Longtown, close to the Scottish border on the banks of the River Esk, even included a foot race specifically for women wearing bloomers (first prize £1)! Word of the blooming British scene evidently filtered across the Atlantic, for an American pedestrienne and bloomers fan – Miss Kate Irvine – decided to head for the old country intent on making an impact in front of a brand-new audience.

Miss Irvine had a point to prove. After an unhappy time in Massachusetts, where her integrity as a walker had reportedly been questioned, she wanted a fresh start and was willing to travel across the oceans to get it. It was a bold and opportunistic move for the times and came in mid-1852, several years before the Seneca Indian 'Deerfoot' made the same journey and dazzled the Brits with his brand of exotic distance-running.

STORY 7: KATE IRVINE – 'LIGHT AS AN ANTELOPE'
The first the British public knew of Miss Irvine and her arrival on these shores was when large posters and placards began springing up across the city of Birmingham in the unusually wet summer of 1852. It was confirmed the American walker would wear her bloomer costume for all appearances.

"The Yankee go-ahead mania is seemingly not confined to one sex alone," announced one newspaper, talking up Kate's visit as something of true novelty value. Keen to impress, Kate's first task, said the posters, would commence in mid-August and be 500 miles of walking in 500 consecutive hours with 500 US dollars at stake. The venue was the popular Royal Albert Gardens next to the Golden Cross Tavern in Aston, Birmingham. *The Era* warned that the folks in Birmingham would regard her with suspicion and might prove as "skeary" as the critics she had left behind in the States. However, public interest was intense and Golden Cross landlord William Jones rubbed his hands at the prospect of an upturn in business at his well-known tavern.

Kate, a tall woman, very chatty and said to be in her late thirties, evidently fulfilled her opening task with few problems. After a break of just over a fortnight, she was up for another challenge of 500 miles for which she would base herself at a pub and bowling green around six miles away in Dudley Road, Wolverhampton. Here the Albion Tavern landlady Ruth Williams and her three daughters took good care of their celebrity visitor who spent three weeks toiling hard to win a £300 purse. Her performance delighted the Black Country locals and the *Wolverhampton Herald* was highly complimentary about Kate's looks, particularly the way she "stepped splendidly as light as an antelope".

Encouraged by her reception in England's West Midlands, Kate sailed back to the United States over the winter of 1852–3, but returned the following spring ready for more mileage in England. This time she would tackle three events – with mixed fortunes – which involved appearances at Birmingham, Sheffield and Nottingham. She returned to the Aston Cross Grounds in May 1853 and was welcomed back by a good-sized crowd for the Thursday start of a challenge to walk 580 miles in as many successive hours. The grounds remained open night and day for spectators to come and go and monitor her progress. It is thought she succeeded comfortably, although details are scarce.

A few weeks later Kate took on 800 miles in 800 consecutive hours at Sheffield's Adelphi Gardens, better known to many as Barrack Tavern Gardens, for a wager said to be worth £500. A crowd of 300 watched her set off with a brisk first mile of 12mins 30secs. Attendances continued healthily as she progressed in impressive fashion – her general well-being monitored by the visits of "several medical gentlemen". One paper commented that her carriage was remarkably erect and she looked very sprightly, seldom betraying any wish for sleep. She again sported her bloomer costume – a straw hat, a jacket of thick black material, a light vest with bright buttons, a tunic silk shirt, and light boots. She maintained an extremely cheerful façade, chatting with spectators throughout. Her early miles were all completed at speeds of between 12- and 13-minute miling, and one paper pointed out: "For a woman, that is considered really wonderful". It was another superb effort and nobody seemed surprised when Kate completed the 800 miles in 33 days.

What would turn out to be her swansong in Britain occurred a few weeks later in November 1853. It was an unusual triple-header for a £100 wager, scheduled to start at Nottingham's Trent Bridge cricket ground, where she was provided with living quarters for the duration. She was to walk in full bloomer costume a total of 600 miles over three successive weeks, divided into three parts. The first 200 would be at the cricket ground, followed by around 36 hours' rest, then a further 200 at Birmingham, a short rest and ending with the final 200 at Wolverhampton. Admission to the cricket ground was set at tuppence and a good crowd waved her off in fine style, only for the whole show to be halted within a couple of days. The borough authorities had been made aware what was happening and decided it should be immediately prohibited in the name of maintaining law and order. It was a disappointing and frustrating end to Kate Irvine's British adventure, but she had certainly made her mark and helped establish the liberating bloomer costume as an important asset for lady walkers.

STORY 8: JANE DUNN – 'NO DECLENSION OF FLESH'

While the glamorous and extrovert American Katie Irvine was taking the Brits' breath away with her elegant walking and talking, a Lancashire mother-of-five began clocking up mileage in more prosaic fashion, determined to earn a crust for her hard-up family. The two women's style and background were vastly different, but crowds flocked to see both perform in their colourful and controversial bloomer costumes.

The Lancashire lass was a tailor's wife called Jane Dunn, who lived in humble Ravald Street, Salford, and had undertaken an epic bid to complete 1,000 miles in 1,000 hours for a wager of £500. She commenced on Saturday 7th May 1853, a few days after handbills had been posted around Manchester proclaiming the event at The Tea and Strawberry Gardens in Seedley Grove, Pendleton, just a few hundred yards from her home. Working-class folk came out in great numbers to watch, with the Gardens packed through Whitsun Week, and the lively atmosphere inspired her to maintain solid and consistent progress.

Jane found herself benefitting from good publicity in *The Era*, a relatively new weekly paper noted for its sports and theatrical content. Launched to cover general news, it had by now evolved into a paper that was regarded as invaluable for reviews and general theatrical information and gossip, devoting plenty of space to pedestrianism as well as assorted advertisements by and for actors, performers and theatrical companies. Discussing Jane's bold efforts in Manchester, *The Era* reported:

"She states her age to be 30, but without being charged with a want of gallantry, we may safely put her down as seven years older... She walks in the bloomer costume and in strong boots laced at the front. She is mother to five, the youngest being only five months. Her ambulation is very masculine, quite in unison with her person and if the midnight vigils have done their duty and she really does walk during the night there is little doubt of her completing the task".

During the course of proceedings, Jane and her helpers issued a public assurance that she was continuing to walk one mile every hour, throughout each night, even though very few people were around to check this in the small hours. If anybody doubted this, the gates of the public gardens were open at all times, they said. A reward of £5 was promised to any person detecting her sleeping when she ought to be walking. As well as a sign of her confidence, this was probably a thinly disguised effort to drum up publicity and extra interest during the quiet periods. Mr John Jones, the Gardens' proprietor, may have kept his gates open at night but apologised for not doing so on Sundays "to avoid the displeasure of the constituted authorities".

As the 42-day event dragged into June, brave Jane seemed to be dealing well with the lack of proper sleep, although it was noted she was making much more use of her parasol to keep the sun off her head, and was clearly going slower than earlier, although not visibly flagging or complaining. "There is no declension of flesh", the public was reassured, and sure enough she went on to complete the 1,000th mile on time during the warm middle weekend of June still evidently in good shape, clearly delighted with her success and ready to consider future engagements of a similar nature.

For a woman to match Captain Barclay's famous achievement was still quite a big deal and Mrs Dunn's efforts made news across the length and breadth of the land. Even the far-flung *John O'Groats Journal* highlighted the event, its pages giving Jane equal billing to hot gossip from Berlin that William Frederick of Prussia was about to announce his engagement to Victoria, the 12-year-old Princess Royal!

The American Miss Irvine was no doubt made aware of the emergence of a rival female attraction in Britain, and maybe this influenced her decision not to return to these shores the following summer (1854). Or perhaps Britain's involvement since March in the Crimean War was a factor in her thinking. For her part, Mrs Dunn was clearly no flash in the pan, for she was making plans to perform even more long-distance feats in her second summer as a pedestrienne.

In early July of that year, a married woman named Davis reportedly started a 1,000-miles-in-1,000-hours attempt in Sheffield, but is not thought to have succeeded. Over the same period, Jane Dunn headed a few miles out of home territory Salford, ready to repeat her efforts over the Barclay distance in front of the people of Merseyside and The Wirral. The chosen venue was an enclosure adjoining the Star Hotel, in New Chester Road, Rock Ferry, Birkenhead. As a young mother making a spectacle of herself, the usual heady mixture of adulation and condemnation awaited her. Disapproval came from the *Alnwick Mercury*, whose correspondent wrote: "We can only say that we think it is a great pity she has not something else to do." Although Birkenhead had recently opened the world's first purpose-built municipal leisure park, complete with attractive lakes and meadows, Mrs Dunn's performance didn't meet with the approval of civic dignitaries, and as such had to be held a short distance away in rather less salubrious surroundings.

Mrs Dunn emerged from the Star Hotel ready for action, colourfully attired in the bloomer costume, comprising a short blue jacket, pink Turkish-style trousers and a straw hat. The *Liverpool Standard* got up close and personal, noting she was a woman of short stature, no more than five feet tall, and "somewhat muscular" in appearance. It was becoming clear by now that not only did bloomers make the walking much easier for wearers, but the costume itself helped draw the crowds. And, on this occasion, as if 1,000 consecutive hours of one-mile walks wasn't enough, Mrs Dunn now took on an additional wager: for £20 she would complete an additional 140 quarter miles in 140 quarter hours directly after completing the Barclay distance. This meant she was in action for a grand total of 1,035 miles over the 44-day period ending Sunday 13th August.

It had been "a most dreary task" reported one paper, referring sympathetically to the repetitive nature of the beast – but there was little sympathy from certain other quarters. An anonymous letter writer to the *Liverpool Standard* had put pen to paper after barely a week of Mrs Dunn's perambulations, expressing outrage at such inappropriate scenes being played out in Birkenhead: "I shall feel obliged by your allowing me to ask, through the medium of your paper, whether there are no means of putting an end to the disorderly scenes taking place on Sunday at Rock Ferry in consequence of the exhibitions of one sort or another being got up in that locality".

Mrs Dunn needed the money badly and it would take more than this sort of complaint to keep her off the streets. Encouraged by her performance at Rock Ferry, if not by the "disorderly scenes" she'd caused, she accepted a new challenge later that summer in faraway Bristol, some 175 miles from home. This engagement was at the Victoria Tea Gardens in Horfield, Bristol, starting Saturday 2nd September 1854, once again involving full bloomer costume. By paying tuppence admission to the popular tea gardens, the public could watch Mrs Dunn walk 1,000 half miles over 1,000 consecutive half hours. Although it was half the distance of a 'Barclay match' the rest periods were half as long too, but Mrs Dunn showed great spirit and fortitude over the three-week period and completed the ordeal with little obvious discomfort. In fact, she was so untroubled that immediately after finishing she launched into another challenge – 150 quarter miles in 150 quarter hours. She finished this on schedule too, meaning she had totted up just over 537 miles in a period of 23 days, with no rest period lasting longer than 15 minutes. It was an astonishing display of strength and stamina, and most onlookers seemed to agree she deserved every penny she made.

Mrs Dunn's decision to perform away from her home territory appears to have been a wise one. While she was in action in Birkenhead and Bristol, two other 1,000-mile treks involving a female walker were arranged on the outskirts of Manchester – and both encountered difficulties involving local police and magistrates. The troubles began when police inspector Walker showed the city's mayor and magistrates a placard that stated a Miss Annie Foster was planning a walk of 1,000 miles in 1,000 consecutive hours at the Ash Inn Gardens, Eaton Norris, a task that would involve "a violation of the Sabbath". The magistrates instructed Insp.Walker to inform the landlord of the Ash Inn, James Turner, that Foster was not allowed to walk for a wager on his premises on a Sunday – and if permitted to do so his license would be immediately suspended. This was apparently ignored by Turner and Miss Foster's walk duly went ahead that summer. Turner was summoned to court, accompanied by his solicitor Hudson, and claimed he was bound by a financial agreement to permit the walking and had been unable to put a stop to it –

although he had done everything in his power to do so, after hearing it was regarded "distasteful" in the eyes of the court. Mr Hudson said his client had never been formally told that walking on the Sunday was disapproved of by the magistrates. There had been no disorderly conduct, he added, and the entry fee of tuppence was for people to view the pleasure gardens and had nothing to do with the female walker. The magistrates found Turner guilty and fined him 40 shillings (nearly £200 in modern terms), including costs. If such conduct was repeated, they said, his license would be revoked and he would face a hefty penalty for taking admission money. They warned other proprietors of tea gardens in the Manchester area they would be treated similarly if these pedestrian events continued.

A few weeks later the annual licensing day in Manchester was told that senior police officer Mr Little opposed the issue of just one public house license renewal – that of Mr Perrin of the Victoria Gardens on Mottram Road. Solicitor Hudson appeared again, this time representing several of Mr Perrin's neighbours who opposed renewal, claiming the pub's activities had become a nuisance to the neighbourhood. Officer Little said a female pedestrian had recently commenced walking 1,000 miles in 1,000 hours in the pub grounds and the landlord knew she should not walk on the Sunday. When visiting the pub himself, officer Little had difficulty getting through the huge throng of people assembled on a footpath nearby who were spectating. They had destroyed neighbouring fences and there were a number of underage youngsters in the pub grounds, some boys playing dominoes, music and dancing going on, and various other activities that disturbed the pub's neighbours. The license application was duly rejected.

*

Although the public image of female pedestrianism had hardly been improved over the course of 1854, there was certainly evidence that the advent of bloomerism and the realisation that money could be made was encouraging newcomers into the sport. Hence it is safe to say these women were not participating with any particular 'Corinthian' spirit. There were no championship titles or medals to be won – earning money was the name of the game.

Derek Martin, researcher of sport and leisure history at Manchester's Metropolitan University, confirms that around half a dozen female pedestrians between 1852 and 1854 walked at least 12 Barclay matches between them. He points out: "They were strictly money-making affairs, promoted by proprietors of pubs, hotels and pleasure gardens, who already provided music, dancing, fireworks and the all-important refreshments. The women were an additional attraction. For the admission fee of tuppence, [spectators] could observe a woman walk, at a set time every hour or half hour, day after day, week after week. Contrary to early Victorian ideology, stamina and endurance were not exclusively male attributes and as interest in [male pedestrianism] waned, several working-class women broke into this very male world, mainly in the North of England."

Meanwhile, variations on the Captain Barclay feat took place in a number of towns for the first time. In Dublin, a Miss Dobson, billed rather bizarrely as 'The Only Female Pedestrian in the World', walked 1,000 miles in 1,000 hours in Victoria Gardens beside the River Liffey and opposite the King's Bridge (now Sean Heuston Bridge). Chasing a purse of £200, she rattled off a trouble-free 500 miles in 500 hours – stopped for a doctor called Stevens to examine and pronounce her in perfect health – and went on to finish the job. The pleasure gardens were said to have been transformed by this event into "quite a fashionable lounge" where officers from the nearby Collins Barracks and other sporting types waited anxiously, fretting over whether they were about to win or lose heavy sums thanks to little Miss Dobson.

Later in the year another American, referred to as 'Mrs Macarte', followed the precedent set by Kate Irvine, arriving by boat from the USA to have a crack at 1,000 half miles in 1,000 half hours on British soil. Thought to have been connected to the 'Macarte Monster American Circus' touring Britain at that time, Mrs M dressed in full bloomer costume, and carried out her task with showbiz flair in a crowded meadow adjoining Milbay Barracks in Plymouth. The *Northern Whig* and other newspapers were not impressed however, and derided her efforts as "a useless exploit".

Women's involvement in pedestrianism then appeared to slowly dwindle in the second half of the 1850s, probably due in part to the fading of the hysteria towards bloomerism, and partly because of the continued opposition from the authorities, the newspapers and the middle classes. Although many aspects of life were changing fast across the land, Britain was evidently not quite ready to accept the sight of women earning money from sporting displays in public.

The odd event would still crop up here and there, almost exclusively in industrial, working-class towns such as Neath in South Wales. This was a market town expanding fast with the arrival of the industrial revolution and new iron, steel and tinplate foundries. In the late summer of 1855 a Scot, Miss Isabella Melrose, walked 500 half miles in 500 half hours and 500 quarter miles in 500 quarter hours at a green spot close to the Cross Keys pub and Neath's railway station. A big crowd watched her on the Mera Field, which would later be known as Corporation Field, home of the Neath Fair, and then developed into the attractive Victoria Gardens. It was said Miss Melrose already had a '1,000-in-1,000' success under her belt from the previous year. She gained grudging admiration from the *Bicester Advertiser*: "She is a representative of the female fast school. She would make a good postwoman".

A few months later, and a few dozen miles further up the Welsh coast, a woman called Margaret Jones, said to be in her late fifties, flew the flag for the Principality with a highly impressive long-distance trek. On a chilly Monday morning in January she set off from the town of Aberystwyth to walk the 80 miles or so inland to the Llangollen Road station, situated on the new railway line which had opened between Shrewsbury and Ruabon. The indomitable Margaret reached her destination late on the Thursday afternoon in good shape, following four days of footslogging, onlookers marvelling at her determination and pluck: "This is very good pedestrianism for an old lady bordering on 60, especially as the road is mountainous and the season is winter", reported the *Wrexham Advertiser*.

That sort of praise – fairly restrained though it was – was quite a rarity for the time. It was certainly in complete contrast to the press treatment in early 1857 of American pedestrienne Mrs Adeline Shaffer (a.k.a Mrs Dallison or Miss Hall) after she issued what was described as "an Amazonian challenge" to male pedestrians Trainor and Kennovan. Adeline, in her late twenties, would be joining Trainor at the 400-mile point of his 1,000 miles in 1,000 hours walk in California, dressed as "a Highland lassie, exhibiting herself to the wondering millions". After keeping pace with Trainor she then planned to go for 1,000 half miles in 1,000 half hours, followed swiftly by 1,000 quarter miles in 1,000 quarter hours on her own, finishing off this series with a match against Kennovan at a distance of his choosing. It sounded outrageously ambitious and the *San Francisco Bulletin* was among those highly dismissive: "Mrs Shaffer is pretty widely known, and few will be surprised at her new freak. When a woman is so lost to the decencies of her sex and humanity as to make such a ridiculous and dangerous exhibition of herself, she cannot expect any sympathy".

SEVEN

'WALKING MECHANICALLY IN A HIDEOUS DREAM'

The general fuss over 'bloomerism' died down after a year or two in Britain, although the costume did remain *de rigeur* for most pedestriennes. The mould had been broken and women no longer needed to feel afraid or ashamed to wear trousers in public.

The pedestriennes clearly shared Amelia Bloomer's drive and determination to try and improve a woman's lot. And it wasn't just about women's rights or usurping male prerogatives. As author Don Chapman reflects in his 2017 book *Wearing the Trousers*:

"In an age before social security it was a case of [a pedestrienne] finding the cash to feed her family. Women who wore bloomers for work did so for equally down-to-earth reasons, not high-minded principles. They were more practical than skirts for many occupations and – as growing numbers realised – for sporting activities too."

So bloomers weren't going away, but during the late 1850s female pedestrianism itself seemed to be fading out of fashion. Occasionally a British woman would feature in an event in America – one example being Miss Lucy Reynolds of Liverpool who was named as one of those racing in Jackson Square, New Orleans in 1858. Via the cotton trade New Orleans forged close links with Lancashire which perhaps explains how runners from both Liverpool and Manchester were known to have competed in America's deep south in the 1850s.

However it wouldn't be until 1864 that any pedestrienne achieved real prominence again in the UK, and the resurgence of interest was all due to the efforts of a Yorkshire-born woman who had returned home having earlier emigrated to join the Australian gold rush.

STORY 9: MARGARET DOUGLAS – GOLD-DIGGER HITS PAY DIRT

The small, slim-built woman who single-handedly ended female pedestrianism's fallow years of the late 1850s and early 1860s was mother-of-seven Margaret Douglas, a native of Doncaster with a colourful backstory.

Margaret had been among the thousands who flocked to Australia to join the post-1851 'gold rush'. There she quickly found work, becoming a paid entertainer in the saloons and music halls that sprang up in areas known colloquially as 'The Diggings'. Her husband also found work in the entertainment business, describing himself as a pantomimist, although his working life over the years was increasingly affected by ill-health.

Having a large family and sick husband had created pressure on Margaret to keep the family above the breadline and although the Australian colony of Victoria was 10,000 miles from home, it had represented a way out of their problems when they took the plunge. Some of the major diggings in Victoria were in the Ballarat area and this is where the family headed.

Before gold was discovered in 1851 only 80,000 lived in Victoria, but more than 600,000 people arrived over the next ten years or so. More than 150,000 of them were women – wives and daughters hoping desperately that Australia could change their lives for the better. Many would regret the trip, finding life uncomfortable and just as difficult as the one they were attempting to escape from. Most of the huge overseas influx were British, and among the most determined to make a success of things was diminutive Margaret Douglas.

The status of women as subordinate to men, combined with Victorian morality, means women are not as well represented as men in historical records. Therefore first-hand accounts from English women who had travelled to Victoria were unlikely to have been available to Margaret, meaning she was stepping very much into the unknown. However, she will have probably deduced for herself that the physical labour of mining and the 'looser rules' of colonial society meant active women like her could prosper. If she hadn't known beforehand, she will certainly have noted on arrival that plenty of women attracted to the goldfields were doing well as shopkeepers, businesswomen and entertainers. She slotted herself into the latter category.

Her plan to tackle pedestrianism bore fruit in the late 1850s. During a period lasting less than two years (1858–60), and by now a mother of seven and approaching her 40th birthday, Margaret is believed to have completed four different challenges of at least 1,000 miles in 1,000 consecutive hours. The first of these was in Ballarat in 1858, followed by another at the Hippodrome in Melbourne in March 1859, and then seven months later at the Black Swan campground in Sandhurst, just outside Melbourne. As we shall see, she then topped these performances with 1,500 miles in 1,000 hours in the Olympic Theatre in central Melbourne during the first few weeks of 1860.

Detail is hard to come by, but we know that during October 1859 she occupied the Long Room of the Black Swan Hotel in Sandhurst, where one reporter noted that after the first week or so of her 1,000-mile trek Mrs Douglas was proceeding at a speed that only a good, experienced male walker could match. In common with other attempts, her routine was to commence roughly 15 minutes before the hour, finish one mile before that hour expired and begin the next at one minute past the next hour. This gave her an interval of roughly 90 minutes to rest before the next outing. It was stated she was averaging about 14 minute miling most of the time although at least once on the first Saturday night she dipped under 12 minutes. It was pointed out that in her previous Melbourne performance the logbook recording her progress was signed by several spectators who were "gentlemen of respectability and standing" and these included Sir Henry Barkly, the Scotsman who was Governor of the colony of Victoria, and the Hon John O'Shanassy, the Irishman who was Premier of Victoria. These two VIPs attended at different times and were only too happy to verify the fairness and legitimacy of Mrs Douglas's performance.

While Mrs Douglas was in action at the Black Swan, there was a simultaneous attraction at the Montezuma Theatre, around 70 miles away in Ballarat, where the Australian Beverley Howard was trying to steal Margaret's thunder by achieving something a little harder – 1,250 miles in 1,000 hours. This meant walking one mile and a quarter during every single hour for 42 days, each session involving 45 laps of a path of about 50 metres. 'Tedious' doesn't begin to cover it!

The *Ballarat Times* and *The Mudgee* expressed astonishment at Miss Howard's feat, recalling the "utterly helpless state" to which male pedestrian star Allan McKean had been reduced when he recently attempted the shorter 1,000 miles in 1,000 hours. For here was a young woman not only avoiding the need to "creep or crawl" but covering the final stages very briskly, with her body not bent but leaning forward, arms and legs moving freely and no perceptible heaviness of step.

The local papers did mention, however, that Miss Howard had occasionally swayed to one side or the other but always recovered quickly thanks to the railings of the stage on which she walked. It was also pointed out that during the course of the ordeal she appeared to have lost a considerable amount of weight. Remarkably, Miss Howard even threw in an extra three laps at the end, which was either an extravagant gesture of bravado, or maybe to cover the possibility of any minor errors by the lap-counters.

After Douglas and Howard had finished their separate epic efforts at around the same time, Mrs Douglas's camp decided to strike while the iron was hot and issued a challenge to the younger walker's representatives. The Yorkshire woman had by now adopted the mantra "there is no such word as fail" and under this headline she published an offer of a match of 1,500 miles in 1,000 hours in Melbourne – or, if this was not accepted, would walk against any other man or woman in the Australian colonies over 1,000 miles in 1,000 hours. Despite the hot Australian summer having now arrived, Miss Howard accepted and the agreement was made for £200 per side, to take place at the Olympic Theatre in Lonsdale Street, Melbourne. It would last six weeks and commence just before Christmas 1859.

Mrs Douglas must have marvelled at how Yuletide in Australia contrasted with the equivalent holiday season back in grimy Doncaster. But she would have to miss much of the seasonal fun in her new hometown Ballarat, for her walk would already be underway when the streets filled up on Christmas Eve, crowds shopping for the next day's dinner, or for 'boxes' to give in memory of the season. The main road would be enthusiastically decorated, the fruiterers, butchers and poulterers and hotelkeepers dressing their frontages in colourful fashion. Turkeys, ducks, and chickens would be seen and heard throughout the town, either huddled in cages awaiting selection or in transit to the oven of the purchaser. Generally Christmas Day itself would be fairly quiet, with most people marking the day with a church service and quiet family gatherings. Much of the excitement and frivolity was saved for Boxing Day when many made their way to the theatre, sports events, or picnics. Pedestrianism, shooting matches, horse racing, quoits, sack races and even climbing the greasy pole were all on offer to entertain the goldfield folk on Boxing Day.

Margaret would miss all this. After saying goodbye to her loved ones she headed the 50 miles or so into central Melbourne to tackle an event that would see her and Miss Howard striding along, day and night, for six hard weeks. Periods of sleep would never last much more than 75 minutes until the task was finished in early February 1860. Admission for this extravaganza was set at one shilling and the match billed as a "Female Pedestrian Pete" that was truly novel, unparalleled and extraordinary.

The Olympic Theatre would be their home for 42 days, a remarkable landmark known locally as 'The Iron Pot'. It was a prefabricated iron building that had been shipped in from England to occupy the corner of Lonsdale Street and Stephen Street (now Exhibition Street). It had opened for business in 1855, but within a year or two found the competition tough and by the time these two pedestriennes arrived the building was said to be "falling prey to gloomy silence, and irreverent bats". A few months after the walk it would be sold and converted into Turkish baths. Its heyday had been short and sweet. However, 160 years later, the site is still a place of entertainment, now occupied by The Comedy Theatre.

The building was temporarily transformed to host the two walkers, and this extraordinary event got underway with plenty of public interest, despite garnering very little publicity in the press. One rare update, early in the new year, reported that 415 miles had been covered by both women at a certain point on the evening of Wednesday 4th January. Both looked confident and determined to finish even though the tiny figure and short strides of Mrs Douglas contrasted sharply to that of the more athletic-looking Miss Howard. Those watching with no knowledge of Mrs Douglas's previous exploits (at least two 1,000-milers completed) will have been sorely tempted to place bets on her failing to match her younger opponent. But as the end loomed neither woman seriously faltered and *The Age* newspaper carried an advertisement announcing in matter-of-fact fashion they would complete their "self-imposed and unheard-of task" the next evening at around 10pm on Friday 3rd February.

Despite Mrs Douglas's splendid performances, the opportunities to gain further fame and fortune from walking apparently dried up after this in Victoria. It would be several years before she was heard of again, after making the bold decision to head back to England for a spell, to try her luck performing in the land of her birth.

It would prove a very timely move. The vogue for distance-walking by bloomer-clad females had faded in the early 1860s in Britain partly because the country got its fill of exotic pedestrianism and theatrics from the touring performer Louis Bennett, better known as Deerfoot, a native American of the Seneca tribe. Deerfoot left the American civil war behind to cross the Atlantic in the summer of 1861, preceding Mrs Douglas by three years. But they both found an England that presented opportunities for someone bold and talented enough to seek a living from pedestrianism. The English taste for gambling was alive and well (despite Lord Liverpool's recent ban on lotteries) with betting popular on foot racing, prize-fighting, wrestling, cock-fighting, bull-baiting, dog-fighting and horse racing. All the gambling and drinking provided a release from the grim reality of life in London and elsewhere. Deerfoot and Mrs Douglas would no doubt feel homesick for some aspects of the nations they left behind, but the potential to earn money was a powerful pull.

It is not clear exactly how long Mrs Douglas had been in Australia – it was probably ten years or more – but both she and Deerfoot had stepped off their passenger ships to encounter a nation basking at the height of its powers in the world. England was a fast growing mix of great prosperity and abject poverty, rolling green countryside and sprawling industrial expansion. By now it had become the first nation in the world to have most of its population living in towns. Immigration from Scotland and Ireland and a staggering rate of reproduction meant England's population had soared to more than 18 million. Both Deerfoot and Margaret Douglas were strangers as far as London was concerned and must have found the city a fascinating but vaguely threatening place. Their first impressions are not recorded, but we can glean an idea of the *zeitgeist* from the recollections of French philosopher Hippolyte Taine:

"I recall Haymarket and Strand at evening, when you cannot walk 100 yards without knocking into 20 streetwalkers, some of them ask you for a glass of wine, they say, 'It's for my rent mister.' The impression is not one of debauchery but of abject, miserable poverty. One is sickened and wounded by this deplorable procession in these monumental streets. It seemed as if I were watching a march-past of dead women". According to another account: "In many [London] streets the city dwellers seemed lonely and unregarded, trudging along crowded avenues with heads lowered, carrying their burdens patiently enough but isolated nonetheless. This was the paradox of Victorian London – there was an appearance of energy and vitality in the mass, but the characteristic individual mood was one of anxiety or dependence".

It is understood Mrs Douglas set sail from Port Phillip, Melbourne, in March 1864 on the wooden clipper ship *Anglesey*, a 1,150-ton vessel built in London in 1852, which was part of the Blackwall Line of Packets and captained by Edward Jones. It is recorded as arriving at East India Docks in London on Wednesday 22nd June, with £48,500 worth of gold included in its cargo. The new arrivals stepped off the ship to find an England suffering from drought over recent months, a situation that would last all summer.

Having disembarked, Mrs Douglas had barely a month to prepare for what would be the biggest occasion of her walking career thus far. News of her achievements in Australia had by now reached sporting impresario George Martin, the man who managed Deerfoot's recent tour of Britain. Martin got together with Mrs Douglas's agent James Ellis and arrangements were thrashed out for her to attempt 1,000 miles in 1,000 hours in the spectacular surroundings of the enormous Alhambra Theatre

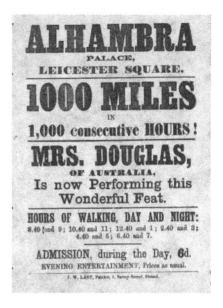

of Variety in London's Leicester Square, a building often referred to as the Alhambra Palace, or Royal Alhambra. Her reward for completion would be £500 (something akin to £30,000 in 2021 terms).

Ignoring the fact she'd been born and raised in Yorkshire, Martin made great play of Mrs Douglas's Australian connections when promoting the event. He knew full well from his experience with Deerfoot that a performer from faraway shores would hold great appeal and novelty for the British paying public.

Margaret must have felt immense pressure and nerves over what lay ahead at the Alhambra. A huge life-changing financial reward was on offer and she had to chase it in awe-inspiring and somewhat intimidating surroundings. Could this tiny but determined woman rise to the occasion again and repeat those gritty displays she had managed in Australia?

By now this theatre had been open nearly seven years, initially as the Royal Panopticon of Science and Art, now converted into the Alhambra Palace with a circus ring installed. In 1860 it was adapted into a Music Hall (London's biggest) with the addition of a proscenium arch and a stage. It became a model for the Parisian music halls where the famous *Folies-Bergere* emerged. Interestingly, the Alhambra building also housed one of the few bars in London that would accept women without the escort of a man. This bar would be described as "the greatest place of infamy in all London". The leading ladies of the stage would descend underground after their performance, where they would flirt, eat oysters, drink Champagne and make eligible acquaintances. When it was later gutted by fire in 1882, the site was said to be cursed because it had housed such debauchery. It would eventually be demolished altogether in 1936 and subsequently rebuilt as the Odeon, Leicester Square.

For Mrs Douglas's epic trek, the Alhambra had erected a raised, circular wooden boardwalk around the main hall, upon which she would have to walk 19 times to clock up a single mile, each lap a shade under 100 yards. She would set off at roughly 20 minutes before the hour and chief timekeeper George Martin, after the 19th lap would bellow out loudly "time up!" at which point Mrs Douglas would stop and rest on a sofa for a few minutes before starting the next mile just as the new hour started. With her short stature and quick, small stride, her planned average pace was 16 minutes per mile. If timed correctly this would allow her around 80 minutes of uninterrupted rest after each of the second miles. Sometimes, when her walking slowed slightly, the rest period could drop to 75 minutes or so. As always, the major hurdle to overcome would be the deprivation of proper sleep, but Margaret had shown she could handle this. The dangling carrot of £500 was a massive incentive for a working-class woman.

As had become *de rigueur*, Martin issued a public statement to dispel the doubters. Mrs Douglas would be walked a mile each and every hour of the day and night, he said, and special arrangements would be made during night-time hours to accommodate any sceptics who needed confirmation she carried on after midnight when most spectators had gone home. Admission to see her daytime walking was set at sixpence (a shilling for a balcony seat), with 'normal' prices in the evenings when the other entertainments also took place. Her competition for the attention of the paying customers would include the Italian Operatic Company, Bond from the Cirque Madrid, Watkins – the Greatest Juggler in the World – and Charles Burton the Transformation Dancer. Spanish gymnasts the brothers Risareli were scheduled to join the fun but were absent due to being mysteriously detained in Paris.

Mrs Douglas soon warranted mention in the theatrical and sporting newspaper *The Era* that had by now established a large readership broader than just the showbiz crowd. Its 64 closely printed small-type columns allowed the claim they were "the largest newspaper in the world". Events at the Alhambra enjoyed good coverage within their pages and one writer was enchanted by the efforts of Margaret after she set off at breakfast time on Tuesday 2nd August

1864. He pointed out that when Captain Barclay walked this distance ("a man with well-proven powers"), many thousands of pounds, at almost any odds, were bet against him achieving it, but now at the Alhambra was this "slight and delicate woman… with a gay and smiling face and the light, elastic step of a wild fawn, going merrily over the apparently endless course with as much ease and *sang froid* as the gallant Captain would have shown walking down Pall Mall!". The correspondent pointed out that he and other *Era* staff had assisted in the first week with timekeeping and other duties and all had become fully convinced "the gallant and plucky little lady" would finish successfully.

Word of the event went around the globe. *The Mercury* told its readers in Tasmania that Margaret was a wiry little woman of 42 years, dressed in gaudy costume with knickerbockers and ankle boots. She walked briskly but seemed a little tremulous in her gait and had completed half her task on schedule, looking as fresh and buoyant as when she started three weeks earlier. Another paper mentioned the fact that when the crowd was large enough to warrant it, Mrs Douglas would make a point of walking to the edge of the stage area to take a bow at the end of each mile.

The colourful columnist 'Flaneur' of the *Otago Daily Times* tried to imagine the ordeal as seen from Margaret's point of view: "She walked briskly enough, but seemed, I thought, a little shaky in her gait… Of all the strange ways to make money, surely this is one of the shadiest. Fancy pacing round and round that ghastly building every hour for six weeks? What different phases she must see it in – at night filled with noise and tobacco smoke, and hundreds of gazers – then empty, but reeking with the fumes of the bygone entertainment; not a creature awake but the watchers, and the timekeeper, and the wiry little woman on her never-ceasing round, and then the day with its weak, half-admitted light and its occasional droppers-in! How she must know every inch of the walls. Or does she never look at them, never sees them, but walks on mechanically in a kind of hideous dream?".

The musings of 'Flaneur' made absorbing reading, as did those of Arthur Munby, a philanthropist, barrister, civil servant and poet, who made a special trip to the Alahambra to study Mrs Douglas. Munby is said to have had a particular academic interest in working-class women, particularly those who performed hard physical labour. He was known to wander the streets of London and other industrial cities where he approached working women to ask about their lives and the details of their work, while noting their clothes and dialects. It all went into his journals, excerpts of which were later published by Abacus and author Derek Hudson. Munby's diary entry for Tuesday 9th August 1864 reads:

"Dined after a warm bath; and went for ten minutes... to see one Margaret Douglas walking 1,000 miles in 1,000 hours. A boarded stage... has been built around the centre of the hall, high enough aloft to exhibit the performer: and upon it the woman was pacing as I entered. A stout, sturdy little woman of 43; dressed in a wideawake, a loose white shirt, a red kilt with a pair of knickerbocker breeches underneath, and red stockings, no petticoats. Round and round she went, like a wild animal in a vast cage; walking about four miles an hour; taking no notice of anyone... She has been walking for a week: a monotonous, almost ludicrous performance: shows powers and last, however, and that is why I went to see it".

Mrs Douglas scurried past the 500-mile halfway stage towards the end of August and the *London Evening Standard* discussed the fact that earlier many folk had suggested "the whole affair was a trick" – but endorsed the organisers' efforts to allow any sceptics to view the whole performance, day and night, and judge for themselves. However, the *Standard* seems to have tempted fate, for shortly after mentioning the "trickery" allegations, there were sensational developments on Friday 5th September when, completely out of the blue, the whole performance ground to a halt.

After completing no fewer than 824 miles, all of a sudden "the game was rudely squashed", reported one paper. After 34 days of toil, Mrs Douglas had apparently been thrown out on her ear, without remuneration and not a word of apology. The so-called 'Undersized Lady from the Diggings' could not believe it.

Initial rumours suggested Mrs Douglas had quit of her own volition, but it soon became clear the Alhambra management had ordered the stoppage and there would be no restarts. With only eight of the walk's scheduled 42 days remaining, the proprietor had, without prior warning, had the boardwalk dismantled during one of Mrs Douglas's rest periods. A notice was quickly slapped on the wall outside the theatre informing the public it was all over. Gossip indicated her efforts had not been generating enough admission money for the management's liking, and this was why the plug was pulled, but it seemed a strange course of action so close to the finish. The *Evening Standard* sought out the full story and they reported the next day:

"Disappointment was felt last night over sudden cessation of the labours of Margaret Douglas... the greater part of her task was performed and everyone looked forward to the completion of it as a certainty and not a little surprise was expressed last evening when the temporary erection put up to enable her to perform her undertaking was found removed and the following notice posted in the hall: 'The proprietors beg to give notice that in consequence of Margaret Douglas having failed to fulfil the conditions of her engagement, her walking is discontinued'. [Her] friends, however, declare there was no failure on her part and the matter is likely to create not a little discussion and amusement in a court of law. The crowd was entertained last evening by the two brothers Risareli, unrivalled gymnasts".

The day after the stoppage, Mrs Douglas, accompanied by her agent James Ellis, appeared before local magistrate Robert Tyrwhitt, seeking advice on how to resolve the situation. The Marlborough Street court was told she had walked night and day for the past five weeks, seven days a week, accomplishing 824 miles, but at about 5pm the previous afternoon, when about to commence another mile, Mr Wyld Jr. – nephew of the Alhambra proprietor – approached and instructed her to cease walking while he took apart the wooden platform and put an end to the match. She wished to know what she should do under these circumstances, as Mr Wyld's conduct had been a source of great [financial] injury to her – and not completing her task would hamper her chances of finding future engagements. Mr Tyrwhitt advised her to consult a solicitor who, if there had been any breach of agreement, would know how to proceed. She thanked him and stood down.

Mrs Douglas and her support team talked through their options and soon decided the only way she could have her day in court and try for compensation would be to pursue the matter of the timekeeper's logbook, which they claimed had been seized from them by the Alhambra management during the walk. And so, a week later, Thomas Wright, cashier at the theatre, appeared before the court after receiving a summons for detaining the logbook, described as the property of Margaret's agent Ellis. Lawyer Mr Lickford was hired to represent Ellis and Mrs Douglas, and Mr Dillon-Lewis defended Wright.

Mr Lickford explained to the court that a summons had been taken out to recover the book which had been originally provided by Ellis as part of agreed procedure to keep a record of every mile walked, to be signed by timekeepers engaged for that purpose. He said Mrs Douglas had complied with the terms of the agreement and walked a mile within each hour, but theatre manager Mr Wyld had only paid one week's money. They had applied for more of the money due while Mr Wyld was attending the office of the Sheriff in Chancery Lane

– but he had refused and alleged the agreement had not been fully complied with, even though entries in the book had been made by his own employees. However, a further £20 was paid to Ellis and an agreement made to allow time for the next payment.

The court then heard those events had been quickly followed by the dismantling of the platform which prevented Mrs Douglas fulfilling her part of the agreement. Magistrate Mr Tyrwhitt interrupted to order the two solicitors to keep strictly to the subject of the seizing of the book. Lickfold said the book was his client's property; it had been purchased by him and he'd never parted with his rights to it. On Monday 1st September, after again being refused money owing to them, Ellis told Mr Wyld he was changing the record-keeping to a new book. Wyld insisted the old book should not be taken away and when Ellis attempted to do so, was obstructed and assaulted by Wyld. Ellis said the book was valuable because it contained private entries and he valued it at £200. Dillon-Lewis, for the defendant, said this amount was beyond a magistrate's jurisdiction and therefore this must bring an end to the proceedings. Mr Tyrwhitt agreed and dismissed the summons, saying only a superior court had the power to produce the book via subpoena.

Tyrwhitt then asked Ellis if he was claiming that Mrs Douglas had managed to walk a mile every hour as agreed, and this was confirmed. The magistrate seemed to have doubts about this, remarking that the feat of Captain Barclay had been "a trifle" compared to what Mrs Douglas had allegedly done at the Alhambra. He said Barclay had been a powerful man and a noted pedestrian while this lady was a small person of no remarkable powers. Ellis objected to this, saying that Mrs Douglas had previously proved her capabilities by walking 1,000 miles in events in Australia. Application was then made by Mr Lickford for a summons alleging assault during the confrontation over the timekeeper's book. Tyrwhitt turned this down, as well as a request for costs. The magistrate was clearly not inclined to sympathise with Mrs Douglas and friends, whatever approach they tried. They were not about to give up, however.

A fortnight later the same cast of characters were back in court again. This time Thomas Wright, theatre cashier, was in the dock answering a summons for assaulting agent Ellis. Solicitors Lickford and Dillon-Lewis again represented the respective parties. Ellis said he resided in Dean Street, Soho and on the night of Friday 9th September went to the Alhambra only to be refused admission. Mr Wright was called to the door and seized Ellis by the collar, threw him against a wall and pushed him into the street. Ellis denied having threatened to create a disturbance. Dillon-Lewis called three witnesses to rebut Ellis' story, and said he regretted occupying the time of the court with all this, but was only doing so because Ellis's solicitor had made misrepresentations which had gone public and damaged the reputation of Mr Wyld Sr., the theatre's proprietor. He emphasised that Wyld had given orders for the dismantling of the walking platform only after finding Mrs Douglas was deceiving the public. The trio of witnesses were called and their evidence persuaded Mr Tyrwhitt that an assault had been committed on Ellis, but only a minor one. He concluded no real violence was used and the defendant Wright was therefore fined a nominal five shillings and costs.

It meant Mrs Douglas came away from court under suspicion of deceiving the public in some way, although nobody had apparently stated publicly the exact nature or basis for this allegation. It was certainly not the first case of a messy ending to a pedestrian event, involving the local police courts, and it wouldn't be the last.

To save her stay in England from becoming a financial disaster, it was clear Mrs Douglas needed to perform another high-profile walk before making plans to return to Australia. Before long agreement was reached for her to commence another 1,000 miles in 1,000 hours, this at the American Opera House in Crosshall Street, Liverpool later in the autumn of 1864.

This grandly named venue was in fact a circus arena built of wood and canvas which had opened two years earlier as Bell's English and American Hippodrome and Circus, later renamed Myers' Circus, and then more recently became the American Opera House. It stood on a spot just yards from what would later become the legendary Cavern Club of Beatles fame. The management ran a tight ship and vocalists appearing there would be fined if they did not adhere to rules such as the wearing of white kid gloves. Mrs Douglas's hourly perambulations would be along an irregular platform around the building, requiring 14 laps for each mile. After her frustrating experience in London, she was good and ready for the challenge and set off on Tuesday 24th October with an opening salvo of a brisk 12mins 30secs for the first mile. Attendance was generally good and a number of heavy bets were said to have been placed on the outcome. After the Alhambra debacle, things were looking up again. One reporter at Liverpool described her "a little, somewhat wizened but muscular woman, who has the utmost confidence in her ability to complete her task".

Her confidence proved well placed and by Wednesday 7th December the *Evening Standard* was able to reassure the public: "Each successive mile was witnessed by persons who have attested its fair performance, and the remarkable woman has gone through the arduous feat with astonishing freshness and vigour".

During the final mile, the Opera House echoed to the rafters with cheering from a good-sized crowd, despite the lateness of the hour, and, several times Margaret stopped walking to perform a little celebratory dance. She looked almost overcome with joy and relief. The crowd loved it and an immense noise greeted her finishing after a final mile that took around 13 minutes, great cheers ringing out. In the delirium of the moment she declared she could have walked at least 200 miles more and would be willing to undertake a challenge of 1,400 in 1,000 hours at some point. After the disaster in London, Margaret and her helpers were no longer on the brink of financial ruin – and she could return to Australia a relieved and contented woman. News spread of her Liverpool achievement and as there seemed no reason to suspect any skulduggery or that the achievement was not genuine, it meant the tiny figure of Margaret Douglas had kick-started female pedestrianism again in Britain.

EIGHT

THROWING OFF THE SHACKLES

The sojourn back in Britain of Doncaster gold-digger Margaret Douglas lit a fire that spread across Northern England. Her efforts in London and Liverpool received heavy publicity and inspired other women to try their luck at this 'walking for a wager' game.

After a few false starts, women's pedestrianism appeared in 1864 to be throwing off some of the shackles holding it back. Before long around half a dozen other British-born women were performing extraordinary feats on a reasonably regular basis and, once the Americans sat up and took notice of this, the die was cast. By now the women's rights movement was making some important advances and the female walker looked to have gained a better level of acceptance than her vilified sisters of yesteryear.

One notable character who was inspired into action after reading of Mrs Douglas's efforts in the papers was fellow Yorkshirewoman Mrs Emma Sharp. A strong, highly active and extrovert woman, Emma had no experience of distance-walking whatsoever, but within a week or two had brushed aside her ironworker husband John's protests and arranged a solo six-week walk at a Bradford sports ground.

STORY 10: EMMA SHARP – GUN-TOTING HEROINE

Emma Sharp was impulsive, single-minded and not a woman to be messed with. When this 30-year-old mother-of-three decided to walk 1,000 miles in 1,000 hours in home-town Bradford, there wasn't a cat in hell's chance of anybody persuading her otherwise. Her husband did his best, but the lady was not for turning.

Emma confirmed later on that her motivation for tackling this huge challenge had come when she read about Margaret Douglas journeying all the way from Australia only to be foiled in her 1,000-mile challenge in London.

"Wah, I could do that mysen!" Emma is said to have cried, the look of horror on husband John's face only serving to strengthen her resolve: "Yes, I can do it, and what's more I will," she insisted. It was not idle talk. Emma was supremely confident about having the necessary stamina to repeatedly walk as long as necessary, surviving on severely limited sleep. She clearly wanted to test herself and try something different to spice up her humdrum life. And the money would come in handy too.

John – a mechanic at the huge ironworks in Bowling Back Lane in south-east Bradford – was aghast. He was cringing as he pondered the embarrassment and humiliation that lie ahead if his wife carried off this absurd idea and made a spectacle of herself in public. His mates wouldn't be getting just a glimpse of his wife prancing around, this would last six weeks! His biggest fear was the anticipated reaction of friends and workmates when presented with concrete evidence of who 'wore the trousers' (literally) in the Sharp household. John couldn't persuade Emma to drop her plan, and it would later emerge that during her walk he often retreated to a dark corner of the Quarry Gap hotel bar for hours on end, searching for anonymity and a place to hide.

Emma was convinced she could achieve the 1,000 miles in 1,000 hours, despite no experience or understanding of organised pedestrianism. She was not even fazed when the event was hastily scheduled to take place within only 10 days of her first hitting on the idea. She was persuaded to get things underway quickly as the summer was almost over. Leaving it too long would risk weather conditions less attractive for both walker and spectators.

Bradford was at this point the world centre of the wool trade and expanding fast. It was the archetypal 19th-century 'coaltown' and among the most seriously polluted places in the British Isles. But this had been the case throughout Emma's lifetime and breathing in what the foundries and mill chimneys spewed out was perfectly normal to her. Six weeks of continuous outdoor exercise in blackened, dirty air probably never struck her as a bad idea.

With her husband washing his hands of the whole affair, Emma enlisted the help of a neighbour when applying to the local Peel Park Gala Committee with a view to their undertaking management of her proposed walk. She wanted it to be in Peel Park, Bradford's first public park, which had opened in 1853 and was named after former Prime Minister Sir Robert Peel. However the committee turned her down, citing the fact they had no power to charge for admission to the park for a six-week period. Undaunted, Emma turned to Alf Hardy, landlord of the Quarry Gap Inn in Dick Lane, Laisterdyke, conveniently positioned less than a mile from her home in Mount Street. The entrepreneurial Hardy was happy to put on the event at his grandly named City Sporting Grounds, which were attached to his pub. The arrangements were quickly thrashed out, with Emma promised a good share of the gate money.

The Quarry Gap Inn – still standing more than 150 years later, having been converted to a café – was in 1864 a classic example of a Victorian-era pub becoming an unofficial centre for the staging of sporting events. It was only three years old and one of around 130 pubs in Bradford, but stood out as a leading venue for staging sporting events, a trend evident in many towns now that the police were intent on driving sports away from open land and off the public streets. The idea of staging money-spinning events appealed to many landlords who had a field or gardens attached to their pub. It was a development that marked the birth of commercialised sporting grounds.

The first large-scale sport on the 14 acres next to the Quarry Gap had been horse racing, although this was in decline by the time Alf Hardy took over in February 1862. The ancient bat and ball game of 'knur and spell' attracted large crowds here, as did cricket, including one memorable match between a team of Greenwich pensioners, all minus an arm, against a team of Chelsea pensioners, each with only one leg. Pedestrianism events staged here included the nine-year-old Australian boy John Day walking five miles in under an hour for a purse of £200, and the appearance of Native American runner Deerfoot – in full Seneca costume – along with his travelling circus of huge marquee and portable track.

The date of Emma's walk was set for mid-September 1864 and one of her main tasks in the short build-up was to find an outfit she could wear. By now the bloomer fad of the early 1850s had begun to fade, but its legacy was the fact that Emma and other women walkers could wear something resembling trousers in public without being regarded as an exhibitionist or freakshow. This was significant in terms of a woman's right to wear whatever she deemed to be practical, comfortable and appropriate. It was quite a breakthrough, although still regarded as scandalous by the less liberal sections of society. Emma, unsurprisingly, opted for 'proper' trousers for her walk – not the flamboyant Turkish-style bloomer costume, although her outfit did turn out to be every bit as colourful and eye-catching.

Rather than the bloomerists, Emma was probably influenced by the many 'Pit-Brow Lassies' of Northern England – working women whose job was to sort and grade coal as it was brought up from the mines, and who wore trousers every day for convenience and warmth while doing their work.

Emma's bold choice was a dazzling man's outfit of red and black checked coat, along with what some newspapers called 'inexpressibles' or 'bifurcations' rather than use the term 'trousers'. She also sported a white waistcoat, laced boots, turned-down collar and scarf, and carried a cane walking stick. The only concession to her own sex was a large droopy straw hat, upon which a white feather and other adornments were pinned. She cut an impressive figure in this outfit, described by one observer as "rather above middle height and possessed of a light and active frame".

However, husband John was not among those showering her with compliments and encouragement. He was a bluff, hard-working Yorkshireman who was plainly baffled by his wife's sudden need to make a spectacle of herself. They had married in 1852 at Bradford Register Office when both were aged 19, Emma already five months pregnant with their first child Isaac. John was then a fitter, living in Sticker Lane, Bowling, and Emma a millhand from just round the corner in New Houses. Emma had been born in Hull in November 1833, one of five children of Mary and Isaac Stephenson, an engine tester. Father Isaac died aged 36 when Emma was 12 and this appears to have precipitated the family move to the Bradford area.

Emma herself would have three children – Isaac, Emma and Abe – between 1852 and 1861. They set up home in Mount Street in the Laisterdyke district, John working at the Bowling Ironworks, just a five-minute walk away. Although eight-year-old Isaac was listed in the 1861 census as a schoolboy, it is known that two years earlier he'd joined the many other children of that era pushed into factory work to help boost family income. At the age of just six, Isaac had started at his dad's workplace, his first job being to chip clay from the iron ore before smelting. Compulsory attendance at school wouldn't come about for another 20 years or so, when the Elementary Education Act quietly overrode the Factory Acts in 1880, dramatically reducing the amount of time young children were allowed to spend in mill and factory work.

Emma's descendants of today say she learned from childhood to be a strong character who would stand up for herself, and they tell tales of her getting up to major mischief as a young girl. One escapade involved climbing up Mitchell's huge mill chimney, and another prank saw her clamber up to rooftops in New Lane to place slates over every chimney pot, before retiring to watch the occupants emerge from their front doors coughing and spluttering due to smoke inhalation. On one occasion, to avoid being caught, she hid behind a wall opposite after doing the deed, not realising she had been spotted. The watcher stayed silent and only revealed this to her many years later, long after she had achieved fame as a pedestrienne!

Emma's great-great-granddaughter Kathy Nicol believes the initial idea to do the 1,000-mile walk was not based on Emma wanting to win a wager or having a strong desire to make money, it was more a case of simply relishing the challenge (ditto the mill chimney episode!): "She seemed to want to put women on the map!" says Kay.

Her chance to do just that would commence on Saturday 17th September 1864. A straight course of 120 yards was laid out and railed off in the sportsground next to the Quarry Gap. Emma's routine would be to make her way down from her room in the pub, accompanied by her loyal little dog, and set off at around quarter-to the hour, traversing 14 times up the path and 14 back, and without stopping walk back to her room, at which point she would have done a total of two miles within two separate, consecutive hours. Each 24 hours would see this happen a dozen times for the next six weeks.

As usual the betting fraternity was attracted to the ground and some good sums were reportedly invested by those predicting a non-finish. The odds were long for good reason – Emma had no background in pedestrianism and had taken on this challenge at short notice with little time to prepare. She was certainly not a highly trained, knowledgeable athlete. But those who knew her were confident: Emma Sharp was no quitter.

Her progress generated great interest in the district, during both day and night sessions. By now it had dawned on Emma that a good payout was in prospect from her share of the gate money, although she was reportedly nonplussed by the frenzy of betting that had gone on. It is said she had little or no understanding of the worlds of gambling and professional sport, and hadn't even realised that people might want to stake money on the outcome of her efforts. The proprietor of the Quarry Gap, on the other hand, knew exactly what was involved and urged Emma to simply concentrate on putting on a great show to keep the punters returning and make sure she didn't peak too early as this would be a long slog.

From the start she looked well in control and any anxiety or nerves were kept well hidden. After completing 250 miles it was becoming clear large numbers of locals were interested in the event and were attending regularly. Alf Hardy would have been delighted to see this become one of his most successful promotions yet, and he no doubt laid on one or two extra entertainments to add to the fun to keep the punters coming in and spending their hard-earned money. Emma duly passed the halfway mark on the morning of Saturday 8th October looking confident and walking easily. Most of the time her little dog scampered alongside to keep her company. There had been no major dramas to speak of and both looked well capable of finishing.

One account of the walk concluded that by now the only real hazard potentially preventing success might be the antics of the betting fraternity: "These were her only enemies". Once she had passed halfway without injury or accident it started to look likely some of the gamblers could lose big sums and a number of them might become intent on spoiling her chances with unsporting behaviour. With this in mind, a public notice was published by Alf Hardy on October 13th, requesting all visitors to behave in an orderly fashion.

Sharp suit! Emma Sharp and her dapper walking costume.

Despite the risk of unpleasant scenes of skulduggery, the *Bradford Observer* was able to report that around the time Emma passed the 600-mile mark "it was clear that no fewer than 5,000 females were watching from the enclosure". Unless this was a gross exaggeration then Emma had surely created some sort of record? Until this day, only the handsome 'noble savage' Deerfoot had ever attracted significant female interest at a pedestrian match before. A lot was made of the high number of women who turned out to watch Emma. Although some of this support will have been spontaneous acts of feminine solidarity, a big factor could have been the reduced admission fees for women.

The scheduled finish date was Sunday 29th October and as the last dozen days ticked slowly by the weather did Emma no favours. It was often stormy and very wet, but with tremendous resolve she was always able to 'come up to the scratch' and performed at roughly the same speed throughout. However, in the final week it was plain for all to see that major fatigue was setting in.

From both a physical and emotional point of view, the last thing Emma needed at this stage of her ordeal was interference from spectators, particularly when it amounted to assault. However, a number of deliberate efforts to block her progress were made. It was said certain spectators tried to trip her up, tamper with her food and disturb her rest periods. These were desperate men, willing to go to great lengths to prevent the loss of stake money. Emma told one interviewer she was even jostled by a man who attempted to bring her down with chloroform.

On top of this, somebody managed to surreptitiously spread red-hot cinders across the track. Emma was not burned but her dog's paws did become blistered and the poor pooch had to drop out of the walk, leaving its mistress to battle on alone. Kathy Nicol, Emma's great-great-granddaughter, says this nasty episode has gone down in family lore: "I don't know the name or breed of the dog. It was only ever spoken of as the poor little thing that dropped out of the walk with blisters on its feet because men threw red-hot cinders in Emma's path in an attempt to stop her."

Emma was no shrinking violet and was never going to give in to this sort of intimidation, and managed somehow to fend off the various attacks in spirited fashion. However, things reached a point where her helpers needed to lay on some extra protection to prevent the whole thing ending in catastrophe. Thus it came to pass that during the final night's walk spectators were greeted by the grim sight of a policeman with loaded musket briskly striding ahead of Emma, who was herself brandishing loaded pistols in both hands. There was a high number of police at the ground by this point, sanctioned by Frederick Grauhan, the Chief Constable of the Bradford City force, who had responded quickly and positively to the request for help.

Over the final 24 hours of walking an estimated 18 officers, most of them disguised as ordinary townsfolk and tradespeople, wandered around the grounds keeping an eye on things. Even so, Emma said later she had needed to fire her two pistols skywards between 25 and 30 times in order to fend off possible troublemakers.

Despite the event being due to finish around dawn, for several hours beforehand all roads leading to the Quarry Gap were thronged with pedestrians and vehicles, reports estimating more than 20,000 had come out to see Emma's big finish. It was also reported around 100,000 had descended on the City Sporting Grounds over the six-week period in total.

Emma's final lap, the last of 14,600 over 42 days, was completed amid a wonderful atmosphere, the crowd drowning out the triumphant strains of the Bowling Brass Band who led her in. The band had been playing since around 4am to entertain the many pre-dawn arrivals. The *Bradford Observer* marvelled at "the vociferous cheering of an immense concourse of spectators". They added that Emma had appeared to have gained weight during the task, and quoted her as saying she would never repeat something like this. Her share of the gate money was estimated to be more than £500 (roughly equivalent to £64,000 in modern terms).

She finished with a flourish at a quarter past five on the chilly late October morning precisely as scheduled. This signalled the start of the day's grand gala of celebrations – a firework display, cannon fire, the roasting of a whole sheep, and of course more music from the brass band. Alf Hardy had organised some lively events in his time as Quarry Gap landlord, but this topped the lot. Emma, although telling everyone within earshot she would never again attempt 1,000 miles, still had enough energy to walk up and down the track several more times later in the day in a short solo victory parade.

Her plan was to remain at the inn for at least a week in order to generate a little more business by selling her 'cartes de visite' [photographic calling card] to her many new admirers. This souvenir had been produced by local photographer William Marsden, a near neighbour of Emma, from his studio in Sticker Lane. Listed as a 'beer seller and photographic artist', William must have been very grateful for the work, having recently been declared bankrupt.

Enterprising Emma certainly had no immediate money worries. It was widely acknowledged she had walked away with at least £500, and years later her granddaughter Ann Land would claim the figure was probably double that. Whatever the true amount, Emma Sharp would never again have to settle for a tedious, poorly paid job in a mill like thousands of her contemporaries in Northern England. Before the walk she had been earning roughly 10 shillings a week at the local mill, now she was returning home to life as a rich woman.

Organiser Hardy did well out of the walk too, of course, and he promised another cash beneficiary would be the Bradford Infirmary, whose windfall was no doubt much smaller than Emma's but no less welcome.

The only physical problems Emma is known to have suffered during the entire event was soreness from swollen ankles during the early stages, an issue that was remedied without difficulty at the end of each session. She had been able to sleep well throughout, albeit in very small chunks of time, and it was said she slept almost continuously for several days after it was all over.

Once the dust had settled, it wouldn't be long before Emma upped sticks and used her new-found wealth to provide the family with a better home, swapping Mount Street for Dick Lane. John continued as a mechanic at the ironworks, but by the end of the 1860s had gone completely deaf in one ear, a common ailment among those working in similar environments.

Meanwhile, Emma kept to her word about never attempting a long walk again and made use of part of her winnings to take over a grocery shop in Napier Street. The 1881 census lists John as a grocer and Emma as a shopkeeper, although at the point it was taken she was living, probably temporarily, at her sister Sarah Taylor's house in Newton Heath, Manchester, presumably on an extended visit of some sort. For a spell she took on some additional work, as a baker for the Bradford Co-operative Society in Hirst Street, of which she was an active member behind the scenes. This did not last long, and during 1882 she and John left the grocery world behind to set up a rug-making business – their speciality being 'stuff hearth rugs' – based at the Perseverance Works in Thornbury, Bradford. The business would become well established, surviving well into the 20th century. The couple would move house again, to occupy 68 New Lane, adjacent to the factory. Several grandchildren would work for her in the rug mill over the years.

Emma and John had a shared interest in collecting and accumulated many specimens of antique china, paintings and other curios. Not long after John died in early 1902, Emma raised a considerable sum to support her life as a widow by having this collection auctioned. She was by now a very well-known Bradford celebrity, and in the summer of 1904 was visited by author James Parker, who would feature her prominently in his book *Illustrated Rambles from Hipperholme to Tong*. She was by now 71, but retained very clear memories of her famous feat of pedestrianism and provided Parker with some nuggets of information that hadn't been included in the sketchy newspaper reporting back in 1864.

She continued overseeing the rug-making business well into her seventies, by now living with son Abe and his family. When somebody paid her the intended compliment of having become "a grand old lady", Emma responded in spirited fashion: "Get out, that's nowt, I am going to live to 100. I am now enjoying the comfort [of the money I made] but I must be careful, because if I live to be 100 I may need it all!" She added that apart from "a gammy leg" she was feeling as well as ever, and her tongue was especially active, for it "never keels"!

As her 80th year approached, she decided to make one final house move, albeit a very short one, purchasing the property next door at No.66 New Lane. This was the imposing 'Woodman House' – which was still standing in 2020. Her presence here represented the final confirmation, if it were needed, that here was a working-class girl who had made good.

Emma lived through the 1914–18 war, dying on September 3rd 1920 at the age of 86 and was buried alongside her husband. Great-great-granddaughter Kathy Nicol has located an interesting cutting from the early 1900s which reflects on how Emma had been a strong and admirable woman who would have made a formidable suffragette if that movement had been alive when she was young and active.

Emma differs from most other British pedestriennes in that she found no need to carry out further walks in order to make money, meaning her period in the sporting spotlight was brief, yet she still avoided the slide into obscurity and hard times. Her wise investments, and her bold and courageous nature saw to that.

NINE

THE NORTHERN NEW-WAVE

The north of England established itself as the region at the forefront of women's walking in the mid-1860s. A new spark of interest had been lit in the industrial areas, West Yorkshire and Lancashire in particular. After a few barren years, a good number of high-profile events would be staged during a 12-month spell covering 1864–5. The Mesdames Sharp, Somers, Wood, Brook and Gawthorpe were five of the main protagonists of this renaissance.

Once again, the newspapers, broadly speaking, failed to treat the new wave of interest with approval. Female pedestrianism continued to be condemned for lacking integrity and decorum. The *Bradford Observer* concluded: "Everything that cunning can devise is produced to feed the love of the sensational… to give a pungent flavour to the almost slake [sic] dish of female pedestrianism". Although the critics were now forced to accept the fact women walkers were proving well capable of performing over long distances and timespans, the timekeeping and lap-counting at their events remained issues that left the sport open to abuse.

STORY 11: MISS ELIZABETH SOMERS – 'REMARKABLY GOOD LOOKING'

Twenty-two-year-old Elizabeth Somers, a native of Exeter who had moved north to Bradford, stepped up to undertake a 1,000-miles-in-1,000-hours attempt at George Martin's impressive 16-acre athletics ground and pleasure gardens known as Royal Oak Park in Oldham Road, Newton Heath. It was a well-organised event and a wager of £100 was offered that she would succeed. The grounds were adjacent to a large pub that gave the new park its name, and the place was regarded as "one of the most superior sporting arenas in England, if not the world" (*Manchester Guardian*), able to accommodate crowds of 20,000. It was all stage-managed by George Martin, the man who masterminded Margaret Douglas's London performance.

Born in southern England, Martin, was a well-travelled athletics promoter and trainer, who had spent his teenage years in London as an apprentice shoemaker. Here he had become immersed in sporting matters, particularly following his marriage to Alice, the daughter of James Holden ('the great stakeholder of Lancashire pedestrianism'). He quit his trade to take charge of The Plasters Arms in Manchester's Deansgate, from where he trained and represented a stable of young pedestrians. Father to six children, Martin competed regularly himself until 1858 and then became a promoter. A snappily dressed if rather rotund man, he was energetic and canny and took to his new role like a fish to water, showing good business acumen. Taking British runners to perform in the USA and returning with the erstwhile unknown Deerfoot would be just one of his groundbreaking ventures. He helped Manchester become a pedestrianism hotbed, turning the Royal Oak pub grounds into a major arena.

Martin invested heavily in the Royal Oak venue, creating ornamental gardens with statues, sculptures and other exhibits. The facilities included a 651-yard cinder track, wrestling arena, bowling green, trotting course and grandstand – not forgetting shower baths that could be used by the public for a penny a time, and a four-wheeled wagon (carpeted inside) that served as a portable dressing room. In the case of Miss Somers it served as a bedroom for the 1,000 periods of rest she would be taking over the 42 days. In circus and travelling show argot these wagons were known as 'living carriages'. The *Ulverston Advertiser* explained that its wheels were "inserted into the earth" for stability, and inside was a fire-grate, a bed, and various pieces of furniture for Miss Somers. Maybe even some of the magic soap which *Bell's Life* reckoned was an essential for all pedestrians: "Rub your feet with yellow soap before you put on your socks or stockings, and take your work easy at first".

The wagon might have been small and draughty, but was probably a more cosy prospect than some of the icy garrets, upstairs in a pub, that other pedestrians were often expected to use. The track was situated near the main road between Manchester and Oldham, renowned as a chilly part of the world, and Miss Somers will surely have been glad her accommodation was positioned so close to the track now that winter was on its way.

Promoter Martin will have noted the recent success of Emma Sharp and had full confidence in Miss Somers emulating her, even though she was also not an experienced multi-day walker. She did claim, however, that she had often walked 42 miles on a single day, and could move at a brisk rate if necessary, having once covered 21 miles in four hours on St Thomas' Grounds in Stanningley, east of Bradford. Elizabeth was said to be aged 22, standing 5ft 5ins tall and weighing a little over nine stone. She admitted she had been "spurred up" to tackle this challenge after hearing of various other attempts by women in Yorkshire.

Her big event started early in the afternoon on Tuesday 25th October 1864 with a very composed-looking Miss Somers setting off in what was described as "a light male costume" topped with a straw hat and aided by a thin walking stick. She will have been relieved at the weather being fine following the rain and high winds of a couple of days earlier. She now had the soul-destroying task of walking 4,000 times up and down a 440-yard straight-line track normally used by quarter-mile runners, with flags marking each end. But she looked undaunted and in the early days most of her miles were timed at around 15 minutes each.

At night lamps were lit alongside the track to help both Miss Somers and any spectators who attended after dark. George Martin, who always rolled his sleeves up and got heavily involved in the events he promoted, repeatedly told the local papers that she was a confident lass, well capable of finishing, and he would pay a reward of £50 to anybody who could prove she had not walked a mile in each hour. The flames of the lamps would surely enable even the most sceptical of onlookers to see she was not cheating by taking extra sleep in her comfort wagon. The only times during the six-week event that the public could not be present was "during the hours of divine service on Sundays".

The thorny issue of monitoring a walker's progress at night in this type of event had by now become a regular topic of discussion. There had been little argument over the authenticity of Captain Barclay's claim to have completed his task, but many of the less well-attended attempts since then had ended with doubts being cast over whether the walker had done their full stint during the night-time sessions. The *Ashton Weekly Reporter* fuelled the fire by suggesting Captain Barclay was the only person who deserved true credit for accomplishing 1,000 miles in 1,000 hours, as although many others completed the distance, the public had no faith in timekeepers or lap-counters. The *Western Daily Press* also implied a level of disbelief as far as women were concerned: "This feat was once considered a herculean task, but recently several women are at least reported to have accomplished it."

It seems that sometimes these doubts over authenticity might have influenced the level of coverage an event would get in the newspapers... over the years a number of walks would be publicised early on, but then inexplicably fail to get a mention during the final climactic stages. One paper went so far as to suggest that the well-organised nature of Miss Somers' walk at Newton Heath meant that if she lasted the course, it was likely to be the only *bona fide* effort since Captain Barclay. Certainly the well-lit and well-attended track here meant Miss Somers and her helpers would have little chance to cut any metaphorical corners if they were so minded.

The Sporting Life gave its attention to proceedings here, taking a close look at Miss Somers herself and concluding: "She is somewhat prepossessing in appearance, and walks exceedingly smart for a female". And the *Derbyshire Times* managed to get even more up close and personal: "She is remarkably good looking, and, as she walks, casts her eyes on the ground. The biceps and pulmonary muscles appear to be well developed from what can be seen through her [style of] dress, which is that of a modern swell in morning costume". Having set off briskly, the young woman's progress over subsequent weeks was seen to be smooth and largely untroubled. One report after a fortnight's walking talked of large crowds both day and night and no signs of fatigue. Elizabeth passed the 360-mile mark by noon on Wednesday 9th November and her steady progress continued. The newspapers evidently lost interest as the days and weeks passed by without incident, and although detail is scant it is thought Miss Somers successfully made it to the bitter end.

In the wake of the walk she relocated from her Bradford address to Jack Lane in Hunslet, near Leeds, along with three younger brothers, all textile workers, and her stepfather John Harper, a labourer and widower. There appears to have been no return to ultra-walking, with census records describing her as the family housekeeper. A few years later Elizabeth would set up home just around the corner in Whitehouse Street, Hunslet, after marrying Leeds forgeman John Richmond.

Meanwhile, having overseen this event, promoter George Martin began suffering serious health issues. He reportedly had to battle "mental afflictions" and was admitted to Wye House, a private asylum high in the Buxton hills which claimed to provide treatment for insane people from the higher and middle classes. He was later moved down to St Martin's Workhouse Hospital in London where he died suddenly in October 1865 reportedly suffering from "derangement in deplorable circumstances". Martin was aged just 39 and his widow and seven children had to be helped out by his many sporting associates as his £2,000 legacy all went to a creditor, the spirits merchant Joseph Fildes. Around a year after Martin's death, the Royal Oak grounds would be sold on.

*

The crowds at Newton Heath for Miss Somers would be matched in West Yorkshire over the same autumn when a Mrs Thorn – a mechanic's wife from Bowling – completed 1,000 miles in 1,000 hours at Bradford. An "immense throng" was said to have greeted the local heroine on her final mile.

Barclay match 'mania' was certainly red-hot in Bradford by late 1864 and one of several other local women to dip her toe into the water was a Mrs Mary Wood. She travelled westwards across the Pennines to the town of Burnley to attempt 1,000 miles in 1,000 hours at the Glen View Gardens. These grounds had recently come under the control of new proprietor Webster, and he was introducing a number of innovations to attract more local townsfolk. He took a punt on Mrs Wood and she certainly didn't disappoint in terms of pulling power. After roughly 10 days of walking Webster reported more than 4,000 people had been to see her in action. It was said a considerable sum was staked on the event, and to keep interest high Mrs Wood – described as "low in stature and of a very pleasing appearance" – agreed she would appear in a brand-new costume on certain days. The good folk of Burnley evidently found it fascinating and showed up in good numbers.

However, this sort of turnout was not matched when a 45-year-old walker by the name of Mrs Brook took on the same 1,000-mile challenge on the track behind the George and Dragon Inn in the busy village of Honley, just south of Huddersfield. Interest from the public was patchy throughout, but Mrs Brook duly started at 12.45, lunchtime on Monday 7th November 1864 and throughout the rest of that month brief reports emerged that she was ploughing on according to plan and remaining in good health.

Mrs Brook had a good track to perform on, but the lack of interest meant it was mostly a lonely affair. Without being able to invest the same sums as George Martin, George and Dragon landlord Joseph Haigh had nevertheless created an impressive track on what was previously the cricket field in Honley. For around four years most of the best male pedestrians would be attracted here and the place flourished. The sport's top names – John Neary, James Nuttall, William Lang *et al* – all trained or raced on the George and Dragon track, but sadly its heyday would be short-lived. At some point in 1864 the pub was sold to mill owner William Brooke, one of the biggest employers in the Huddersfield area. Acting on behalf of the previously ousted cricketers, Brooke was a teetotaller who disapproved of pedestrianism's sleazier aspects, and before long he would close the pub and track, the former becoming a working men's club that did not serve alcohol. It seems Mrs Brook's fine performance, which only pulled in reasonable crowds on the Sundays, was probably the last pedestrianism at this once thriving venue.

By the time this doughty woman completed her task on the Monday before Christmas 1864, it was clear her remuneration would be poor. There were no wagers, and she'd been relying purely on taking a proportion of the meagre gate money. To rub salt into her wounds, the *Huddersfield Chronicle* called the whole episode "an undignified and useless feat". Perhaps it is no surprise the name of Mrs Brook would not be heard of again in a sporting context.

STORY 12: EMMA GAWTHORPE – THE NO-NONSENSE GREENGROCER

Lancashire lass Emma Gawthorpe deserves her place in the pantheon of pedestriennes, but will be chiefly remembered not for athletic excellence but for being confronted in two different events by gun-brandishing lunatics. On the second occasion her assailant was charged by police with intent to inflict grievous bodily harm.

Emma was born in 1835 in the South Yorkshire village of Thurgoland, arriving with twin sister Anne. Her large family of nine boys and six girls subsequently settled in the Dukinfield district of Stalybridge. By the time Emma was 16 she was working as a cotton weaver and living at home with mother Mary Ann and father George, a corn miller. During the year of her 30th birthday her talent for pedestrianism would see her break out of the daily grind that trapped many young women near or below the poverty line. The extra earnings from walking would enable her to establish herself as a greengrocer, running her own business on the outskirts of Manchester.

Her first taste of serious pedestrianism came in 1864 at various Yorkshire locations. Her local fame soon spread and by early 1865, supported by a small circle of friends and helpers, she undertook a challenge involving 1,000 miles in 1,000 consecutive hours on the main cricket field in Stockton-on-Tees, more than 100 miles from home. The weather was appalling, with severe gales battering the NE coastline the night before the walk started, temperatures then plummeting overnight so that Emma was greeted on the start line on Saturday 28th January by a severe frost and icy pathways. Youngsters around the region gleefully found ponds to skate on, but Emma's careful walking still attracted a steady stream of spectators after commencing at noon.

The field, nowadays known as Ropner Park, resounded to their hearty cheers, but the noisy support was not universally endorsed, the *York Herald* commenting: "If she receives a sufficient amount of patronage to make [this] speculation a paying one, we can only say there must be a great dearth of popular amusements in Stockton".

Stockton was a fast growing industrial town of around 20,000 people at this point, with heavy engineering providing employment to many of those who turned out and handed over threepence to watch Emma in action. She walked in what was still widely described as "male attire" on a ground recently set up specifically for pedestrian events and partly covered for the purpose. One account states she accomplished her task eight hours early, completing 1,000 miles by 4pm on Saturday 11th March. Little else was reported of the event, although it would emerge later that a gun was brandished at Emma at one point in a bid to frighten or injure her and therefore save certain gamblers from losing a small fortune. The ploy didn't work and the 1,000-mile club had a new member.

It would be a full year before Emma Gawthorpe hit the headlines again, tackling another 1,000-miler near to home, at the Mona House Grounds in Bolton Road, Elton, near Bury. The venue was formerly the Wellington Gardens, recently revamped by new proprietor Matthew Weston. Emma was performing for a wager of £200, and set off on the warm afternoon of Saturday 14th July 1866. The Gardens were open day and night with admission threepence per adult, with children half price during the day and not allowed in after dark. Weston insisted the gardens be cleared every evening around 9pm at which point parties wishing to enter or re-enter to test the accuracy of Emma's walking would be admitted at sixpence each, to be paid to the watchman. The venue was only five minutes' stroll from two railway stations, refreshments were available and public interest was good. The place looked smart and attractive and Weston was keen to point out in his adverts that any visitor "plucking or otherwise injuring the shrubs or flowers in the park will be rigorously prosecuted".

Although the list of British women who had by now completed 1,000 miles in 1,000 consecutive hours was slowly growing, the *Bury Times* commented that this was still "a somewhat novel feat – at least for the softer sex". They reported that Emma was dressed in a light cloth suit of clothes and a grey wideawake, garments which allowed her to perform the allotted mile with apparent ease [and] with quick firm step".

Her progress was indeed smooth and largely untroubled – far too smooth, in fact, for the liking of the unscrupulous types who had placed big bets on her not succeeding. It seems the first serious problem Emma encountered on the entire walk did not present itself until Sunday 12th August, some 29 days after starting with nearly 700 miles already under her belt. It was an incident that left her fearing for her life and in a badly shaken state.

It occurred around mid-morning just as she set off on her sixth and final lap of the course in order to clock up another mile. Her agitated brother-in-law John Brierley, who appeared drunk, suddenly appeared from nowhere pointing a gun at her. The weapon jerked and made a loud crack, apparently misfiring. With Emma reeling back in shock and the place in uproar, Brierley quickly applied a match to the nipple of the gun in a ham-fisted attempt to get it to fire, but fortunately failed. The gun was wrestled from him and Emma regained her poise and kept walking as the shouting and chaotic scenes gradually died down.

The police arrived and 30-year-old Brierley was removed to appear before magistrates at the Bury Petty Sessions the following morning. With much money resting on the outcome of the walk, Emma was determined to press on – even though she would be needed as the key witness in the court proceedings. Remarkably, her solicitor Mr Anderton was able to persuade the senior magistrate to hear the case at precisely 12.30, so that she could complete one of her miles, get herself to the court, and then be released in time to do the next mile. It is tempting to view this changing of the court schedule to suit a mere pedestrian as perhaps a small sign of a growing acceptance among the ruling classes that not everybody in the sport was a dishonest scallywag deserving of no respect.

And so, at precisely 12.25 on the morning of Monday 13th August, Emma bustled into the courtroom, no doubt perspiring in unladylike fashion after dashing directly from the track at the Bolton Road grounds. It was a bizarre and almost comical scene; some might have thought it was all part of her six-week athletic entertainment. One court reporter eagerly passed on details of her appearance: "She arrived, attired in her walking costume: male attire of a light plaid loose coat, trousers of a similar pattern, a white vest, and Dundreary scarf, paper collar and felt hat. Her coat had blue silk slashings and was braided".

Her choice of scarf was named after the Lord Dundreary character in the stage play *Our American Cousin*, hugely popular at that time. Dundreary was an extrovert dandy with a very characteristic look and colourful, stylish clothes. Choosing such an item as part of her walking outfit illustrates Emma's confidence and willingness to put on a show. It was noted in the courtroom, however, that in the witness box she appeared "somewhat hard-featured and a little jaded with her work, but quite self-possessed".

The court heard that Brierley was charged with attempting to shoot Emma, and if there was intent to kill he should be sent for trial at the higher assizes court. Emma took the stand and stated that Brierley, appointed as a watchman to observe parts of the walk, had early that day left the track to meet and escort another of her helpers – Miss Jane Meaney – who was travelling by train from Stalybridge. But Miss Meaney arrived by herself with Brierley nowhere to be seen until after Emma's walking was underway.

Emma said she then noticed him kicking the door of an outbuilding nearby, shouting and demanding the key, and then heading off towards her private room. She was on her fifth lap of six that session when he suddenly appeared again and pointed the gun directly at her. She heard the cap go off before Miss Meaney attempted to pull the gun away from him. She added that she had been very afraid. Her solicitor Anderson said it was scandalous that a woman who had taken on this huge task of walking 1,000 miles could not be allowed to complete it without molestation by such men as the prisoner. He said Brierley had been induced to commit the offence by men who wished to win large bets. In trying to stop him, Miss Meaney had been kicked in the body very violently. Brierley admitted he had been drunk at the time but had a right to be in possession of the gun as it went with his job as the walk's watchman.

Miss Meaney told the court she had made her own way to the sports ground that day as Brierley hadn't turned up to collect her at the station. He first appeared when she was eating breakfast in Emma's room. When he took a gun from the room and left, she followed and saw him point the weapon at Emma, shouting: "I'll stop her bloody walking. I'll stop her bloody game altogether. I'll make you all fall like sods." The gun misfired, she said, and he took a match from his pocket to fire it up again by means of lighting the nipple. She tried to prevent this and the gun was wrestled from him by Jane Mahoney, an employee at the grounds. Mahoney managed to take the gun away by promising Brierley she would put another cap in it for him. He fell for this ploy, saying, "Yes do [that] and I'll then have a good fire, and it shall tell a tale!" The gun was instead taken straight to proprietor Matthew Weston who hid it in a bedroom and called the police.

The walk was able to continue, but before too long Brierley was on the rampage again and confronted Miss Meaney in threatening manner, saying he still intended to "do the job" and then go away. She said he appeared sober by now and knew what he was doing, and she suggested he should instead go home. At this point he flew at her, kicking her arms, legs and body.

Weston was asked why it had been necessary to have a watchman [like Brierley] employed to protect a female walker. He replied: "Because a similar attempt to stop her was made at Stockton-on-Tees and it was at her request. A friend also loaned me a dog. From what I have heard, I fear some person in the town is combining with the prisoner to stop the walk." Police Constable Ralph testified that on being apprehended Brierley said: "Tell Dick Ainsworth he's won his prize, this bloody woman's not walked it." Brierley offered no defence, was committed for trial at Manchester Assizes and bail refused.

At the subsequent trial he was charged with maliciously shooting Emma Gawthorpe with intent to cause grievous bodily harm. His solicitor Ernest Jones said there was no intent to seriously hurt her as the gun only contained coarse gun powder and wadding and not ammunition that would have caused injury. The gun had been provided for his job as watchman, so that he could scare off any undesirables while Emma walked at night. The incident had been a drunken practical joke for which the prisoner had already suffered severely having been imprisoned since then. The jury retired and returned to acquit Brierley.

Having by now completed at least two high-profile 1,000-mile challenges, Emma Gawthorpe was unlucky to have found her achievements somewhat overshadowed by all the fuss surrounding the gun incident. But it is evident she did make money from her efforts, as by 1870 she had established herself as a greengrocer, operating from premises in Princess Street in the middle of busy Stalybridge.

Over the years Emma remained proud of her walking feats, and was quick to mention them when appearing in court in 1870 as a witness in a fraud case. Harry Edwards, a 28-year-old hawker, was acquitted of a charge of passing counterfeit coins in Dukinfield. Much amusement was had in court when Emma was asked about her occupation and background and declared she was a greengrocer and former professional athlete. She said she had covered 1,000 miles in 1,000 hours and was still capable of walking it all over again "by any watch they could bring"!

STORY 13: EDITH PARSONS – DAUGHTER OF THE REGIMENT

For years Preston mother-of-six Edith Parsons worked as a pot hawker, meaning her daily treks around industrial Lancashire left her ideally conditioned to take up the sport of pedestrianism. Irish-born Edith was one of many new names who jumped on the bandwagon over the winter of 1864–5 following Mrs Douglas's headline-grabbing performances in London and Liverpool.

Edith enjoyed being billed as 'Daughter of the Regiment' before her events – a reference to the popular comic opera of that name. She was an energetic, outgoing character who thrived on public attention and put in a series of notable walking performances over a relatively short period.

One of these, in Accrington, saw her achieve the so-called 'Barclay feat' in spectacular style, covering the 1,000 miles twice as quickly as the famous Captain had! According to reports from the cricket ground in Peel Park Gardens, Accrington, Mrs Parsons set off on Saturday 14th January 1865 to cover 1,000 miles in only 500 hours. The *Preston Chronicle* could only find space for a brief confirmation that she finished the task successfully in early February while *The Era*, supposedly well versed in matters of pedestrianism by now, said she had managed "a sensational feat" which suggests she did indeed cut the usual 1,000-hour time schedule in half. *The Era* had mentioned earlier her passing 670 miles after only a fortnight of walking. A substantial number of people defied the cold weather to visit the track to watch Edith, who was described as a middle-aged woman very well known in the Preston area.

She was certainly not a complete beginner, having twice completed 1,000-milers beforehand, in her native Dublin and in Blackburn. In fact, at the latter, which finished on Sunday 11th December 1864, she 'accidentally' covered a total of around 1,030 miles thanks to a course measurement blunder that was only discovered afterwards. Hosted by the Royal Park Gardens in Blackburn, along with other music hall acts she pulled in large crowds and the atmosphere was noticeably good with much cheering and cordiality. She walked in a bloomer-style costume, topped by a fetching woman's hat trimmed with blue ribbon. Afterwards she declared she was not excessively tired and could do the same all over again. It was presumably a tongue-in-cheek remark but it delighted a crowd who seemed far more entertained by Edith than by the 'serio-comic' and male Scottish vocalist who also performed that night.

Edith's fourth engagement would be a few weeks after Accrington, 1,000 miles in 1,000 hours at Borough Gardens in Ribbleton Lane, Preston, starting on Saturday 4th March 1865. Admission day or night was tuppence per person with adverts proclaiming "the working classes and children half price". A reward of £20 was offered to anyone spotting Edith breaking the rules and she was closely monitored during daylight hours by a female watcher and at night by a man. By now very well known among the Lancashire sporting fraternity, Edith, sporting her bloomer costume, was able to again pull in some very good attendances and, inspired by the goodwill, never seemed to flag or show obvious weariness throughout. The *Preston Chronicle* pointed out that she was starting each new mile on the hour mark, whereas Captain Barclay had been free to cover his mile at any time within the hour. The *Lancaster Gazette* reported that she hit the 1,000-mile mark in late April and the following day celebrated by setting off on another session during which she confidently strode two miles in every hour to the noisy approval of a good crowd.

The 1860's pedestrienne renaissance saw the 1,000-mile distance prove a mainstay event, but occasionally other formats were tried. Edith Parsons had pulled in good crowds partly due to her reputation as a real entertainer and crowd pleaser, while other events of the period were not likely to be such crowd-pullers. An example was the December 1865 effort by 30-year-old Jane Toner, who decided to walk the 42 miles between her home town Darlington and the Newcastle district for six successive days in very testing weather conditions. And let us not ignore the non-competitive efforts of one Phoebe Cartledge, whose daily routine throughout the 1850s and 1860s involved walking from her rural home in Ollerton, Nottinghamshire to her job at Thoresby Hall gardens every single day. By the time Phoebe was in her early 40s somebody calculated she had done this for 17 years without a break, and at seven miles a day that amounted to 43,435 miles in total (not far short of twice around the globe).

After the Civil War ended in 1865, foot racing for women began to make small advances in America. But, as in Britain, women-only events were often not taken seriously in sporting terms. For example, a race in Pittsburgh between the American Fanny Brown and Madame Jazete from France saw the pair depicted in the *National Police Gazette* as glamorous, attractive, buxom beauties, the whole event described from an erotic rather than athletic viewpoint. And, at a women-only event at New York's Gilmore Gardens, the participants described thus: "A queer lot, tall and short, heavy and slim, young and middle-aged, some pretty and a few almost ugly". There was even an instance in Buffalo, NY, where a pedestrian found herself forced to take out a licence to have the privilege of wearing 'male clothing' when walking.

TEN

A MASTERPIECE OF MARKETING

The women who made a success of pedestrianism invariably had someone on their team who knew a thing or two about how to market them to the public. Occasionally that person would be the walker herself, but more often a promoter, agent or pub landlord. In the case of Margaret Atkinson it was her husband Joseph.

Not averse to being a little flexible with the true facts, Joseph seized on his wife's status as a person of mixed race and vigorously promoted her as 'The Mulatto Lady from Calcutta' and later as 'Madame Angelo'.

The idea was to create a mysterious aura that would get the punters excited to come and watch a performer from a faraway place. Pale-skinned working-class lasses from the North of England who took to pedestrianism were just as worthy and deserving of attention of course – but the public were more captivated by the idea of an exotic foreigner, the like of which wouldn't normally be seen anywhere near Pudsey, Pontefract or Pocklington.

STORY 14: MARGARET ATKINSON – A STALWART OF SHOW BUSINESS

From the moment the first posters went up proclaiming a proposed walk by "The Mulatto Lady of Calcutta" the people of Yorkshire's smoky industrial towns were intrigued. What they didn't know was that the Calcutta claim was false, for Mrs Margaret Ann Atkinson was a mother of seven, born in a workhouse and raised in the north of England. However, after digging a bit deeper it is clear Margaret's true background is actually more complex and interesting than even her stage name suggested.

Margaret was raised largely by her maternal grandmother Ann Harris, a 'free coloured woman' from Demerara in South America, who in June 1812 had crossed the oceans to Britain at the age of 20 to seek a new life. Ann carried the official status of being 'free coloured' which indicated she was of mixed race but not one of the thousands enslaved in the Dutch colony that is nowadays known as Guyana.

Unmarried Ann arrived in England with a young daughter, Eliza, the result of an extramarital relationship with Captain Henry Iles Underwood, an important merchant with business interests in London and Demerara. According to research published by Edinburgh University in 2015, it was common for 'free coloured' women like Ann to form relationships with the powerful (usually married) Europeans who ran things in Demerara, for it allowed the women to exercise a high degree of 'sexual leverage' in order to advance themselves and their wider families. It seems likely that Ann's trip to England was organised and paid for by Underwood, who already had a wife and another 'free coloured' lover called Emily Le Brun who was considerably older than Ann, and as such would expect to be named in his will when the time came.

Ann and little Eliza set sail from Demerara alongside Underwood's three sons, at least one of whom was bound for a boarding school in the village of Startforth on the Yorkshire-Durham border. The Underwood connection with this school – Galland's Classical, Mathematical and Commercial Academy – seems to have been the deciding factor over where Ann and Eliza should start their new life.

Ann's exotic background and mixed-race appearance made her stand out in the tiny village of Startforth, but she evidently settled quickly and would subsequently spend the rest of her life in the area. At the age of 23 she was baptised in a local church, and then at 26, after becoming pregnant, married Englishman Edward Lawson in June 1817, giving birth to a son two months later. Edward was from a respectable family and grandly described on a census return as a "landed proprietor".

The second of Ann and Edward's seven children came along in 1819, also named Ann. This new arrival would suffer a sometimes troubled life, becoming an unmarried mum herself at the age of 21 and evidently living for a time in the Durham Union's Crossgate workhouse at Barnard Castle. It was at this workhouse that Ann Lawson junior gave birth on Sunday 26th September 1840 to a girl she named Margaret Ann. This baby would grow up to be the so-called "Mulatto Lady" of pedestrianism fame.

The arrival of the illegitimate child clearly led to much family discussion, the outcome being Margaret would largely be brought up in Startforth by her grandmother Ann who was by now benefitting from payments of £50 per annum (equivalent to around £5,000 in modern values) bequeathed by her former lover Underwood in Demerara, who had died aged 51. Much of Underwood's fortune had been made via ownership of a cotton estate in Berbice, and Ann was described in his will simply as "a coloured woman formerly of Demerara".

And so Margaret Lawson grew up without her biological father and also lived apart from her mother, even though the latter was based locally and worked barely a mile away in Demesnes Flax Mill in Barnard Castle. Margaret found herself in the care of grandmother Ann, who was regarded in the language of the day as a 'mulatto'. This term would later be regarded by some as offensive or derogatory, but it seems Ann carried her status with pride and strength among the pale-skinned folk of 19th-century Teesdale. Her influence meant Margaret would be happy to describe and promote herself as 'mulatto' when performing in public later on.

Predictably, on leaving school Margaret found work in a local mill as a weaver. Shortly before her 20th birthday, in the summer of 1860, she married Joseph Atkinson, a grocer's assistant two years her senior, born and raised in Armley, to the west of Leeds. The wedding took place at St Peter's Cathedral, Bradford, and they started a new life together in that fast-growing industrial town where there was work aplenty in the many textile mills. Their new home would be a small dwelling at 42 Captain Street, just yards from the cathedral where vows were exchanged.

The couple's marriage certificate reveals that Margaret was probably illiterate, for she signed her name with an 'X'. Additionally, a little white lie may have been responsible for her (absent) father being identified as a "gentleman". The couple's first child arrived in December 1861, born at home and named – in rather flamboyant style – Julius Caesar Atkinson. Over time Margaret and Joseph would have six more children – but none of those had arrived by late 1864, which was the point when certain sporting events changed Margaret and Joseph's lives forever.

The high-profile 1,000 mile walks of Margaret Douglas in London and Liverpool and, more importantly, of local Bradford woman Emma Sharp, clearly had an impact on young Mr and Mrs Atkinson of Captain Street (soon to move to Priestley Street). The couple would have been among the huge crowds who witnessed the Emma Sharp event over its six weeks, taking inspiration from those remarkable night-time scenes when Emma completed her walk to the joyous cheers of up to 25,000 fellow Bradfordians.

During autumn 1865, the Atkinsons had their second child, Violette, born at Birstall near Dewsbury, but this doesn't appear to have curtailed the serious planning that was underway for jumping aboard the pedestrianism bandwagon. Margaret was to be the performer and Joseph her manager/agent. They dreamed of earning the sort of money that would significantly raise the standard of living of their growing family.

It was clear by now that a fit and determined pedestrienne teamed with a hard-working and entrepreneurial manager could, with a little luck and following wind, earn a good living by travelling from town to town to perform long-distance feats. Margaret and Joseph reckoned they fitted the bill as a duo and were determined to give it a real go. Although they had no background in either pedestrianism or show business, they understood the importance of maximising the impact of a new player's arrival on the scene. They were astute enough to see that Margaret's mixed race background could be a major asset, for it made her very different from the rest, an exotic curiosity almost, thus providing huge novelty and marketing value.

Athletics historian Andy Milroy confirms this: "I suspect that Margaret Atkinson enjoyed being seen as exotic – being of mixed race among the pale inhabitants of Durham and Yorkshire would have made her distinctive from an early age. The fact she chose to name her first child Julius Caesar adds further to that impression".

It hadn't escaped the Atkinsons that individuals whose appearance differed from the norm would be regarded as fascinating by the masses who would stump up the cash to see them at close quarters. In terms of using skin colour as a novelty, showman P.T. Barnum had set the precedent when sending African-American slave Joice Heth out on tour in 1835, billing her as a black-skinned curiosity who was 161 years old and had once nursed US President George Washington. Thousands paid to see her, even though the age claims were clearly ridiculous.

Joseph in particular was convinced his wife performing as plain 'Mrs' or even 'Madame' Atkinson would be far too mundane and uninteresting. Her predecessors in attempting the Captain Barclay feat had been content to use their own names and let their feet do the talking, believing the sheer size of their walking challenge would be sufficient to pull in paying punters. Joseph sensed a bit more was needed to achieve real success – and so the idea was born to create a 'brand' that made full use of Margaret's unusual ethnic background.

The British Raj in India had come into being fairly recently, offering yet another angle to increase the exotic appeal and utilise Margaret's skin tone. And the recent excitement generated by Native American runner Deerfoot will have been recognised by the Atkinsons – he raced in Bradford and many other northern venues in 1862 – providing further proof the British would come out in droves to watch a dark-skinned performer from a foreign land. The Atkinsons weighed all this up and decided Margaret's billing should be 'The Mulatto Lady – a native of Calcutta, India'. Some male pedestrians of the time had unusual sobriquets, but this was the first time a female emerged with such a billing. It was certainly an attention-grabber and canny piece of marketing. Later they would embellish it yet further, to: 'Madame Angelo the Mulatto Lady'.

The more striking the name the better. The blossoming British music hall scene had seen to that. Acts offering all sorts of entertainment would give themselves bizarre monickers in order to gain maximum attention. The *Norwood News* gave 'The Mulatto Lady' a mention, and added her to a list of weird and wonderfully named performers who were doing the rounds at the time. This list included intriguing acts such as Lady Ceiling Walker, The Elastic Kickapoos, The Bone-less Wonder and Man-Snake, and The Peculiar Black Cloud.

Margaret Atkinson's first public performance was arranged for the summer of 1866, an attempt at the pedestrienne staple of 1,000 miles in 1,000 consecutive hours, to take place not far from home, at the Park Hill grounds on the outskirts of Wakefield. A good proportion of those who heard about Margaret's intentions no doubt scoffed or even railed against the very idea of a young mother planning such a venture. Didn't she have more important things to do with her time? But the world was changing fast: at exactly the same time the Atkinsons were putting in place arrangements for the big show, the MP and philosopher John Stuart Mill was presenting the very first mass women's suffrage petition to the House of Commons, complete with 1,500 signatures of women demanding the right to vote.

With Margaret a complete unknown, and limited funds available, securing a suitable track for her event posed a problem for Joseph, particularly as he needed a space that was securely enclosed in order to charge admission fees as well as keep his wife reasonably safe. Eventually he settled on Park Hill field and got to work at setting up a temporary track for the duration of Margaret's six-week trek. He also hired a band of musicians to entertain the hoped-for crowds. He appears to have copied the set-up used by Deerfoot's travelling show of four summers earlier, putting up canvas sheeting held in place by tall wooden stakes to enclose the 220-yard circuit his wife would be walking. The venue, near a large colliery, was also the home of Wakefield Gun Club, which might have proved useful given the weaponry Emma Sharp had needed for protection in 1864!

Following a recent heatwave, the weather when 'The Mulatto Lady' set off briskly on Tuesday 24th July 1866 had become dull and overcast, which was to prove quite portentous. The event as a whole was well short of the rip-roaring success the Atkinsons hoped for, even though Margaret did manage to trudge valiantly for six weeks to the bitter end on Tuesday 4th September. The whole affair was overshadowed by allegations of cheating. As we have seen, such claims were far from uncommon at this type of event, but, in this case, the allegations received extra attention by being aired in the Wakefield magistrates court. Frustratingly for the Atkinsons, this meant the scant newspaper coverage of the walk was mostly negative, even though nothing untoward was actually proven against them.

The *Sporting Life* certainly didn't beat around the bush, describing the sight of Margaret in action being "as lively as witnessing a horse grinding clay". This was not the sort of endorsement Joseph had expected, and worse came elsewhere in the same report, the suggestion being the public had been conned and her walking had not always been continuous during night-time sessions. Local papers opted to cover the court case in detail but not the walk itself – although the *Bradford Observer* did at least acknowledge that Margaret had finished her 1,000-mile task a few days prior to attending court as a witness.

What the *Sporting Life* called "a neat little exposure" unfolded at the Wakefield Court House in a case actually brought by Joseph himself, who accused three men of assaulting him. They were John and Charles Bainbridge and Frederick Morton, musicians in the band recruited to perform at the event, who he claimed attacked him shortly after he had dispensed with their services. The court heard that in the middle of the night, when Margaret was walking as usual but no spectators were present, Joseph heard noises from outside the canvas fencing which enclosed the track. He investigated and discovered one of the bandsmen lying on the ground, peeping at proceedings from under the canvas and making notes with pencil and paper. Told he was trespassing, this 'spy' allegedly jumped up and struck Joseph several times, his fellow band members egging him on. The bandsmen claimed there was considerable doubt among the people of Wakefield over whether Margaret was walking her full allotted laps during quiet periods at night – so they had crept into the field in the early hours to check this. They claimed that in one instance, after Margaret had done just a quarter of one of her miles, they heard a man shout: "That will do, Mary Jane!" This caused them to laugh out loud, leading to their discovery by an enraged Joseph. Margaret was called to the witness stand and corroborated her husband's side of the story, but the magistrates were not impressed and dismissed the case on the grounds that any assault on Joseph had only been "slight".

The Atkinsons must have walked away from the courthouse ruing their decision to prosecute – not only had the case been thrown out, but the accusations of cheating, flimsy though they were, had now been given the oxygen of publicity. This had been a real baptism of fire in the world of pedestrianism for them, but they were determined not to be knocked out of their stride. With barely time to bathe her tired feet back at home, Margaret was being lined up for a second 1,000-mile challenge – this to be staged in Gateshead later the same month.

There was no let-up in the Atkinsons' heavy duty advertising either. For the Gateshead appearance, Joseph booked newspaper adverts that proclaimed: "Go and see one of the greatest miracles of the present day, Mrs Atkinson the Mulatto Lady, a native of Calcutta, walking 1,000 miles in 1,000 hours". The event came just three weeks after Margaret had finished at Wakefield, and involved travelling up to Gateshead for an early morning start on her birthday, Wednesday 26th September 1866, just after dawn. It would be staged in what was known as Gypsies Field. This was not the biggest or most popular pedestrianism venue in the Newcastle area, but these were early days and it was important to get Margaret known and acknowledged as a talent so that big financial rewards might follow. Joseph wanted his wife in action before the winter arrived and as Margaret was not a 'one-trick pony' in performance terms, they could examine various options once she had a couple of major walks under her belt.

There is little or nothing on the record, but Margaret appears to have achieved her goal at Gateshead and it would be surprising if they returned to Bradford out of pocket in November, despite the timespan of the task. Admission to the Gateshead public over the six weeks had been threepence on the gate, and three times a week a "grand gala" was staged on the field as an added attraction. The *South Shields Daily Gazette* described Margaret as 26 years old and "about the middle stature and slight, but well made".

Having displayed her capabilities twice over 1,000 miles, Margaret had now earned herself a degree of local and regional fame, and it was decided the time was right to now extend her repertoire. The plan was for the pair of them to make a full-time living from 'show business' – with the long-distance walking serving as either a launch pad, or maybe the mainstay of her repertoire if enough opportunities arose. Emma Sharp had made a mint from her one-off walk in Bradford, but Margaret had more strings to her bow than just sturdy legs, lungs and stamina. Consequently the Atkinsons worked out a little stage-show routine and decided to promote her as available for appearances on stage as well as track.

This being late 1866, the first great music hall boom was by now well underway, many performers earning a living on the stage. Within a year or two there would be more than 30 large halls listed in London and almost 400 elsewhere in the country. To climb on the bandwagon and stay there, Margaret needed to be aggressively marketed, and Joseph set to work on this aspect with a vengeance.

Before long an advert appeared in *The Era* announcing a portrait of 'The Mulatto Lady' could be purchased by calling on or contacting Joseph at 2 Priestley Road, Bolton Road, Bradford. This type of postcard-style souvenir was unusual at this point in time, but the Victorian public loved the new world of show business and music hall, and consequently a market would grow for keepsakes or collectibles depicting the celebrities of the day. Margaret's new career had barely begun but already she and her husband were intent on developing the Mulatto Lady persona. In terms of pedestrianism they were pioneers. The sale of portraits of pedestriennes ('cartes de visite') did not become generally common until much later, in the early 1880s.

The combination of this marketing allied to her completion of two 1,000-mile walks duly bore fruit when Margaret launched a music hall career in late 1866 as a novelty act, walking a mile around the stage as quickly as feasible while singing "her great walking songs". The idea was to present frequent, manageable performances by Margaret that would bring in earnings and wouldn't involve the hardship of multi-week performances at the mercy of

British weather. However, the 1,000-mile walks could continue separately, as and when opportunities cropped up.

The following year, 1867, saw Margaret tackle just one 1,000-miler as far as we know, and this would prove another occasion where the performance was hampered by happenings beyond her control. The venue was the Royal Park Gardens in Blackburn, a pub run by John Smith, who had also created a music hall on his premises. Margaret's hopes of a smooth and trouble-free journey over the six-week period were dealt a blow when it emerged that proprietor Smith was allowing a series of special meetings to take place at the venue at the same time she was in action. These were no ordinary gatherings: William Murphy, a controversial spokesman for the Protestant Electoral Union, was to hold anti-Catholic rallies at the Royal Parks Gardens as it was the only local venue that would allow him to rent a hall for his activities. His so-called 'lectures' nearly always sparked trouble, often leading to scenes of violence.

In normal circumstances the Atkinsons might have been pleased to share their workspace with something bringing in hundreds of extra spectators and therefore potentially more money – but these rallies were known to be explosive affairs and the personal safety of anybody in the vicinity couldn't be guaranteed. *The Illustrated Police News* said Murphy's meetings were little more than a mask for stirring up xenophobic rioting and disorder.

Newspapers of the era often sneered at female pedestrianism, but on this occasion it was Murphy and his followers who took the brunt of the disapproval. The *Blackburn Standard* was highly sympathetic towards Margaret having her walk "almost eclipsed" because proprietor Smith had chosen to ignore the ban on Murphy imposed by local magistrates. The *Standard's* lead writer set out his thoughts:

"The peculiar entertainments of the Royal Park Gardens have been subjected to a congenial variation. Pedestrianism, in however a wonderful guise, has among other things been almost eclipsed. It was unfair of Mr Murphy to take possession of the premises while the 'Mulatto Lady from Calcutta' was engaging attention by her astonishing feats. If there is honour among knaves, why not among mountebanks? A thousand miles in a thousand hours is an awkward feat to be interrupted because the performer cannot by breaking off place the number completed to the balance of past or future performance... Maybe [Murphy] is not [here] to 'cut out' the Mulatto Lady or draw away attention and coppers from her thousand-mile feat. Perhaps Mr Smith, the enterprising landlord of the public house where both attractions are [underway], has engaged Murphy in addition to, and not permitted him to come as a rival of, the Mulatto Lady... [If] the engagement proves a hit... the frequenters of this tavern have an additional enjoyment, and the treasury of the establishment a profitable investment".

On Monday 14th October, with Margaret Atkinson's walk well underway at the premises, the ban by magistrates was ignored by Murphy and his rabble-rousers, and landlord Smith made no attempt to stop them gaining entry into the music hall building at the RPG. Around 400 turned up to hear the speeches, with 30 nervous-looking policemen keeping an eye on proceedings. It passed off relatively peacefully and the following two days saw further lectures delivered, witnessed by a bumper 1,300 or so. Although there is no record of Margaret abandoning her walk, it seems highly unlikely she escaped interruptions during this period, even though the expected rioting failed to materialise. She may well have chalked up 1,000 miles , but probably not in the intended 1,000 consecutive hours.

The Blackburn authorities dealt with proprietor Smith by fining him £5, plus costs, for allowing their ban to be breached. Local police were kept busy during Margaret's walk as Murphy and his men marched around the town, their Orange procession featuring flags, banners, swords, maces and pistols – the latter fired menacingly into the air on many occasions.

*

From the tail end of 1867 until summer 1873 Margaret would only do a handful of 1,000-mile walks over this six-year period, concentrating instead on appearing on stage at music halls, where her speciality became circling the stage for a mile in around 11 minutes, while singing comic songs. This act was highly popular, going down well in the lively music hall atmosphere, audiences fascinated to see a woman at close quarters who had chalked up incredible feats of athleticism. From 1873 to 1877 she would then renew her status as the most prolific British pedestrienne with another batch of 1,000-milers in various towns, the music hall appearances continuing in between. Her final long-distance walk would be completed in January 1881, an epic 2,000 miles in 1,000 hours.

During the 1870s Joseph and Margaret will most likely have seen the way sport and leisure was going. Properly codified sport was gaining a foothold, thus limiting earning opportunities, and generally the police and magistrates were exerting an ever stronger grip on things. Throughout the 1860s fines for permitting gambling, breach of peace and other misdemeanours had been viewed as occupational hazards, but by the 1870s publicans who staged pedestrianism faced a higher chance of being put out of business.

Margaret's increasing dependency on her music hall appearances prompted her to change her billing accordingly, placing a little less emphasis on the 'Mulatto Lady' persona and leaning heavily on a new name. This one was also designed to emphasise to the paying public her exotic foreign connections – hence the choice of 'Madame Angelo'. Although she was, of course, born and bred on the Durham/Yorkshire border, the new name implied an Italian background and seems to have emerged in the summer of 1868. It appears to have gone down well with music hall proprietors and audiences alike, and it wouldn't be long before some adverts announcing her upcoming engagements and availability would be describing her as 'the female Deerfoot'.

Her music hall 'turns' were, of course, underwritten by her success as a 1,000-mile performer. What she did on stage was not spectacular or especially difficult, but the pulling power came from the novelty of who she was – i.e. one of, if not the most, prolific 1,000-mile female walkers anywhere in the world. Most people in her audiences would be well aware of how walking even one mile non-stop could be a tiring affair for an ordinary mortal, so were fascinated to see at close quarters the mother of a young family who was capable of marching a mile every single hour for six weeks. Variety was the name of the game and music hall provided it in spades.

She would be placed at the top of the bill for most of her music hall appearances and would give audiences a rendition of popular ditties of the day with the lyrics adapted to tell of her adventures as a walker. A regular was 'Hop Light, Loo' of which there was more than one version. Margaret favoured the one with a comma after the second word, which indicated it was an address to a woman called Loo, to jump and skip as she walked. The song was said to have been composed in 1860 "for black-faced minstrels" by George Ware, a singer-songwriter who also managed the celebrated Marie Lloyd.

Typical of her regular engagements were those at the Museum Concert Hall in Bolton in March 1870 and at the Parthenon Music Hall in Great Charlotte Street, Liverpool a week or two later over Easter. At Bolton her show reportedly involved circuiting the stage no fewer than 110 times to complete a single mile, while singing songs "in a manner both surprising and pleasing", according to *The Era*. With an 11-minute mile to aim at, this was not especially easy on such a tiny track while singing lustily.

At the big Liverpool venue, the proprietor John Stoll boasted of "an unrivalled company of dancing and vocal talent" on his bill, listing Madame Angelo (Margaret) as the main attraction, rather misleadingly calling her "the only lady who ever walked a thousand miles in a thousand hours". Among her supporting cast was a Madame Bousfield, adopting various classical Grecian poses on a revolving pedestal with beautiful limelight effects, the 'old favourite' Long Barney, the 'original' Lazy Sam, vocalist and dancer Emma and a musical burlesque show by Mr and Mrs Bousfield. Entry was sixpence for the Upper Hall and threepence downstairs.

The public memory can be short, so the Atkinsons found it necessary in 1870 to head for the West Midlands and add another 1,000-miler to her *curriculum vitae*, in order to ensure the music hall crowds knew they were watching a genuine performer. So she stepped out at The Chuckery cricket ground, at the top of Pool Street in Walsall. It created plenty of interest and one local lad bunked off school to go and see her, producing a remarkable pencil sketch which survives to this day. Billy Meikle was around ten years old at the time and fascinated by what he saw: "She wore her hair in a chignon, topped off by a turban-like hat with a feather sticking out of it. She was dressed in a white silk blouse, over which was a black velvet bolero; below were black satin knickers [breeches] and white stockings. On her feet were elastic-sided shoes".

The costume was a colourful variation on the 'bloomers' theme and its exotic, continental flavour encouraged the Atkinsons to describe it as her "native costume" in their ever-changing advertising. Clearly showmanship had been added to the exotic persona. The sight of Madame Angelo covering all those miles for all that time was to stay with Billy Meikle for the rest of his life in the Walsall area, where he became a very well-known character. Fortunately he preserved the sketch he made as a boy.

Madame Angelo at Walsall's Chuckery Cricket Ground, as drawn by admiring spectator Billy Meikle.

Over the 1869–70 period business was booming as the popularity of music hall grew, and although Margaret became pregnant twice during this two-year spell, her touring schedule remained hectic. The fact she gave birth to her third and fourth children, Annie and Angela, in Leeds and South Shields, respectively, illustrates how the family had by now adopted a peripatetic lifestyle, living as lodgers in various northern towns according to where and when Margaret's music hall bookings were located.

The marketed persona was proving successful. The combination of athletic feat and singing proved popular and profitable, making all the difficult travelling arrangements worthwhile. Census records show the Atkinsons lived as boarders at a number of addresses, and not all their children were necessarily always with them, presumably being looked after by friends or relatives.

Margaret would often perform for a number of successive nights at the same theatre, and early 1870 saw her on stage at places like Manley's Circus in Glasgow, the Alexandra Music Hall in Barrow-in-Furness, Walsall, Hull and Ashton-under-Lyne. As soon as any free days appeared in the diary Joseph would place an advert in *The Era*, offering a complete package that included the supply of posts and brass chains to mark out the stage, as well as coloured posters.

In April 1870 she signed up for a week to perform her one-mile act and songs on stage nightly at Ashton-under-Lyne, placed at the top of the bill by William Revill, proprietor of the People's New Concert Hall in Stamford Street. She was regarded as an even bigger attraction than 'The Great Italian Hercules Napoli, the strongest man in the world'. Revill saw these two acts as a real coup for his theatre and proclaimed: "A great change of talent and novelty – wonders never cease! Madame Angelo and the Italian Hercules". A number of dancers and singers made up the rest of the bill, notably Professor Calderwood and his wonderful 'dioramic' views, which involved a magic lantern projecting images dissolving into one another, which would cause audiences to gasp in amazement at such unseen wizardry.

From here the family travelled back over the Pennines to Bradford for a spell, agreeing a six-night residency at Pullan's New Music Hall in Brunswick Place where an audience of 3,000 could be accommodated. It was a popular new venue, constructed mainly of wood, which would prove its undoing in a fire some years later. As well as their individual performances during the week here, the entire company was asked to come together to perform a spectacular *Comic Ballet d'Action* called Donnybrook Fair, featuring an auxiliary troupe of

40 local children. Margaret was used to walking around tiny stages by now, but sharing the platform with dozens of others would have been a new experience.

Sheffield's Royal Pavilion Music Hall staged a grand gala in the city's Queen's Running Grounds during the summer of 1870 and Madame Angelo appeared, apparently with a spring in her step; she is said to have walked her mile in about 9 mins 30 secs instead of the usual 11 minutes, despite being at least four months pregnant. Immediately afterwards arrangements were announced for an attempt at another 1,000 miles in 1,000 hours, this time in the Victoria Gardens in Wilford Road, Nottingham, commencing in the first week of August 1870. Attendance was good, at least 1,000 watching her at the weekend sessions. During a rest period she was presented with a silver medal by what was described as a group of Sheffield gentlemen, and much praise was heaped upon her for her recent 'graceful walking' in Sheffield which had gone down particularly well. After completion early on Tuesday 13th September she had less than a week's rest before moving on to Stockport, resuming her music hall act for a six-night stretch at the People's Concert Hall.

By late autumn 1870 and now around eight months pregnant, Margaret ploughed on regardless, for the family had to be fed and the lodgings paid for. She fulfilled a booking at Thomas Batty's Grand Model Circus in Belfast, where the splendid new circular building in Oxford Street was hosting a six-month run over the entire winter of this spectacular show. The residency was reportedly the most successful on record and pulled in a grand total of 368,000 people. The acts were top rate, including gymnasts, flying trapeze artists such as Fraulein Laura 'the Queen of the Lofty Wire' and equestrian stunts that involved Prince ('the Fire Dog') riding on horseback and leaping through hoops of fire and jumping banners and bridges. Other stars were Signorina Annetino performing somersaults on horseback and a curiosity known as 'The Man Serpent'.

The 1870–1 winter proved to be very cold, the severe weather lasting well into February. But the Atkinsons pressed on with their plans and headed across for a stay in north-eastern England where they had several dates to fulfil and would remain for several weeks over the Christmas period. First commitment was a short season not far from Margaret's place of birth, the Oxford Music Hall in Green Dragon Yard, Stockton-on-Tees, a 1,500-capacity venue where she helped draw good crowds.

For this period the family took up residence at No.37 Ivey Street in Westoe, South Shields, renting roomy accommodation within which it appears Angela, their fourth child, was born on Christmas day. Just a week or two before giving birth, six nights had been undertaken at the New Theatre Royal in North Shields, the venue management boasting that Madame Angelo was among the cream of the entertainment profession and had been engaged "at enormous expense". Perhaps the fee Joseph negotiated was inflated by the fact his wife was within days of giving birth? He was a smart man and this was surely taken into consideration.

Within weeks of Angela's birth Margaret was back in 1,000-mile action at Worcester. She embarked on yet another 'Barclay match' on the bowling green beside the Saracens Head in the main street known as The Tything. She was no doubt heartened by good turnouts throughout the subsequent 42 days. During her trek, on Tuesday 21st March, to coincide with the wedding of Queen Victoria's daughter Louise to the Marquess of Lorne, a huge bonfire was lit and there was dancing as a band played. It created a stirring atmosphere for Margaret to continue totting up her miles. She finished on Wednesday 26th April and reports of the walk appeared in newspapers as far afield as the USA and Australia. She was now known across the globe.

The 1871 census was collected around now and shows Joseph, Margaret and tiny Angela as boarders at the Saracens Head in Worcester. Margaret was inaccurately listed as a pedestrian born in Calcutta, while Joseph is described as a theatrical agent. Coincidentally the pub in question was positioned just a few short steps from another landmark with strong athletics significance – Ferneley's dispensing chemist was the workplace of the great Walter George, who lived and trained in tiny rooms upstairs. It was here he developed his innovative indoor exercise routine prior to becoming the fastest miler in the world.

The following month saw a return to nightly music hall shows, including a lucrative, lengthy residency at the Alhambra in Gloucester. Watched by an eagle-eyed timekeeper, Madame Angelo had to circle the tiny stage space a dizzying 98 times to achieve her 11-minute mile while singing to the audience. She was top of the bill, supported by "celebrated negro minstrels and dancers the brothers Edwards, trapeze artist Madame Frantz and a range of others". During her spell in Gloucester she and fellow performers The Sisters Gunniss were both granted special benefit nights – this would involve a purse of sovereigns being handed over by Lieut-Col. Sir William Guise of the Royal South Gloucestershire Militia and his brother officers. This would prove a lucrative engagement.

Big, noisy crowds were in attendance for Madame Angelo's main summer appearance that year, 1,000 miles in 1,000 hours at the Spring Cottage inn gardens in Holtshill Lane, Walsall, a district known as The Chuckery. Reportedly 8,000-plus gathered to see her finish the walk. The pub (still going strong in modern times) witnessed some ugly scenes during the event, leading to arrests and a hearing at Walsall court in early August. Landlord Edward Jones was found guilty of permitting drunkenness on the premises during night-time sessions of Margaret's walk. A police sergeant had visited the gardens at 2am and found about 150 persons in various states of inebriation. Jones' claim that no drink was served after midnight and the drunks had broken a fence to gain entry was not accepted, and he was fined 20 shillings plus costs.

With a good number of walks and stage performances having been well received in the West Midlands and Potteries region, the Atkinsons decided around now this was an area where they could settle and continue to make a decent living. They took steps to base themselves here, the biggest of which was Joseph taking charge of the Red Lion pub in Hanley for a spell. Being an enterprising fellow, Joseph didn't plan to merely tick over in steady fashion as a landlord, he wanted to develop things further and make the best possible use of his wife's popularity and talents.

The year of 1872 – one of the wettest on record – would prove pivotal in the Atkinsons' story. It got underway with Margaret appearing on stage at the Provincial Theatricals Royal Star Music Hall in the heart of the Staffordshire Potteries district, at Longton. For once, it appears she wasn't top of the bill, this accolade going to Swedish gymnasts Monsieur and Madame Erato. Also making the good folk of Longton smile was Mr and Mrs Leonard White, described as 'Negro comedians', and Mark Floyd, a female impersonator and transformation dancer.

At the tail end of January Margaret was due to appear in South Wales – billed grandly (and misleadingly) as 'the female Deerfoot' – at the Prince of Wales Amphitheatre in Wind Street, Swansea. It appears this show had to be cancelled as there are reports the venue went bust the same weekend. It was a wooden amphitheatre which had replaced a demolished pub on the same site a few years earlier. Sadly it never lived up to its grand name and there had been regular calls for its closure after a female impersonator called Ernest Boulton appeared there and apparently caused great offence.

The problems at Swansea represented just another day on the road for Madame Angelo, who simply moved on to the next engagement – in this case the Royal Hotel and Oddfellows Hall, Halifax, where her one mile on the stage "was met with great approbation". It was an up and down existence, and, true to form, things soon turned sour again. In early April, the court reports for Bradford showed complaints of an assault on Margaret. She was unable to attend the court – recorded as "absent having to fulfil a music hall professional engagement". The Swansea theatre going bust had been one type of occupational hazard and, it seems, common assault was another.

Her name and reputation meant she usually bounced back from these minor setbacks and sure enough in June of 1872 at the Oxford Music Hall in Burslem, proprietor Hurley proclaimed that his popular family resort was being very well attended, justifying his engagement of Madame Angelo "at great expense".

She added another 1,000 miles to her impressive tally in Birmingham around this time, an event that would be clearly remembered decades later by a member of the family who owned the land she performed on. The huge pleasure grounds in Duddeston, known as Vauxhall Gardens, had been cleared for housing by the mid-1800s but a small chunk of the site was not built on, and this would be the spot where Madame Angelo walked. Around 60 years after the event the *Birmingham Gazette* published an interview with the elderly Clifford Gretton, whose father James owned the land. Clifford remembered clearly watching Madame Angelo in action as an awestruck youngster. He explained that a small piece of land between the railway line and Dollman Street had been left open when the area was cleared, and this continued to be called Vauxhall Gardens, even though the green pathways and trees had gone. James Gretton would subsequently sell it to the railway company but not before Madame Angelo arrived to give the local public one of their last entertainment treats at the site.

Recalled Clifford: "Her particular stunt was to walk 1,000 miles in 1,000 hours. She and her husband hired a portion of Vauxhall Gardens for that purpose. So that there should be no suspicion of jiggery-pokery, the Gardens were open all night so interested parties might drop in during the small hours and see for themselves that Madame Angelo was still walking. Towards the end she got so tired her husband used to walk beside her and let off a pistol to keep her awake every time she showed signs of going to sleep."

By now Joseph Atkinson was desperately seeking new ideas to increase the family earnings. It was now more than four years since they'd created the Madame Angelo persona and although the aim of making her a well-known name in the North and Midlands had been achieved, the financial rewards had fluctuated. In recent years it seems even some of the well-attended events didn't necessarily result in a handsome payday. This became a constant worry, for they didn't have other jobs to support the walking, it was their sole source of family income. Athletics historian Andy Milroy points out:

"Most pedestrians had a backup job. For example, John Phipps Townsend who won the 1837 London to Brighton, was a lamplighter. He reputedly competed under the pseudonym Ironsides to conceal his pedestrian sideline from employers. George Seward, one of the great sprinters, was a silver plater. From the 1800s through to the 1850–70s pedestrianism was a cycle of boom and bust, with money coming in for a couple of years before drying up again. Few peds survived over more than one cycle. Once out of the spotlight, the chance of a benefit was slim. Margaret Atkinson kept going for 20 years, a remarkable length of time".

Milroy also points out: "The music hall performer's pound had to go a long way: it had to pay for lodgings, food, rates, clothes, costumes and possibly family expenses. In the heyday of the Music Hall most acts were booked on a weekly basis, which offered minimal job security, and even for this short time contracts were impossible to enforce. If a booking was arbitrarily cancelled, there was no redress. If additional performances were demanded, there was little choice but to comply; artists who refused or asked for extra pay were not rebooked. If they were badly treated, they could not afford to go to court. As an example, in June 1887 Gus Elen – a major star – wrote to *The Era* detailing a long-standing contract that had been cancelled with a telegram: 'Shall not expect you; business bad'. Elen received no compensation. No wonder the Atkinson children would rapidly acquire performing skills too. There was no room for any passengers".

*

By the summer of 1872, in a bid to boost their unreliable income, Joseph made considerable efforts to get himself established as a pub and entertainments proprietor in addition to managing Margaret's affairs. The couple moved into the Red Lion inn in Broad Street, Hanley, aiming to settle here permanently and develop this rather rowdy 'spit-and-sawdust' pub into a proper music hall venue. They thought about calling it 'Angelo's' and began making big plans for the future. Unfortunately they found themselves up against disapproving magistrates and the strict licensing laws of the day.

At the Hanley Borough Police Court in July, with the mayor Edwin Powell chairing a two-man bench, Joseph applied for a transfer of the license of the Red Lion into his name from the outgoing tenant Levi Wakin. Joseph was cross-examined and the court heard he'd unsuccessfully tried to obtain the license some time earlier in the name of 'Angelo'. It was stated that since he and Madame Angelo had arrived to take charge of the pub, things had been badly conducted and numerous complaints made. These allegations seemed to be based on the first day 'the Angelos' took possession of the premises, when a band had played loudly in a large room attached to the premises. Mayor Powell and fellow magistrate Mr Walker went into a huddle to consider the matter, and after a long discussion the mayor announced a difference of opinion between them that couldn't be resolved, and therefore no judgement could be immediately given.

Joseph's frustrated representative suggested resolving the deadlock by granting a temporary license, which would allow the court to act at short notice if there were further complaints about the pub. Things then took a sudden turn for the worse, the mayor deciding the application should be rejected. He said he felt Joseph was not a fit and proper person to be in charge of the pub and if he became licensee he would create a source of considerable future trouble for the court and the public. Joseph's representative protested strongly, pointing out the other magistrate was of the opposite opinion, and said he would return to the court after preparing a brand-new application on Joseph's behalf.

Back they came to court a week or so later, Joseph announcing his intention was to have live music at the pub to attract custom, but only via a single piano for sessions known as 'free-and-easies'. He explained that he had already prepared a stage for the performers to use, and promised that on Sundays only 'sacred music' would be played. He then submitted a petition supporting his plans, signed by 42 people including 15 fellow publicans and beer sellers. This was countered by a second petition, opposing the Atkinsons, signed by 40 people including various clergy and churchwardens, and other prominent people. The latter stated that since Joseph's arrival, the pub had been badly managed and was a great nuisance to local people. The bench was sympathetic to this and rejected the license transfer.

It was a financial blow to the couple and underlined how life in the relatively new Victorian world of show business, and as a pedestrian, could be full of uncertainties. Most professional athletes in the nineteenth century had an occupation to fall back on in hard times but the Atkinsons had been fully committed to show business for nearly ten years by now. When life got tough, it was not uncommon for a benefit event to be held for a needy pedestrian, either initiated by other performers or by a promoter. And in September 1872 it was reported that Madame Angelo intended to give six grand comic concerts as a farewell benefit due to having suffered severe recent losses.

Use of the term 'farewell' was probably only loosely applied to the situation, for the couple were not about to quit their chosen career, and pushed on as best they could to make ends meet. By March of 1873 there would be another mouth to feed with the arrival of fifth child Henrietta. Perhaps it was a sign of the times that during an 1873 residency at The People's Music Hall in Hanley Margaret found herself mentioned only in the small print on the posters, instead of being trumpeted at the top of the bill.

But Joseph was nothing if not imaginative. He tackled the financial pinch by coming up with a brand-new venture, a travelling show they would call 'Shah's Temple of Wonder'. As with 'Madame Angelo', Joseph was keen for a name that would sound exotic, foreign and intriguing to the entertainment-hungry public. The 'Temple' project involved using a sort of demountable structure – little more than a hut really – which provided, when needed, a place at trackside for Margaret to sleep and recover between walks. It could save the potential cost of being based in a pub and having to share takings with a landlord. It could be erected in parks and fields and when illuminated could act as a stage or centrepiece for the music hall act. Sometimes they would have to pay rent for the field or land they used, but at least this meant the Atkinsons could keep the gate money and control things better. It was not the first time Joseph had copied the type of arrangements the native American 'Deerfoot' made when he travelled around Britain displaying his running prowess on a nightly basis in 1862. Joseph had clearly learned a lot from that Deerfoot tour, even promoting his wife on occasions with the sobriquet 'The Female Deerfoot'.

Just a few weeks after the birth of Henrietta, Margaret announced the show must go on and returned to action. In June of 1873 she was to be found at the Spring Cottage pub gardens in Walsall, alongside a full brass band while locals danced and sang the night away. Later that summer the new 'Shah's Temple of Wonder' made its way on a rare visit to the capital, opening for business at Charlton Pier, Woolwich, SE London. It was another 1,000-miles-in-1,000-hours demonstration, which got underway at the end of July.

Presumably to avoid confusion with a London pianist known as Madame Marie Angelo, Margaret was this time billed as "the only Madame Angelo travelling in her line of business". And just to emphasise her credentials: "She is patronised by all the mayors, nobility, clergy and gentry in every town and city in which she has appeared". She set off at Charlton Pier at 5.45am on Tuesday 29th July on another six-week extravaganza, which would be watched by an estimated total of more than 20,000, paying tuppence each for the privilege, or threepence on the twice weekly appearances of a brass band playing alongside. A good number came from other parts of London, travelling to the venue by boat along the Thames.

On the evening of Monday 8th September a huge gathering cheered Margaret over the final mile, carrying baby Henrietta in her arms. The celebrations involved a procession through local streets led by the Woolwich Band, just ahead of a wagonette drawn by four grey horses with postillions, containing the so-called 'Great Female Deerfoot' and her husband waving to the crowds as if they were royalty. Behind their carriage came the 9th Kent (Plumstead) Artillery Band, the two bands playing alternately.

The level of interest had been high throughout this walk, and Joseph hadn't been slow to cash in. The public were invited to enter the Temple of Wonder for 3d per person over the three final days, which were billed specifically as a 'benefit' period for his wife. The last evening ('The Night of Nights') featured a baby show for the finest-looking baby under nine months (6d entry), a one-mile bicycle race for allcomers (entry 1s each), a one-mile foot race for allcomers (1s) and a sack race (1s), with separate silver-plated cups for each winner. To cap it all, the Temple was illuminated in spectacular fashion and there were fireworks and balloons. Thousands of Londoners had a great night out and newspaper coverage was plentiful, one report even digging out the information that Madame Angelo was "a 32-year-old mother of 11 children – five of whom were still alive".

High on the success at Woolwich, the couple had to make their way quickly down to the West Country for a booking in Exeter. Mr E Francis, calling himself 'the people's caterer' had announced two days of extraordinary open-air amusement in addition to the usual programme of athletic sports, military bands and fireworks. He said the celebrated Clown Cricketers team would play for prize money against a local side while wearing their full clown costume, throwing somersaults and going through marvellous acrobatic performances, while 'Madame Angelo of Calcutta' would appear and walk her usual sing-song mile in under 11 minutes. Novelty acts like the cricketing clowns were proliferating and grabbing the headlines, and this must have underlined to Joseph and Margaret the need to up their game to stay in business.

By early 1874 the adverts Joseph placed in *The Era* and elsewhere, seeking new bookings for Madame Angelo, clearly needed to be refreshed in order to emphasise her uniqueness and her earlier successes. One that appeared in March told of her triumphs in Cardiff, Swansea, Sheffield (twice), Stockport, and Bradford (twice), calling her "the original" and a "sure success" on stage. Posts and brass chains, 'cartes de visite', circulars and coloured posters were all available to anyone wanting to book her. The address given for enquiries was now 52 Cawney Hill in Dudley, where the family was now based. The adverts continued to appear despite Margaret being heavily pregnant with the couple's sixth child. She was obviously planning another quick return to action after Cyrenious's arrival in mid-April.

Large families were of course the norm in Victorian England and it was just a question of working around the logistical problems of having small children. While just a few months old, the Atkinson babies would actually be paraded at the end of mum's 1,000-mile walks to generate extra crowd interest; once they were old enough to perform, having been raised in the peripatetic lifestyle of the pedestrian/music hall performer, the older ones would even develop their own acts. Julius Caesar was trained as a distance walker by the time he was ten and one of his sisters by the time she was seven. When the family were travelling as the Shah's Temple of Wonder, two of the girls developed a remarkable act where they would lift members of the audience inside barrels, by way of a rope attached to their plaited hair or gripped by their teeth! In a later census young Violette was actually described as a 'travelling strong woman'. Julius Caesar branched out, learning circus skills, first as a tightrope walker and then, before he left the troupe, as a trapeze artist.

Presumably the older Atkinson children would have looked after the younger ones when Margaret and Joseph were away or indisposed. According to her great-great-granddaughter Kay Nestor, Margaret was the type who would have been pragmatic and simply just got on with navigating the issues presented by pregnancies and childcare: "I think she probably just got on with things. All the women in our family are of that nature, you just have to get on with things."

By the middle of 1874 Margaret had been taking on the 1,000-mile challenges for ten years or so – and in that time had averaged almost two per year. This puts her firmly among the most prolific of the pedestriennes. She was now approaching her 34th birthday, had six children, but was far from finished yet. Much of the summer would be spent in the city of Norwich, where she performed her six-week speciality at the Hop Pole Inn's gardens in St Faith's Lane. Proprietor William Harper welcomed Margaret to the Hop Pole, a venue that had staged a number of other walks and athletic events with success, and would soon be holding popular bicycle contests. A small track of 14 laps to the mile was laid out for her at this city centre location.

Although the first music hall and variety entertainments put on in Norwich had flopped in the 1850s, things had recently picked up now the leisure-time activities of the working class had become more diverse. Pubs, even those without pleasure gardens like the Hop Pole, became meeting places for societies and clubs formed for working-class folk who were gardeners, cage-bird fanciers, anglers and cyclists. This mirrored the middle-class association between hotels and inns and the societies and clubs that first sprang up in the early 1800s.

Despite all this, magistrates and police remained unhappy over certain aspects of the new pub scene. During Madame Angelo's Hop Pole walk, when landlord Harper could see the event was likely to finish on schedule he put in for an extension of licensing hours over the final weekend. But the Norwich magistrates were unimpressed, stating simply they could see no good case for granting this. According to *The Era*, the walk attracted "very fair numbers of spectators" throughout, although the best crowd – on the final day – suffered a minor disappointment when it became clear Margaret was struggling badly and in no fit state to make a grandstand finish by carrying baby Cyrenious over the final mile as promised. With her agreement, and due to popular demand, it was decided the infant, less than three months old, would instead be handed to her close to the finish line, at which point she could compose herself and finish safely.

The magistrates may have taken a dim view of proceedings, but the local papers praised Margaret's efforts. She never failed over the entire six weeks to be ready to start each mile, it was reported, and she had to overcome great hardship during the final seven days – "her limbs swelling, and considerable difficulty experienced in keeping awake". It also emerged that Margaret was rewarded for completing the 1,000 miles with a handsome gold medal and dress ring, paid for and presented by a handful of respectable gentlemen of Norwich.

One report suggested an agreement made beforehand allowed Madame Angelo to pocket all gate receipts. This would have yielded a good return, allowing Joseph to splash out on a large display advertisement in the press afterwards, which, unusually, featured a line drawing of his wife walking around a fenced-off circle. This represented something of a revved-up PR campaign and included some of Joseph's best lines: "[She is] the only lady who has been patronised by all the nobility, mayors, clergy and gentry in every town and city in which she has appeared... the only lady who has given satisfaction to the public at large... the only lady given permission to walk on licensed grounds by the Norwich Magistrates". And more.

Interestingly, Joseph now issued an appeal for other walkers (gender not specified) to come forward and contact him: "Wanted, wanted, wanted! One-thousand mile walkers, those who do not care about too much sleep at nights". Anybody interested was urged to write to Joseph ('Mr Angelo') at the Cawney Hill address in Dudley. It seems he wanted to assess the possibility of staging a new type of event involving multiple walkers, and was considering head-to-head races involving his wife. Ever the restless entrepreneur, Joseph was looking for new opportunities, possibly management and promotion of other acts, and new venues. However, little appears to have materialised in the short term, which at least allowed Margaret good time to recover from the Norwich walk and its very uncomfortable finish.

By the following year of 1875 things improved a little and the Grove Inn – virtually next door to the Atkinson's home in Dudley – was able to host several 1,000-mile walks by Madame Angelo. To give its full name, The Cromwell Grove Inn and Pleasure Gardens at 57 Cawney Hill, a site that would be cleared to make way for the South Staffs Waterworks reservoir. The premises was at the time being run by Tom Davies, previously a 'butty collier' [freelance coal miner] and was said to be one of Dudley's nicest pleasure grounds. It was laid out with flower beds and regularly welcomed large numbers from far and near. All manner of activities might take place here, some – such as cock-fighting – illustrating how landlords didn't hesitate to bend the rules in the desperate battle to make a living. Getting caught was an occupational hazard and at the Grove, Tom Davies would come a cropper on one occasion for selling ale and tobacco from an unlicensed tent in the gardens. He was fined a sum of £17.10s that he could ill afford.

A Dudley newsletter, issued many years later, recalls tales of Madame Angelo's walks at this venue, quoting the memories of an elderly local woman called Frances Mulley, who remembered the stories told by Lavinia, her late mother. Lavinia, who had 14 children, had witnessed Madame Angelo in action, and had been horrified by the sight of the poor woman being pricked with a needle in order to keep her awake and alert during the tougher parts of the task.

Madame Angelo and her family based themselves in Dudley for much of the mid-1870s, and in addition to the 1,000-milers, we can be sure she appeared at the town's Alexandra Music Hall, a venue the couple used as a correspondence address in order to receive bookings arising from their advertisements. Margaret's extended stay in Dudley would make her something of a local legend – she was mentioned in *Edwin Blocksidge's Dudley Almanac* which described in detail the entertainments staged outside the Cromwell Grove Inn, where admission was gained by passing through the pub itself in Watson Street, or by means of an adjoining passage. There were pigeon shooting contests for generous money stakes, and a large room adjoining the pub where the cockfights secretly took place for considerable sums too, plus a dancing platform on the green where a band would play. But greatest attraction of all would always be the amazing walking feats during the tenancy of Tom Davies. Large sums were taken at the gates for the 42-day performances, usually ending with a brass band playing while driven around in a brake, triumphant Madame Angelo sitting up front. It was generally tuppence or threepence to gain entry with the track marked out by ropes lined with big crowds, even at night when the scene would be artificially lit. Posters advertising the event were printed by Blocksidge, publisher of the almanac, at his office in Union Street, with Margaret's husband rolling his sleeves up and assisting in the 'lithographic department' on a regular basis. The Almanac commented: "Angelo was a woman of athletic appearance and wore striking costumes, and we understand she netted a considerable sum as reward for her labours".

In the spring of 1875 Joseph did a deal with Joseph Clewes, owner of the Victoria Pleasure Gardens in Leicester, to stage a 1,000-mile walk at his venue. They would use the portable, wooden 'Shah's Temple of Wonder' trappings as the walk HQ and Clewes would add in a three-day 'gala' to pull in extra punters. Clewes, well known in Leicester as landlord of the Coach Makers Arms in Church Gate, placed an advert in *The Era* for talent of all descriptions to come forward for the gala section. A varied cast was assembled and the public responded in great numbers throughout. Weekend crowds were put at between 3,000 and 5,000, while the final Monday, with its bonus attractions, was said by police to have involved a bumper 15,000 spectators.

Clewes hired a high-wire walker and a balloonist to add to the grand spectacle, but he had to bring these acts to a speedy halt when it was realised potential customers could stand and watch them from outside the grounds without paying to come in! The grounds, along with the Temple of Wonder, were situated fronting Welford Road near the Toll Gate. Nowadays the site is occupied by University of Leicester student accommodation units, and a DIY store. Many local people evidently loved the spectacle but, as was so often the case, the local press seemed unimpressed by what went on. A *Leicester Chronicle* editorial brought up the old chestnut of disrespect being shown by staging events on Sundays:

"One naturally wonders by what strange inconsistency it is that while the inhabitants of Leicester find themselves on Sunday not only denied the Free Library but are also turned away from our Town Museum, [when] there is no compunction in permitting them to witness the elevating spectacle of a strange female pedestrian [Madame Angelo] wearily trudging around a narrow circle, in discharge of the self-imposed task of walking a thousand miles in a thousand consecutive hours... [yet] upon almost the very day the commencement of a similar performance is threatened in Belgrave, the Brighton Aquarium Company are remorselessly fined £200 [for] abuse and profanation of the Lord's Day".

Meanwhile, writer Guy Dart gave his verdict in the *Leicester Daily Post* of the final day's activity on Monday 24 May 1875: "A good many people appear to have been keeping Saint Monday [absenteeism from work]. Between two and three in the afternoon the London Road, Granby Street, Belvoir Street and other thoroughfares were thronged by thousands of persons, who apparently preferred lounging about to being at business. Many people wondered what it was drew the concourse together, and led to such a suspension of business, and asking: 'What went ye out for to see?' were told that it was to see Madame Angelo... parading the town in costume in a brake and four greys and with a band of music. Verily a most important reason to assemble by troops in the streets, mothers to leave their children, and workmen their business. Shoals of people visited the ground to witness Madame A complete the 1,000 miles, a great many riding thither in brakes and other vehicles. It is stated that the gate money during the 42 days the affair has been on has amounted to several hundred pounds, and that on some Sunday mornings as many as 3,000 persons have been present, whose admission money would amount to £25. No preacher in Leicester can draw so large a congregation and a walking woman appears to have a greater hold over the popular mind than a talking man. It is surprising that exhibitions of this sort should obtain so much attention, but it no doubt arises from the fact that amusements of a more reasonable sort are somewhat discouraged by the powers that be".

Despite the controversies, it was clear Madame Angelo's fame and reputation was still growing some 11 years after becoming a pedestrienne. A letter in June 1875 to the *Leicester Chronicle* complaining about the shortcomings of Leicester Corporation stated: "I wish earnestly the Corporation had the energy, the determination, and perseverance of Madame Angelo!". And then, as if to counter-balance the positive with a negative, it was reported that when landlord Joe Hallam of the Victoria Grounds beerhouse appeared in court to renew his license, objections were raised as he'd been spotted selling beer to spectators in the field where Madame Angelo was walking. The magistrates considered the case carefully and chose leniency, granting Hallam's license with a caution.

There were several outbreaks of trouble during the Leicester event, perhaps inevitable with such large crowds involved. William Clayton, employed as a 'clicker' at the entrance to the Victoria Grounds, was ordered to pay £2 or do 21 hours of hard labour by local magistrates for assaulting a police officer. The scuffle had started after Clayton left the arena to fetch a drink from the nearby pub. When he was not allowed immediately back in, he struck a fellow employee and threw the contents of his beer jug at the policeman. Superintendent Moore told the court: "There were nearly 15,000 on the ground at the time. Madame Angelo was finishing her walking of 1,000 miles in 1,000 hours. I have [dealt with] a good deal of trouble during the time she has been walking." The chairman of the magistrates seemed baffled by it all and enquired whether Madame Angelo was still alive after such an almighty effort? Moore replied: "Yes I believe so!"

Madame Angelo's second big walk of 1875 would be another 1,000-miler, this based at the Volunteer Drill Hall, Millbay in Plymouth, starting in unseasonably rainy mid-July. Large crowds gathered on the final day of the walk after it was announced she would complete her 999th mile just before 10pm and then cover the last three laps cradling baby Cyrenious in her arms. She was cheered home enthusiastically by a crowd that also enjoyed a baby show, sack racing and a shorter-distance walking match for women.

Margaret was at the peak of her fame around now, but there were signs that other pretenders were emerging with claims to her crown as queen of the UK pedestriennnes. Madame Willetts and Miss Richards were two such performers, while in the Potteries, young Emma 'Mademoiselle' Bailey spent a considerable chunk of the early summer of 1875 impressing fellow citizens of the Hanley area, totting up the awe-inspiring total of 1,500 miles in 1,500 successive hours. Crowds were rather thin for much of this walk, with a notable exception being the day of the customary local ceremony of 'well dressing' at Bucknall. In addition to admiring the flowers decorating the well, the crowds watched Emma – between walks – being paraded in a six-horse open carriage, accompanied by the Old Borough Band. There was also maypole dancing, and skittle and shooting matches.

Emma Bailey and the other up-and-coming pedestriennes will have learned a lot from Margaret and Joseph about the art of marketing and communications – 'PR' as it would subsequently be known. Indeed, the year of 1876 would prove significant as far as communicating in general was concerned: Scotsman Alexander Graham Bell patented his newly invented telephone in March of this year, proudly speaking the first intelligible message to his assistant ("Mr Watson, come here, I need you!").

This year saw two more high-profile walks of 1,000 miles by Madame Angelo. At the end of May a return visit to the Hop Pole Gardens in Norwich culminated with her final stages being serenaded in spectacular fashion by the splendid Band of the Caribiniers (Dragoon Guards). A month later she set off on another six-week trek, based this time at New Holland, the village that served as a ferry and rail terminal on the southern banks of the River Humber. The *Belfast Telegraph* waxed lyrical about the latter walk, praising her for being "a dainty walker". After finishing the 42-day stint she performed for two extra days at a special gala staged for her benefit.

Having demonstrated once again her remarkable staying power – at the age of 36 she'd now completed around 20 walks of 1,000 miles in 1,000 hours – Margaret was in a stronger position to secure more music hall bookings for the next few months. Joseph fixed up dates throughout 1877 for her, including, among others, a lengthy visit to Scotland. She performed on stage at several venues north of the border, including Aberdeen, Dundee, Glasgow (Britannia Theatre in Trongate) and Greenock (Moss' Varieties Theatre), and was also part of a highly successful show at the Prince of Wales Palace in Middlesbrough. On occasion, part of the evening programme would feature on-stage walking matches over half a mile and mile, and even a novelty hopping race, with "beautiful gold rings" put up as prizes.

A one-off return to 1,000 miles was fixed up for the summer of 1877 in the bustling resort of Brighton. Margaret completed the feat on the evening of Monday 16 July in the gardens of the Allen Arms in Lewes Road. Despite inclement weather for much of the last week or two "she walked with apparently unabated vigour, and performed the feat in a really genuine manner", according to the *Brighton Herald*. The event seemed to encourage rowdy behaviour, particularly at weekends, and the police were kept on their toes.

While in Brighton, Margaret posed for a new portrait photo in the Lombardi & Company studio in King's Road, which meant Joseph could create a brand-new and improved 'carte de visite' for publicity purposes. There were other distractions away from the walk, too: during the second week of the event, a middle-aged woman called Fuller, employed to spend every night waking Margaret up to do her hourly miles, decided she'd had enough and quit her job. The unhappy Mrs Fuller described the six-week walk as "an unsavoury event" and went to court to claim payment of 11 shillings from the Atkinsons for the 11 days she completed before quitting. Joseph was refusing to pay, claiming she breached her contract by walking out and therefore forfeited all wages owing to her. With Madame Angelo unable to leave the walk and attend court as a witness, the case was adjourned until after the event had finished. By the time of the rescheduled hearing Joseph and Margaret had already left town. The bench took a dim view of this and ruled the pair of them should be ordered to pay the full amount plus costs.

A 'carte de visite' souvenir postcard depicting Madame Angelo.

By the start of 1878 the competition was definitely hotting up for Madame Angelo, with the Londoner 'Madame Anderson' by now performing walks of differing distances instead of sticking to the tried and trusted 1,000-milers. The impressive Anderson issued advertising which posed the question 'Who is the champion female pedestrian?' which was a thinly disguised dig at Joseph who regularly called his wife a champion in her publicity material.

This would be a busy year in terms of music hall appearances. Attendances were very good during her residency at the Circus of Varieties in Burnley and a "great and glorious success" was registered at the Theatre Royal in Farnworth, near Bolton. Madame Angelo had become a well-established favourite in Lancashire by now, and Joseph made the most of this. He would use several of the county's venues as a mailing address when offering her services via adverts. He continued to work hard on new gimmicks and by now theatre managers could obtain life-sized posters of Margaret to help publicise her shows.

Not long after a series of appearances at Wolverhampton (Prince of Wales Theatre), Oldham (Adelphi Music Hall) and Sheffield (Alhambra Palace), the end of May 1878 heralded a return to the 1,000-mile treadmill for Margaret. The Shah's Temple of Wonder took up residence in Rochdale Old Road, near Huntley Brook, Bury, and then later in the summer on a field near the Fox Inn, Milnrow Road in Rochdale. Once more Margaret put on superb shows of consistency and reliability, and as she neared the finish at Rochdale, organisation swung into action of a grand procession to celebrate the efforts of 'The great female Deerfoot' through all the principal streets of Rochdale in an open carriage drawn by four grey horses and headed by two military bands. The usual attractions were on the main field, plus some novelties not commonly seen, such as silver-plated cups for winners of a donkey race, sack race and bicycle race. The sparkling illumination of the Temple of Wonder was this time accompanied by "the novel flight of a fiery pigeon". Then came the magnificent ascent of what was described as "an Angelo balloon, plus a monster balloon containing Mr Wilder's new patented electro-magnesium light and the newly invented Serpent Meteors, the wonder of the age". These special effects dazzled the wide-eyed crowds watching from below.

Rochdale had certainly been one of the more lively fixtures for Margaret, and proved a real money-spinner, but Joseph wasn't resting on his laurels. He remained keen to keep things ticking over, as there was no guarantee when the next good payday would come along. Christmas 1878 was on the horizon and they still had six of their seven children to feed and clothe, and even though the weather would be unfavourable for walking and for spectating alike, Joseph found himself with little alternative but to fix up another 1,000-miler.

This one would test his wife, by now aged 37, to the full, for the location was bitterly cold and unwelcoming. With winter moving in, the task of going outside to walk every single hour for six weeks would not be a comfortable one. The event would be on the edge of the moors, enclosed in a field at The Nook just outside Oldham. The main hazard might not be conquering a lack of sleep this time – Margaret was well practised in that art – but more likely to be battling against the cold and the razor-sharp winds. Snow was another potential problem, and so it would prove.

The walk commenced in October and during its early stages attracted decent enough crowds. But, as was so often the case, it was not universally popular among those living and working in the locality. It was condemned as a vulgar pursuit that shouldn't be happening at all, let alone on Sundays, according to one angry local, who hit out via the letters column of the *Manchester Examiner*. Francis Fielding of Mumps, Oldham, called the scenes at the walking venue a disgrace.

Fielding wrote: "The scenes I wish to draw your attention to are taking place in an enclosed field, where there is a lady engaged in performing the feat of walking 1,000 miles in 1,000 hours for which admission is 2d each; and I can assure you the scenes that take place are a disgrace to Oldham and the people who live there. It is a well-known fact that large numbers of the sporting fraternity from all the surrounding towns come here to indulge in their favourite sport and their presence in the district is anything but agreeable to the inhabitants… It strikes me the parsons and ministers are not doing their duty in not raising their voices against such scenes taking place on a Sunday".

Criticism of this nature is unlikely to have troubled the Atkinsons, but the arrival of shocking weather did present an unwelcome development. Shortly after the walk had passed its halfway stage in November, heavy snow fell in the area, and drifts of about four feet were seen all over Lancashire. Later a storm struck, with reports of huge hailstones, and there were many blocked railway lines and roads. These were the worst storms for decades in Lancashire. It was not a time to be trying to walk a mile every hour for six weeks. The *Manchester Evening News* reported that many workplaces and public events had ground to a halt and "much distress is beginning to be felt among the labouring population. In the Manchester area thousands are suffering from poverty to an unwanted degree".

Things were so bad in northern Britain that Queen Victoria and Princess Beatrice could only venture out from Balmoral if they used a sleigh and not their normal well-appointed carriage. In Oldham, Madame Angelo had no such luxury of choice – she either plodded on with her task through the snow and slush, or she quit altogether and took the financial hit. It was a stark choice. Confirmation that she was able to finish the 1,000 miles has proved difficult to locate, but there is evidence much effort went into keeping the walk alive. Joseph reportedly worked relentlessly night after night to keep his wife moving in safety, and stayed awake himself to ensure she kept to her schedule in the difficult night-time sessions.

The weather was hugely inconvenient – but there was more bad luck to come. During the walk news broke that a big chunk of Oldham's working population – and thus part of Joseph's potential paying audience – had been plunged into financial turmoil when 15,000 local workers went on strike at the cotton mills. They were protesting over pay cuts and their action would last fully six weeks. It meant the hard-up families of the area suddenly found themselves having to survive on even less than usual: "The coming yuletide will be fraught with misery and wretchedness", lamented one report.

As if all this wasn't enough, there was worse news just around the corner for the Atkinsons. The same week the area was hit by storms, a major local bank collapsed, leaving more than a thousand customers frantic and potentially penniless, the total liabilities well over half a million pounds. To the horror of Joseph and Margaret the bank in question was Fenton's of Rochdale, of whom they were an important customer. Their losses were said to be severe. The bank operated under the name of Messrs John and James Fenton and had been well established in Rochdale and Heywood, serving customers of all types. Its sudden failure was reportedly caused by "the non-success of transactions that were not of a strictly bank character" into which the firm had entered during recent years… the upshot of which had been "distress and almost desolation" for around 1,200 depositors. These included tradesmen, charities, clergymen, medical men, members of building and benefit societies, and ordinary working people. The *Heywood Advertiser* was able to confirm local speculation that a certain entertainer by the name of Madame Angelo was one of the more severe victims of the bank's failure.

Ultimately the bank's shareholders would be forced to sell their homes and goods, including the Fenton family estate of Crimble Hall, in a desperate bid to satisfy creditors. But this would take some time to sort out, and in the immediate aftermath of the crash Madame Angelo and hundreds of others faced uncertainty and serious hardship. One report commented that "several splendid fortunes" had been thrown away by the bank, due to "sheer stupidity or something worse". Disastrous dealings in stocks and shares were said to be responsible for what happened.

Although Margaret appears to have bounced back from her bad weather ordeal, the general stress and trauma of the period had a serious effect on the health of husband Joseph. Shortly after the Oldham walk and the bank going bust, he suffered a serious stroke that left him paralysed. Then, three weeks after his initial collapse, he died on Thursday 30th January 1879 in Oldham, aged just 38. He and Margaret had been married for 19 years and their seven offspring were aged between 15 months and 17 years old.

An acquaintance of Joseph related the background to this bad news to the *Heywood Advertiser*, revealing exactly how significant a role the Oldham walk had played in his sad demise: "[Joseph] imprudently exposed himself to the full severity of the weather, at a time when the snow lay thick upon the ground and bitter frost prevailed, in superintending night and day the arrangements for the pedestrian feat. When the excitement that kept him up was at end, paralysis set in with the reaction".

In other words, Joseph had worked so hard ensuring his wife's 1,000-mile walk succeeded despite the dreadful conditions, he ended up losing his life as a result. The report continued: "[Joseph] seems to have made light of the attack at first, and it was not until he had lost all power of motion and the use of speech that he agreed to have medical advice. Doctor Howard was sent for, but he pronounced the case almost hopeless, and recommended his removal as soon as possible to the Manchester Infirmary. By the time the recommendation was procured however, the man had become so exhausted that the doctor would not sanction his removal. Great sympathy is felt for [Madame Angelo] in the neighbourhood – the more so as she is known to have been a severe sufferer by the Rochdale bank failure. She is the bearer of popular marks of athletic appreciation in the shape of medals and crosses and it is stated that she is about to be similarly complimented by her Oldham admirers".

Joseph had been heavily involved from the start of her career – indeed his flair for marketing and promotion had shaped it – so his sudden and tragic absence will have left a huge gap. Needing to press on and earn money will have been tough enough from a practical point of view, let alone coping with the emotional implications of losing her life partner. But Margaret clearly had an inner strength that extended further than just athleticism.

With a big family to provide for, Margaret could not afford a lengthy period of mourning, as was currently the case with Queen Victoria following Prince Albert's death. Margaret got back on her feet – in every sense of the phrase – by remarrying barely six months after Joseph's sad demise. One can only imagine the surprise and raised eyebrows that will have been prompted by her tying the knot so soon after being widowed, to a man nearly half her age – 22-year-old Lancastrian John Ashworth.

The pair were married in the Parish Church in Makerfield, Wigan, in the summer of 1879. John had been born in Ramsbottom and worked in a cotton mill on leaving school, but had his eyes on improving his lot and that meant taking over as Margaret's manager and developing her earning power just as his predecessor Joseph had done. Before long, Ashworth was describing his occupation as 'travelling showman'.

Having experienced financial problems in the early 1870s, only to suffer again from the Rochdale bank crash of 1878, Margaret took new directions in the volatile, risky world of event promotion. The relentless calendar of 1,000-mile walks interspersed with music hall performances would now be modified, an important new aspect being the involvement of one or more of their children in their touring show.

Across Northern and central England the popularity of the female 1,000-milers seemed to be on the wane and as Margaret neared her 40th birthday it was clearly time for a more imaginative approach. In 1880, she tried to change the tune, to provide a fresh novelty. The peripatetic 'Shah's Temple of Wonder' brand name would stay on the road, but Margaret experimented with different walking formats, such as a mile and a quarter every consecutive hour for 500 hours.

Interestingly, a few weeks before she married Ashworth, Margaret had been publicly challenged by a new face in the pedestrianism world – 20-year-old Emma Jane Bailey from Hanley in Staffordshire. Emma styled herself 'Mademoiselle Bailey' and already had a number of long walks under her belt. In May of 1879 she undertook another in Gidlow Lane, Wigan, that involved 1.25 miles every hour, night and day for three weeks, finishing on Whit Monday. Hosting this well-attended event was the popular Pagefield Inn, named after the nearby iron rolling mills whose workers made up much of the clientele. Alongside news of this walk, an announcement was placed in the *Wigan Observer*: "Notice to the public at large – Mademoiselle Bailey is not a pupil of Madame Angelo's, but will walk Madame Angelo any length of time or distance she likes, or any other female in the world".

Such a direct challenge was unusual as far as Madame Angelo was concerned, and could well be the result of the new involvement of John Ashworth. A duel between the veteran and the young pretender would have had crowd-pulling potential and great novelty value. A week or so after Emma threw down the gauntlet, the response was made public: "Madame Angelo is prepared to accept the challenge of Mademoiselle Bailey and will walk against her in an eight-day competition for any amount she thinks proper".

It seems by now Emma and Margaret knew each other well and before long would both be appearing at the Shah's Temple of Wonder promotions. It seems unlikely they had an intense rivalry, but it would have been good for business for the public to think so. The acceptance of Emma's challenge was made public by Margaret during her latest solo walk, a promotion based on the Recreation Ground at Ince on the outskirts of Wigan. Music, dancing, balloon and firework displays surrounded the festivities which were said to be in aid of Wigan Infirmary. This walk finished on the last day of June and amounted in total to 1,060 miles. Margaret's final triumphant yards around 10.15pm saw her accompanied by one of her children, prompting huge cheers from the good-natured crowd.

By now, Margaret had a hard-earned reputation to maintain as the top female pedestrian in Britain. As such, she will not have welcomed a scandal that blew up concerning her new friend and rival Emma Bailey. The 21-year-old was an unmarried mother, and details of her private life made an unwelcome appearance in the public domain during summer 1880, courtesy of a court case in her native Staffordshire.

Newspapers reported how the young star of the local pedestrianism scene had summoned a man from Bucknall in Stoke-on-Trent called William Baddeley to "show cause why he should not be adjudged the father of her illegitimate child". She told the court that Baddeley had promised marriage and presented her with the gift of an umbrella during their courtship, before seducing her during 1879. Baddeley, who was a 15-shillings-a-week colliery worker, denied keeping company and having undue familiarity with her. During cross-examination Miss Bailey was accused of "being familiar" with two of the attendants employed at her long-distance walks – young men named Buller and Brunt – which she firmly denied. Her status as a celebrity in the Midlands meant there was considerable interest in the case.

While Emma was going through her courthouse ordeal, Madame Angelo was performing just a mile or two away in Stoke's Finney Gardens, her daughter Angela – billed as 'The Little Champion' – walking alongside her for certain sections of the event. This event would climax in front of a good crowd which enjoyed extra attractions such as bicycle races, a sack race, a military band and illuminations. A grand baby show was held, the winner qualifying to be carried to the finish line by Madame Angelo at the conclusion of her performance.

In fine weather on Tuesday 7th September 1880 a Shah's Temple of Wonder promotion in Rochdale got underway in Shade Walk, Ramsay Street, on what was basically a large piece of wasteground behind the Trafalgar Hotel. It was the challenge of 1879 finally come to fruition – a match between Angelo and Bailey, billed grandly as a contest for the 'Championship of the World' that would involve 1.25 miles being walked in every successive hour, night and day, for three weeks (500 hours). Posters had gone up throughout Rochdale and interest was high. The two women set off during the Tuesday afternoon and by early Friday evening were locked together on a tally of 92.5 miles. Special trains brought in weekend spectators who thrilled at the sight of the beautifully illuminated Temple building and the stirring sound of a military band, all for a maximum admission fee of threepence. It seems the experienced Madame Angelo subsequently forged a good lead and came out on top, although some early newspaper reports gave Bailey as the winner. This was later corrected at the behest of Angelo's husband/manager John.

The defeated Bailey left Rochdale in a hurry to prepare for a 1,000-miler shortly afterwards at the Pickup Croft Mill, off Yorkshire Street in Burnley. Meanwhile, Madame Angelo, having just celebrated her 40th birthday, showed she still had what it takes by also diving straight into another event. This was at the Holme inn at Todmorden, and again involved walking 1.25 miles every hour, day and night, for three weeks (630 miles in 500 hours). Predictably, she employed a system of walking roughly 40 minutes at a time, beginning 20 minutes before the hour and finishing 20 after, to complete 2.5 miles, thus fulfilling the rules and giving herself 80 minutes in every two-hour block for rest and recuperation in the cosy Temple hut.

With October 1880 drawing to a close, the *Todmorden Advertiser* reflected that the early days of this latest outing had passed off with little public support – "the affair has not created very much interest" – although on the weekends when added attractions were laid on, around 2,000 paid to get in on a single day, which will have ensured John and Margaret didn't endure losses.

By now, daughter Angela, whose tenth birthday was Christmas Day 1880, was being groomed to perform as a walker too. She would appear for short spells alongside Mesdames Angelo and Bailey at a number of events, including when the Shah's Temple of Wonder ventured into Wales with Emma top of the bill. It meant little Angela made her debut as a sporting entertainer at a far younger age than her famous mother, who had started at 25.

Margaret and her husband of one year continued experimenting with shorter events. At the tail end of 1880, in what was shaping up as another severely cold winter, she took on an indoor 300-miler in Bradford, at the

Coffee Palace in Alderson's Grand Concert Hall in Bridge Street. This involved walking 50 miles each day for the best part of a week. The first day saw 300 spectators inside the hall with Margaret hitting the 50 mark at around nine in the evening, accelerating so that the final two miles took just 22 minutes. This increase in hourly steps was good preparation for what was to follow – a successful attempt at the mammoth total of 2,000 miles in 1,000 consecutive hours at the same venue in Bridge Street. This was double her specialist distance but within the same time frame, and would keep her occupied well into the new year of 1881, ending on the final Saturday of January. The first week or two passed in helpful, mild weather conditions, but by the time she was approaching the 1,500-mile mark things deteriorated outside the hall with snow and severe frosts hitting the Bradford area in a big way.

Even the lake in nearby Manningham Park froze solid, but there was no stopping Madame Angelo. When doubts were cast that she was continuing to walk during the unforgiving winter nights, a statement was issued in the *Bradford Daily Telegraph* to reassure the cynics: "During the Christmas holidays thousands of persons paid for admission to witness this lady's performance during the night-time. Persons making the above assertion ought to come and see and let their own eyes be their own judge… [for she is] still going on with the greatest vigour".

Margaret completed the 2,000 miles on schedule and although there were no reports of any physical problems resulting from the gruelling endeavour, it does seem likely she treated this mammoth task – privately at least – as a final hurrah for her walking career. In this year of her 41st birthday enough was enough, it seems. She would take a back seat from hereon in, doing little or no high-profile walking herself, concentrating instead on earning a living with husband John by promoting various events for others to participate in.

The 1881 census was taken on Sunday 3rd April and pinpointed the family as staying at lodgings in a street known as Beast Market in central Huddersfield. They may have been here due to 25-year-old John needing to revert to more conventional work for a spell (for he now gave his occupation as 'corn miller'). Margaret stuck with her story that she was born in Calcutta, and again listed her occupational status as 'performer'. None of the four children – Violette 15, Angela 10, Henrietta 7 and Joseph 4 – received the conventional listing of 'scholar' against their names, instead described as 'professional performers' like their mother.

The odd music hall appearance continued to be part of Margaret's schedule, occasions where she would be given top billing and the performances might also see her rewarded with a benefit night. This was the case in Barrow-in-Furness during a very hot period of July 1881 when the Star Theatre of Varieties in Forshaw Street was crowded on a regular basis to see Margaret's stage act, along with various burlesque dancers, 'serio-comics' and stand-up comedians. Her post-1881 appearances were scarce and not long-distance affairs, typically exhibitions of race walking with other pedestriennes such as the one on an indoor sawdust track at the Public Hall in Hindley, Lancashire in March 1882.

How closely John and Margaret remained involved with the Shah's Temple of Wonder travelling show is unclear, but it would pitch up in South Wales in the autumn of 1881 with Emma Bailey again top of the bill. At the Gelli Hotel in Ystrad, and then at the Star Inn in Dukestown near Tredegar, Madameoiselle Bailey performed walks of just under 630 miles in 500 hours, assisted at intervals by an 11-year-old described as 'The Little Wonder', which is likely to have been Margaret's daughter Annie.

In early October, John and Margaret put on a promotion in the large Carriage Repository building in Paragon Street in the centre of Hull. It was a six-day walking tournament in which four men had to 'walk fair heel and toe' for 12 hours a day on a tiny track. Cash prizes to the value of £30 were put up and the winner would be hailed Champion of Yorkshire. Robert Carruthers, regional representative of *Sporting Life*, was appointed referee and measured the track at a fraction under 35 yards per lap, meaning 51 laps were needed to complete a single mile. The four men put up a good show despite the cramped surroundings and poor condition of the track. A couple of days earlier a two-mile walking handicap involving six contestants pulled in a good crowd half a mile away in Brook Street at what was described as 'Angelo's Recreation Buildings'. The name suggests the enterprising couple had managed to hire and rename the place for the duration. Later the same month they staged a four-hour walking handicap contest in the Carriage Repository building.

The Ashworth six-day promotion had gone well, and with a good number of such events already being laid on for men, slowly the development of women's six-dayers gained a little ground too. This would culminate with a major event being set up at the Bingley Hall in Birmingham in March 1884. At stake would be the 'Championship Belt of the World' plus big cash prizes. Less than a month before the scheduled start, the *Sporting Life* published an appeal for a number of named pedestriennes to get into contact urgently, with a view to them taking part. The fact the nation's leading sporting publication should put Madame Angelo at the top of this wanted list underlines both her enduring box office appeal and also the esteem in which she was held. As it turned out, Margaret chose not to take part, but did recommend a substitute – her daughter Violette! Now 18 years old, Violette had proved her pedigree by winning a six-day race in Bradford fairly recently. The full story of the championship is covered later in Chapter 17.

What happened to Madame Angelo post-1884 is uncertain. Margaret's name disappeared from prominence, although her daughters continued in show business and it appears the peripatetic lifestyle was maintained by the family as a whole. The girls had more than walking in their repertoire, for they could perform feats of great strength for the delight and amazement of provincial theatregoers: in February 1885 *The Era* announced that "Sisters Violette and Annie, the talented daughters of Madame Angelo, the well-known female pedestrian, are performing feats of strength to very satisfactory audiences". In a circus managed by 'Lord' George Sanger, known as Sanger's Jubilee, "striking, though brief, proofs of strength were given by the 'iron-jawed ladies' Violette and Annie… these young persons lift tremendous weights from the ground by the 'air of their 'ead and carry a heavy man astride a barrel, the edge of which they grasp in their teeth".

In the 1891 census, Margaret and her family were recorded as living in a 'show van' which was parked up at St.Mary's Place, St Andrew, Newcastle, next to the Eye Infirmary. John, by now 35, was described as 'living on his own means' accompanied by Margaret, Annie and Violette, and teenager Olivinson. The latter is recorded as John's son, possibly from an earlier relationship, or this could be a clerical error and the boy was actually an employee.

Margaret must have felt her dog days were over as far as performing was concerned. Her name was still well known enough to obtain bookings here and there, but having passed her 50th birthday and the children just about grown up, her energy and motivation will have been dwindling. John was still a mere 35, of course, but it was clear their days in show business were numbered. Before long Angela, Henrietta and Joseph would find themselves working in the mills and factories of Radcliffe, near Bury – although Angela remained linked to the world of music hall by marrying a stage manager called Peter Lomas in 1894 and settling in Thornley, Durham. Of the other children, Cyrenious became a painter and decorator, and lived for a spell in the USA before returning to settle in Essex, while Julius Caesar left show business early at the behest of his wife. Annie continued into the early 1900s working with her husband John in their Cottrell's Swimming Show.

Margaret and John settled in her native County Durham and she died during the summer of 1911 at the age of 70, a victim of an extraordinary record-breaking heatwave that hit the UK and other parts of the world. Heatstroke was recorded as one of the causes of her death. Temperature records were set around the country over this period, including one of 98.1°F which would not be exceeded in the UK for 79 years. The relentless heat caused cotton mills to temporarily close and there were countless cases of entire workforces walking out of factories due to intolerable conditions. The death toll was high among elderly folk such as Margaret, and *The Times* even began running a daily 'Deaths From the Heat' column.

Margaret's place of death is not entirely clear. Several sources say it occurred at Crossgate, Barnard Castle, her place of birth, a site that was by now no longer simply a workhouse, but also housed an infirmary and hospital wards too. Other records say she died at the home of daughter Angela in May Street, Durham. What is certain is that she outlived her much younger second husband, John Ashworth, and was interred in St Margaret's cemetery in Durham in September 1911, just as the heatwave was receding.

Although she had been relatively well-off at certain points during her career as a performer, her great-great-granddaughter Key Nestor says it appears there was no great financial legacy passed down to Margaret's descendants after her death, which is probably a result of the difficult period she experienced in the late 1870s.

Andy Milroy, athletics historian, has studied the question of how significant Madame Angelo's contribution to pedestrianism was, and, more broadly, women's sport in general. He says her career should be seen in its social context. He says her significance lies in the fact that as a woman of mixed race she was seen as the first female black professional athlete. The manner in which she unhesitatingly took the sobriquet of 'the Mulatto Lady' shows she was proud of her ancestry. Milroy points out that it is interesting a black pedestrienne should emerge in England but apparently not in the United States where there was a larger black population: "In Victorian England the upper classes seemed to view the Indian rajahs and the African tribal chiefs as equals whereas the English working classes were regarded by them as the lowest of the low. So the segregation in England was social rather than racial. This suggests that Margaret claiming to be from Calcutta was another astute move. In America, with the wounds of the Civil War still raw, there was more overt discrimination. Black male athletes did contest six-day races but they were very few in number.

Interestingly it was Frank Hart who was to be the most successful black six-day performer and he, like Margaret Atkinson, came from an Afro-Caribbean background, being from Haiti. Exotic and not from the USA".

Margaret's descendant Kay Nestor says further confirmation of the mixed race background has come via references to Margaret's siblings. One was a sister who emigrated to New Zealand and is mentioned in an old newspaper clipping as "a pretty little half-caste", while the other was a brother referred to as a "a man of colour".

So was Margaret effectively the first black female athlete to perform in Britain – and one of the first in the world? This seems highly likely, because no black female runners or walkers from the USA have been found in 19th-century sport, although there were a number of black female pro boxers. Even black male athletes were a real rarity in Britain throughout Margaret's era. In 1883, at the very tail end of her walking career, a pedestrienne described as "a lady of colour" and calling herself Madame Green, champion walker of South America, arrived on British shores looking for competition. After disembarking at Liverpool, various challenges were immediately issued but nothing appears to have materialised and little more was heard of her.

Andy Milroy points out: "Margaret Atkinson was important in a more subtle way. Her 'mulatto' sobriquet was part of a marketing strategy. It is the way that Margaret and Joseph sold the black pedestrienne package, through clever use of an engaging, intriguing strapline and the dissemination of portraits that mark Margaret out as unusual and as a pioneer. She even had life-sized portraits produced for sale at venues. This astute marketing enabled a relatively long career and by travelling the country, she greatly raised the awareness of female walking throughout Britain. But Margaret was far from being a one-trick pony. As a music hall and sometime circus performer, she needed to be versatile. She developed her raw talent into a show business package, to capitalise on her fame as a walker."

Before Joseph's untimely death the Atkinsons seem to have made a good living from pedestrianism and the music hall, having operated shrewdly to maximise her background and her talents. They could even afford to commission large oil paintings of themselves. Life was not so rosy after the Rochdale bank crash was quickly followed by Margaret becoming a widow, but for a pedestrienne she had a remarkably long career lasting nearly 20 years. She was certainly an influence on many others, among the very first to bill herself 'Madame' instead of plain 'Mrs', and successfully incorporating singing and stagecraft skills into her repertoire.

ELEVEN

LONDONER KATE
THRILLS THE KIWIS

All the British pedestriennes deserve to be recognised as remarkable women of their time, but the case of Mrs Kate Wiltshire (nee Rider) is strikingly unusual.

Kate was one of just three British-born women to make a success of professional pedestrianism on foreign soil. She shone brightly, if briefly, in the 1870s, having become New Zealand's first nationally known female sports star. Then, more than 100 years later, she attracted unexpected attention all over again after being identified as the great-great-grandmother of Jacinda Ardern, who became New Zealand Prime Minister in 2017.

STORY 15: KATE WILTSHIRE – A STAR IN 'TOPSY-TURVEYDOM'

Born in the St.Pancras district of London in April 1853, Catherine Sarah ('Kate') Rider was just seven years old when her father William, a private in the Army, died prematurely aged 36. Before long her widowed mother, a dressmaker also known as Kate, married joiner John Fox, whose work required the family to settle for a time in Yorkshire. They returned south during the 1860s and the younger Kate went into domestic service. She soon decided this was not for her, and aged just 19 hatched courageous plans to make a brand-new life for herself in far-off New Zealand.

Although its famous 'gold rush' was just about over, New Zealand represented an attractive prospect, not least because of the high number of Europeans who had already made a fresh start there – by now totalling around 300,000 and far outnumbering the indigenous Maori population.

Unaccompanied and no doubt highly apprehensive, Kate boarded the immigrant ship *Pleiades* on a pleasant, sunny day in September 1872 to embark on the adventure of a lifetime. As the vessel headed south on a journey of nearly four months, the passengers had ample time to form new friendships and Kate soon encountered the man who would change the course of her life for ever. Over the course of the 106-day trip, romance blossomed with fellow emigrant Joe Wiltshire, a 30-year-old railway platelayer from Berkshire. Originally from Truro, Joe had already proved himself a promising 'weekend' pedestrian, but had not been enjoying his day job and was heading south for a fresh start, determined to find a better life. His on-board liaison with Kate proved to be more than just a romantic interlude during a long voyage, for after disembarking shortly after Christmas 1872 at Lyttelton, near Christchurch, the couple immediately made plans to marry.

The passenger list shows a good number of single men and women, several of them domestic servants like Kate, although at 19 she was one of the youngest. No doubt most knew very little about their new home on the other side of the world, although when booking their tickets were encouraged by the shipping line Shaw, Savill and Company to find out more from a new edition of the *New Zealand Handbook* costing one shilling.

These migrants were taking advantage of assisted passages to their new lives, courtesy of a relatively new NZ government initiative led by Premier Julius Vogel. Kate's £13 ticket for the voyage would be taken care of, although she would have to contribute £5 after arrival via a promissory note. Joseph had to pay £4 cash in advance, and contribute £8 later, according to his promissory note. His previous working experience on the railways will have stood him in good stead when applying for the assisted passage, for New Zealand's new railway system was being expanded and needed fit and healthy workers like him. However, it seems Joseph had grander schemes in mind and didn't see his long-term future in work such as this.

So how did the epic journey unfold? Thanks to the captain's log and other shipping records, we can discover some details of Kate and Joseph's 15-week voyage. They were aboard the impressive 210-feet-long full-rigged iron sailing ship *Pleiades*, first launched on the River Clyde in Scotland in 1869, and now under the command of Captain David T. Roberts.

On Friday 13th September 1872, with Kate and Joseph safely aboard, the *Pleiades* spent time in the Export Dock at London's East India Docks before setting off down the Thames from Greenhithe, then parting company with its pilot off Dartmouth. In his log, Captain Roberts noted that among his passengers were "some old colonists" as well as many younger migrants, the latter a healthy group who looked well suited to the requirements of the province they were headed for. Kate and Joseph's last sight of their birth country would be on Wednesday 18th September as the *Pleiades* passed Bolt Head on the Devon coast and headed towards the French island of Ushant and the North Atlantic beyond. Many migrants of this era would be regarded as 'running away' from something they wanted to put behind them for ever. The last glimpse of England will have been a highly significant and emotional experience for the many single young women and men on board.

Progress was not fast and it would be nine days after the final sight of England that those on board were able to catch a glimpse of the island of Madeira off the NW tip of Africa in the distance. There was further excitement on board when it was announced they were crossing the equator, exactly four weeks since waving goodbye to the Devon coast. Real drama followed 48 hours further on, Captain Roberts responding to distress calls from the vessel *Jorawur* – a barque converted from the steam frigate HMS *Vulcan*. Its journey from Dundee to Calcutta had been hit by fierce storms causing loss of masts and yards, and serious injury to a crew member. Aid was provided with a doctor and some provisions sent across to the damaged ship.

The *Pleiades* was hit by the worst weather conditions of the trip during the final few weeks. There were heavy storms in mid-November and again over the first weekend of December and the final few days were no smooth passage either. It must have seemed ironic to those on board only familiar with British climes – for here they were in December, the height of New Zealand's summer, and the weather was just as bad as back home.

The 'promised land' came into view in Christmas week, the weather continuing to prove troublesome as they progressed up the coast, past the spectacular rugged scenery of Taiaroa Head, finally sailing into Lyttelton Harbour, close to Christchurch, at breakfast time on Saturday 28th December. In time-honoured fashion a group of excited and grateful passengers wrote out and signed a testimonial, thanking and praising the work of Captain Roberts in getting them safely to the other side of the world. The whole thing had taken 106 days.

Immigration procedures dictated that the passengers be grouped together and disembarked several hours after arrival, to be taken from the port to the Barracks by special train. The local Health and Port Officers boarded the ship and found everything to their satisfaction, with a clean bill of health among the passengers. Kate Rider and the other unmarried young women had been under the charge of matron Mrs Westcott who reported in glowing terms of their conduct during the voyage. A reporter who inspected the ship said it had brought over some fine livestock, with a good number of sheep all in excellent condition, in particular one ram described as a 'magnificent fellow'. Captain Roberts was pleased to record that only one animal had failed to survive the long passage.

Joseph Wiltshire and Kate Rider had boarded in London as unattached individuals, boldly but anxiously beginning new lives. They stepped off the ship together 106 days later having found a partner for life. The prospect of what lie ahead must have now seemed far less forbidding. Coincidentally it would be exactly another 106 days further on that they were married – at St Mary's Catholic Church in Merivale, Christchurch in April 1873. The ceremony was two days before Kate's 20th birthday.

Adjusting to his new surroundings Joseph began planning in earnest. Although the gold rush was largely over in this part of the world, he felt he had a chance of finding his own pot of gold by flying the flag for pedestrianism. He had been an accomplished long-distance walker in England and knew he could impress his new countryfolk by doing something never before seen in New Zealand – a solo 1,000-mile walk in 1,000 hours. It was a feat he'd apparently not attempted before himself, but was confident of managing.

Joseph's ideas were not fanciful or unrealistic. Just a year earlier English runners Frank Hewitt and A. E. Bird, along with Australian J. G. Harris, had arrived in Auckland to perform a tour of NZ. These pioneers sparked what one newspaper called "a perfect mania for pedestrianism" in the country. Foot racing had begun to catch on here in the 1840s and by the time Joseph and Kate Wiltshire arrived, prize money had increased, competition become intense, timing and measuring methods improved and the best performers could acquire national reputations.

Mr and Mrs Wiltshire would become the most famous of the lot for a spell, part of a competitive scene that gained prominence through the 1870s. The best-known pedestrians set up contests between themselves, or via publicans and other entrepreneurs, often for stakes provided by gambling backers. Things developed much as they had done in Britain, meaning Joseph and Kate would be performing for working people in circumstances that were sometimes a little rough and ready, often attracting the disapproval of officialdom.

By the 1870s New Zealand's newspapers were providing coverage of long-distance walking exploits from elsewhere in the world, thanks in no small part to the Wiltshires' emergence among the first to tackle the sport seriously in New Zealand. The couple had set up home in Oamaru, an expanding sea port on the eastern side of South Island, popular with European settlers for its pleasant climate and scenic views. Barely six months after arrival they had become well known in entertainment circles. Kate was never one to take a back seat, and before long the couple cooked up a plan for her to perform alongside Joseph, initially tackling shorter and more comfortable distances, her mere presence as a woman creating much interest and boosting their earning power.

Fully aware of her appeal and happy to exploit its crowd-pleasing potential, she adopted a costume described as resembling a trapeze artist's outfit. It was eye-catching and she became a popular figure, attracting more attention than Joseph even though he tackled longer and more impressive walking tasks. Kate's appearance drew many a compliment from the local papers, one of whom described her as a petite woman of just seven stones (44kg) with "beautiful jet black curls that shook in the sunshine as she walked".

Joseph was savvy enough to realise that getting their name established quickly needed something momentous – so he made sure his debut public appearance would be the first-ever attempt in New Zealand of Captain Barclay's famous 1,000-mile feat. It had been done twice across the Tasman Sea in Victoria, but never elsewhere in the colonies. His confidence at tackling the distance was impressive, for he'd spent the preceding few months earning a conventional living as a labourer rather than training for foot races. He needed a regular wage to tide things over as he and Kate settled into their new home, and also needed to meet the cost of setting up his big event. There was little or no opportunity to train or compete in

Popular Kate Wiltshire, an ancestor of New Zealand Prime Minister Jacinda Ardern.

advance of the big day. However, back in England he'd managed 800 miles in 800 hours at Wednesbury without much difficulty, so his confidence seemed well founded.

On the evening of Wednesday 14th May 1873, a month after the wedding, his event got underway in Christchurch, South Island's largest city some 140 miles up the coast from the Wiltshire's new home. It took place on a paddock near the main railway station, where Joseph had built himself a paling fence enclosure with a roof over the track, lights so he could be seen at night, and a sheltered area for his rest breaks. The event was well publicised, two timekeepers and a gateman hired. Admission was a shilling, or £1 for a season ticket, and Joseph also stood to gain from wagers against him succeeding, with at least £150 staked on the event. Attendances fluctuated and were disappointingly low on many of the 42 days, although predictably picked up at weekends and towards the end.

The *Wanganui Herald* described Joseph as a medium-sized man, powerfully built, with a free, springy style. The course was a circuit of around 200 yards meaning a total of 8,000 laps were required in all. He doggedly accomplished the task, apparently without serious difficulty, right on schedule as the end of June approached. Although it didn't prompt the excitement levels in Christchurch the Wiltshires had hoped for, Joseph did gain publicity and learned enough to make more informed plans for future events. He gamely declared his keenness to do it all again 'for an adequate consideration' and was promptly challenged by a man known as 'Young' Austin for a stake of £500 a side. This came to nothing, probably because Joseph couldn't come up with a backer.

In the wake of Christchurch it was clear some extra ingredient was needed for his next major outing, in order to drum up more interest and earnings. It was decided Kate should also get involved 'front of house', instead of quietly helping out behind the scenes. This time an agent was involved in helping the couple arrange and promote the event in mid-1874 in Dunedin, and things were carefully set up inside a large marquee next to the Princess Theatre in High Street, where admission would cost a shilling per spectator.

Joseph was to repeat his 1,000-mile feat while Kate's task was to walk 500 miles over the same period by doing half a mile every single hour, and she would take the full spotlight by walking during her husband's rest breaks. It was a clever manoeuvre as it meant spectators had twice as much entertainment as a conventional 1,000-miler, and the added novelty of a woman in action. It was advertised as the greatest pedestrian feat ever staged in the southern hemisphere and it worked a treat.

Kate Wiltshire was dressed in a "very neat walking costume", reported the *Otago Daily Times*, "and occasionally shook her beautiful jet black curls as she advanced on her journey… [she carried] a knobby little stick which she occasionally makes good use of by knocking the heads of little boys who endeavour to peep through the canvas".

Things generally went well over the first 25 days or so, but the remainder of the event was plagued by trouble. Minor crowd disturbances repeatedly broke out in and around the marquee, needing visits from Dunedin police, and then towards the end of the fourth week potential disaster struck: having just passed the 630-mile mark Joseph became ill, reportedly feeling dizzy and suffering several seizures or fits. He appeared to recover, but occasionally displayed a very unsteady gait. It was soon evident Kate was struggling too, mainly suffering the effects of sleep deprivation. One particular occasion saw her helpers fail completely to wake her after a rest period, eventually having to carry her into the arena and rather roughly force her into action.

The couple's struggles only intensified the interest of the local press, and the *Tuapeka Times* adopted an optimistic outlook: "I called at the marquee today and saw Mrs Wiltshire do one of her half miles. She is a slight, rather nice-looking little lady, and walked with a vigour and elasticity I was hardly prepared to see after reading the late accounts of her performances. They have now accomplished their 800th mile and half mile respectively, but will no doubt be unable to finish their respective tasks without any breakdowns".

A local doctor was made aware of events, and volunteered his services free, his professional interest piqued by the unusual nature of what was occurring. Spectators will have shared his fascination, although an *Otago Witness* columnist was not at all impressed and wrote that while Kate was fainting and Joseph was getting dizzy, the only person to benefit was the doctor, "who will be able to inform the public in a neatly got-up pamphlet how many miles and half miles it takes to kill a man and a woman in a given time".

With more than 100 half miles still remaining, Kate decided enough was enough and withdrew. As she had become the main attraction the weary Joseph soon dropped out too, despite having passed 800 miles and walking well again. He told the press the whole thing had left him penniless and to have continued would have only benefitted others. The Wiltshires later suffered a further blow when they were summoned to court for non-payment of the printers' bills for posters and other publicity material.

The last completed project of NZ-based historian and athlete David Colquhoun prior to his death in 2018 was an essay on Kate Wiltshire published in the *Turnbull Library Record*. Colquhoun tells how the disappointments and problems surrounding their first two outings, at Christchurch and Dunedin, certainly didn't deflate the Wiltshires' enthusiasm. They turned instead to shorter pedestrian performances, more suited to the professional theatre and music hall circuit:

"Quite likely inspiration came from the benefit concert organised for them after their Dunedin failure by sympathetic local thespians. The Wiltshires took part, each walking a timed mile for the audience's entertainment. The next month Joseph organised a similar two-night variety show at the Masonic Hall in Oamaru, their home town. He headed the bill, doing a three-quarter mile in 6.25 minutes, with support acts of singers, comedians and dancers. On the second night Mrs Wiltshire, in a suit of tartan, joined in with a five-minute half mile. The local paper gave it a very mixed review, but it was the start of the Wiltshires' unique brand of theatrical pedestrianism".

As for pedestrianism generally, interest was slowly increasing in New Zealand and elsewhere, although the Wiltshires did little for the best part of a year, probably due to Kate becoming pregnant around the end of 1874. She gave birth to their first child, Charles, who sadly died at the age of just four months. It was a sad period for the couple and Joseph continued to make ends meet with manual work, regularly advertising his services for excavating, fencing and well-sinking. But he pressed on with his pedestrianism, performing a 250-miler in 100 hours – two and a half miles each hour – at the Oamaru Volunteer Hall in August 1875.

By now, Joseph was seen as something of a local hero and excellent crowds turned out to cheer him on in shorter-distance matches with another British-born immigrant William Edwards and then 'Young' Delaney. Joseph triumphed in the latter thanks to a very fast last mile and after the celebrations was carried home shoulder-high still sitting on a couch he'd been using in the Volunteer Hall after the race!

Just weeks after giving birth, Kate had a successful solo debut at St George's Hall in Milton, a gold-rush town around 100 miles from home. She successfully walked 12 miles in two hours which, encouragingly, attracted a large and enthusiastic attendance, reported the *Clutha Leader*. Backed by the Milton Brass Band, she finished with a "splendid spurt" over the last mile, which carried her home with a minute to spare.

In early 1876 the couple stepped up their walking by means of a new act combining the two feats they had separately trialled in Oamaru and Milton – Joseph would do his 250 miles in 100 hours, with Kate joining him in the evenings to demonstrate her speed, usually with some kind of musical accompaniment. In addition there were even discussions about setting up a match where Kate took on star name William Edwards in a head-to-head battle, with his task being to match her with seven laps to every one she completed. A man-versus-woman contest was rare in pedestrianism and these talks underline how potentially entertaining the involvement of Kate had suddenly become.

These showpiece events presented the local population with a robust combination of sport and theatre that was perfect for the times. They would take place in well-populated towns and go down well with audiences. The first was in Timaru, followed by Christchurch, the capital Wellington, Napier and Auckland. These regular tests sharpened Kate's speed, strengthened her stamina and boosted her confidence – and by the time April 1876 came around she was fit and ready to put in the performance of her life.

The couple had always believed she was capable of achieving impressive feats in her own right and would be capable of far more than just being an eye-catching sideshow to Joseph's walks. This confidence led to the idea of her travelling to Auckland to have a crack at 100 miles in 24 hours – widely thought to be the first time a female had ever attempted the feat, let alone succeeded. On the evening of Friday 5th May 1876, a good crowd gathered at the City Hall on Auckland's Queen Street for an entertainment rather different from their usual night at the theatre. An indoor circuit was carefully marked out that morning with an inside circumference of only 62 yards. It meant Kate must walk a daunting 2,833 laps in 24 hours, a mind-numbing task, although she will have understood the size of the track was dictated by the nature of the premises and the need to pack in a good-sized audience to witness the feat. The *Auckland Star* billed it a feat "never before attempted by any female inhabitant of our planet" and the imagination of the public was captured.

Few men had achieved 100 miles in 24 hours and the best known male time in history at that point was 109.5 miles in 24 hours, meaning on paper it appeared an impossible task for any woman. Kate's abilities were already known in Auckland as two weeks earlier Joseph had walked 250 miles in 100 hours here with Kate doing several single miles with piano accompaniment –

her best a remarkably brisk stroll of under eight minutes. The *Daily Southern Cross* concluded she was the fastest female walker to appear in the colonies, although many still believed 100 miles in 24 hours required a level of strength and stamina that would be beyond such a petite figure as Kate. Nevertheless, well-known Queen Street jeweller F. H. Lewisson was happy to dismiss the doubters, and advertised his willingness to bet on her success. In response, the publican of the Occidental Hotel put up £25 that she would fail. Inevitably Kate's good looks and charisma added to the pre-walk interest and a *New Zealand Herald* comment was typical: "She is both graceful and pleasing, and of good figure".

At 8.30pm on the Friday, Kate was introduced on stage by her husband. She didn't disappoint the eager crowd, sporting her much-discussed and colourful walking costume, and as she prepared to start the Artillery Band began to play. After she set off, circuiting around the seated audience, there was huge initial enthusiasm, but inevitably many began to politely melt away after an hour or two when it became clear there was little else of interest to see until the latter stages next day.

A Friday night in Auckland's Queen Street was evidently a lively affair in the 1870s, with or without a big walking event, and inevitably some of the usual revelry outside would spread into the City Hall. At some point a drunken sailor appeared from nowhere, singing loudly and carrying a flag, who walked along ahead of Kate, serenading and chatting to whoever would listen. Nobody stopped him and this lasted for several hours. It seems unlikely Kate was very amused by this, for by then she was struggling with ankle pain and lack of sleep.

She had twisted the ankle at roughly three on the Sunday morning and this caused a considerable slowing. Reaching halfway at breakfast time, she slowed to around 2mph and there were concerns the injury would ruin the attempt, but she bravely pushed on, finding the pain subsiding and by the afternoon was back on pace. The rowdy sailor had meant well with his intervention, but it was clear Kate much preferred the more respectable company of Mrs Dennis, wife of a prominent Queen Street businessman, who gave her an arm to lean on and walked with her for 20 miles during a very difficult patch on the Saturday morning.

Throughout the day spectators appeared in dribs and drabs, but by 6pm the place was nearly full. By now Kate looked in great shape again and at 6.30pm, with roughly 2.5 miles left, was able to take a break, and prepare herself for a strong finish knowing the hall would be packed to its 500-plus capacity by the big climax. The Artillery Band were signalled to strike up and she set off again looking like a woman inspired, striding out at an estimated 6mph. Her backer, Mr Lewisson, tried to keep his promise and walk alongside her for the final few miles, but found to his astonishment and amusement he couldn't keep pace simply by walking: "He had to make short runs to avoid being distanced altogether and had to divest himself of his coat, collar and necktie... the perspiration streaming from his face", according to the *Daily Southern Cross*.

The last few laps were a riot of noise and excitement, according to the same paper: "The constant clapping of hands and waving of hats and handkerchiefs, as Mrs Wiltshire successively appeared at each corner, culminated at the last few rounds into a perfect furore of excitement". The band struck up Handel's 'See the Conquering Hero Comes', and Mrs Wiltshire processed amid deafening applause". It appears that the lap counters on duty had registered a mile for every 28 laps, whereas a full mile was actually the awkward distance of 28 laps plus another 30 yards or so. This meant Kate would be required to walk for roughly another 25 minutes after '100 miles' had been indicated, in order to ensure the full distance was genuinely done. She apparently knew this would happen and seemed quite happy, the general excitement generated by the crowd having temporarily killed her pain and fatigue. She was eventually timed in at around 8.10pm, giving a splendid finish of roughly 23 hours and 40 minutes.

Kate was hailed the first woman ever to have completed 100 miles on foot within 24 hours and it would prove her finest hour. The Aucklanders were proud, the British expats were proud, Joseph and her backers were proud and – more than 140 years later – her great-great-granddaughter the Prime Minister would talk of her immense pride too!

A 'purse' was made up for Kate from a collection in the City Hall and resulted in a good sum, according to the local papers, which were full of talk of Kate's "gigantic feat of endurance". The Wiltshires announced she had suffered no ill-effects and sent heartfelt thanks for all the support, particularly to Mrs Dennis for walking with her for 20 miles, thereby playing a key part in keeping her going to accomplish what no other woman in the world had ever done.

News of the magnificent feat spread first throughout Australasia and then further afield. There would be the odd occasion doubts were cast about its authenticity – notably after the German walker Bertha Von Hillern failed by a long way to match it in Boston, USA, one journalist writing: "I am quite aware that Mrs Wiltshire was said to have completed the 100 miles in 24 hours, but a great deal of that performance had to be taken on faith".

Kate's backer Lewisson was thrilled by her achievement and had no such doubts, and decided he must alert the British press, posting off a photograph of Kate in her walking costume to the popular London-based weekly *Illustrated Sporting and Dramatic News*. The staff at the *ISDN* were enchanted and one of their columnists made a drawing of the photograph which appeared in the paper's July 22 issue. He wrote:

"The costume in which the fair pedestrienne dressed, with that love of ornament natural to her sex, is another curious thing connected with [the feat], upon which you may comment for yourself inasmuch as I present you with a little drawing I made from the photograph in question… the climate of Auckland has been compared to that of Greece and if Mrs Wiltshire's example is followed, the costume also will be very Greek. You remember Byron's line: 'Half-naked, loving, natural, and Greek'".

The *ISDN* agreed with the spirit of Lewisson's assertion that Kate was "the best bit of pluck that ever wore petticoats" but pointed out that from the evidence of the photo she went about her business without such garments! The paper's British sense of fair play was drawn to reports that Kate had broken rules by receiving assistance during the walk, but it was accepted this so-called help had been "more of a cheering nature than of much physical assistance". They added rather waspishly: "In topsy-turvydom the spectacle of an enterprising tradesman [Lewisson] faithfully executing his advertised promise to walk with her is considered an example of correct athletics".

Kate's walking costumes were sometimes construed as daring or revealing by 1870's standards, particularly when seen through British eyes – not because inappropriate amounts of bare flesh were on show, but because there was no bulky or billowing fabric to disguise the shape of her figure or legs. David Colquhoun points out that she did not always appear in such revealing costumes, and through her career any innuendo or salacious comments did not come from New Zealand newspapers: "Her attire was accepted [in NZ] as necessary for such physical feats. Her good looks were an attraction, but her status as a married woman, always appearing with her husband, helped maintain propriety".

British- and USA-based pedestriennes often gained an unwanted reputation for being involved in something perceived as rather sleazy and daring, but Colquhoun believes Kate was always aiming for higher ground than that. He points out that when the Wiltshires' first variety show, in Oamaru was criticised for having some unseemly content, they quickly toned down the offending act for the second night and did all they could to maintain a good reputation.

Colquhoun adds: "Later reviews and accounts of [the Wiltshires'] various performances suggest their shows were seen as a more respectable entertainment, suitable for ladies, compared with the arenas of male pedestrianism. Their performances were even seen as morally improving. The *Herald* review of the opening night of the Auckland 250-miler, for example, praised the Wiltshires for their endeavours to direct the attention of all to the desirability of improving the mental as well as the physical powers. We would much rather have our young men animated by a desire to emulate and excel in this way, than to see them lounging about the bars and billiard halls of public houses".

New and different challenges for Kate came along throughout 1876 and one that really caught the public imagination was her proposed match-up with William Edwards in Wellington – the only known example of a man-versus-woman match-up in the early years of New Zealand sport. It took place in the Oddfellows Hall on Lambton Quay, watched by a big and noisy Saturday night crowd. The level of interest was great news for the Wiltshires, particularly as they received all gate takings. Kate was to walk six miles to Edwards' seven. She set off first and recorded a brisk 57 minutes, but the experienced Edwards managed to complete his task 15 seconds quicker. Pedestrianism enthusiasts were highly impressed however: Despite her "somewhat slender" appearance, commented one reporter, there was an air of determination about her which showed she was capable of great things.

Kate had certainly given Edwards a tough task. This was a strong man who would walk 100 miles within 24 hours on a number of occasions, even exceeding 110 miles later on. He was a fellow migrant, having been born in England 25 years earlier, sailing south in 1869 to make a big name for himself as a pedestrian throughout Australasia. His chequered career would involve several run-ins with the police before he decided to return home, taking charge of a pub in Essex where he died aged only 35 from heart disease.

A mere three weeks after her 24-hour success, Kate responded to another challenge from a male walker, this time Mahon, an Auckland man of lesser ability than Edwards, for £20 a side, over six miles. Over 600 crowded into a small Lorne Street hall to enjoy the rare prospect of a woman beating a man. Mahon went first, starting fast and finishing in 65 minutes. Kate set off steadily, finding herself well behind schedule at halfway but soon visibly upped the pace. The crowd roared its delight at the sight of this, wrote the *Auckland Star*, and she showed some "sprightly tripping in the last two miles". Sadly it came too late and she finished three minutes slower than Mahon's time. Popular opinion was echoed by the reporter who commented that she would have fared much better had she waited at least another week to recover from her 100-mile effort. Kate apparently agreed, for she immediately challenged Mahon to compete over the same distance again, this time for a bumper £100 a side. Mahon decided to get out while the going was good and turned her down.

The Wiltshires failed to find a winning formula for their final Auckland engagement too. The promoter of the Ellerslie Gardens track, the main venue for professional foot racing in Auckland at the time, hired Kate to perform a demonstration walk outdoors. She was backed £20 to walk a mile in seven and a half minutes, and £30 to manage two miles in 16.5 minutes. She had already achieved such times on a hard hall floor, but had never walked against the clock on a rough and damp outdoor course before, and could only manage a highly disappointing 12 minutes for the mile. Embarrassingly, most of the small crowd left before she even attempted the two-miler.

This called for a rethink. For Kate the options were limited as there were no other female walkers in New Zealand to compete against and her experiment of competing against men didn't seem likely to prove lucrative. The time seemed right to harness the popularity gained from Kate's earlier heroics and focus her performance skills on something new: they called it Wiltshires' United Pedestrian and Comedian Troupe and, broadly speaking, it was an improved version of the theatre variety show they had staged in Oamaru earlier.

The new version opened in mid-1876 in the small gold-rush town of Thames, not far from Auckland, and along with Joseph and Kate performing timed walks, an Irish comedian, vocalists and dancers, came the first appearance of 'The Little Wonder', which appears to have been a dramatic piece featuring Kate's singing debut.

After extensive research into the Auckland events, David Colquhoun feels there could only be one conclusion – the Wiltshire Troupe idea was not a winner: "No doubt the plan was to hone the act in smaller towns [around

North Island] before offering it to city theatre promoters. It was not to be. From Thames they went to New Plymouth for a three-night season, where the local paper gave a positive if slightly bemused review. That was as good as it got. At Waitara the crowd was enthusiastic but very small. By then debts were outrunning income and the troupe attempted a quick getaway by local schooner".

Endeavouring to slip away unnoticed in such circumstances was certainly not something new in the world of pedestrianism, although using a schooner was certainly a novel way to attempt it. But it proved an unsuccessful ploy by the Wiltshire Troupe. It was reported in the *Taranaki News* they had been intercepted by a vessel normally employed "to avenge unpaid washerwomen on cheating sailors". This time the vessel did a favour to unpaid printers and others by driving the fugitives back to Waitara. It is thought the debts in question were paid and the troupe disbanded, although the Wiltshires did have at least one more engagement to fulfil before heading homeward to South Island.

Without their supporting acts, Joseph and Kate ended their tour by offering a show at the Town Hall in Greytown, near Wellington the following month, which would be staged along with a quadrille ball. The local paper urged attendance ("Mrs Wiltshire's pedestrian powers are really splendid and require to be seen to be believed") but turnout was low. The following day there was a two-mile match between two male walkers, the loser going up against Kate afterwards. It was reported: "As a matter of course, he permitted the lady to win", leaving it unclear if this was gallantry or Kate was just too fast for him. Either way, it was entertaining fare for the locals.

Although the Wiltshires hadn't quite called time on their pedestrianism at this point, the Greytown event would ultimately prove to be Kate's swansong, and Joseph would start his own final walk of note in August of 1876. For him it was one last 1,000-miler, his track being a tiny one inside a wooden enclosure next to the Waterloo Hotel at Kaiwharawhara, a seaside suburb of Wellington. There was added interest for spectators via short running races staged on the Saturdays, which Joseph supervised during his rest breaks. The races proved popular although southerly winter winds caused a few problems and eventually forced the whole event to move across to the more sheltered Victoria Grounds on Abel Smith Street for completion. Joseph completed the 1,000 miles in an exhausted state in early October, having suffered considerably in the closing weeks but showing great determination to finish.

Kate was there to help out but didn't walk herself. Around the halfway point she witnessed an alarming series of events that led to her husband being charged in court with using a loaded revolver against a man who allegedly threatened him during the walk. The contretemps ended without serious injury and the walk continued, but Kate was required to appear in court on Joseph's behalf. She unwittingly caused mayhem among officials when waving the offending revolver around while giving her evidence! The charges would subsequently be withdrawn, but the court case itself provided great entertainment, not least via the reports published afterwards. The *Nelson Evening Mail* wrote:

"An assault case, which came before the [Wellington] Resident Magistrate's Court created some fun. Wiltshire, the pedestrian, was defendant, but did not appear, his wife appearing for him. Mrs Wiltshire had this pistol. It caused some uneasiness round the Court. It was loaded in six barrels, and Mrs Wiltshire was carrying it about in a kind of way which suggested the painful thought that it might go off and kill somebody. It is stated that this revolver was at one time seen pointing in the direction of the Magistrate's head, and that he winked. Within five minutes the revolver had pointed around the compass about 50 times and the effect of its presence there was shown. The passage between the witness box and the wall cleared quicker than it ever was before by the bailiff. Mrs Wiltshire went to advise her counsel, Mr Buckley, about the case, and he took a deep interest in her words until he found himself looking down the muzzle of the revolver. Eventually the weapon was got rid of, being placed in the care of the clerk, who put it away carefully".

Afterwards Joseph told a local reporter of new plans, which included a 1,500-mile walk in Melbourne. But, for whatever reason, this would never come about, and instead the couple moved from Omauru to Marton on North Island, started a family and looked at their options away from pedestrianism and show business. Within a year or so they had plunged into the hospitality business, opening a hotel in their new home town. Having lost baby Charles around two years earlier, Kate felt the time was now right to restart a family. It remains unclear exactly how many children they would ultimately bring up, but more than one source suggests she gave birth at least ten times, although maybe not all survived beyond childhood.

For the Wiltshires and many other New Zealanders the 1880s would prove a tough decade financially. After the gold rush of the 1860s and the 'Vogel Scheme' assisted passages of the 1870s, immigration slowed in the 1880s and there was a long economic depression. This seriously affected Joseph and Kate's earning powers, but they stuck at it, brought up their large family and lived productive, interesting lives. Once settled in Marton, Joseph started up a small theatrical agency and also served as official town crier, while Kate was heavily involved in local church affairs and also gained renown as a singer. After a few years they moved house to nearby Palmerston North City, where Joseph continued his agency work and his appearances as a town crier.

In 1891 Kate gave birth to a daughter, Lydia, who would one day marry a man called Sam Ardern – hence the surname all these years later of the country's Prime Minister. Not long after Lydia's arrival, Kate turned 40 and to mark this milestone was only too happy to sign a suffrage petition calling for women to be allowed to vote. Some 25,520 women – one in five of the population – signed, and as a result of the campaigning New Zealand became the first self-governing country in the world to grant women the vote, well ahead of Britain and the United States. Jacinda Ardern would proudly refer to Kate signing the petition in a speech about women's suffrage after becoming Prime Minister more than 125 years later.

Joseph Wiltshire died at the age of 62 in 1906. His obituary in the *Manawatu Standard* referred to him completing several 1,000-milers in 1,000 hours and specialising at the more rarely seen 250 miles in 100 hours, but there was scant mention of widow Kate. Two years later she would remarry, her new husband a Danish-born carpenter and fellow European immigrant called Frederick Conrich Leopold Olsen. Kate would also outlive Frederick and in 1915, having just seen her two sons head off to Gallipoli to fight in the 1914–18 war, she tied the marital knot a third time. John Thomas Lound was a London-born former plumber who played with a brass band and held a prominent position in the Ancient Order of Foresters.

Kate and John, both in their early sixties, went to live in retirement in Taihape, a relatively new town founded by European settlers just a few years earlier on a natural clearing in dense native bush. Kate died three days after her 72nd birthday in 1925. She was buried alongside first husband Joseph in the Terrace End Cemetery in Palmerston North.

After taking office in 2017, Prime Minister Jacinda Ardern spoke of immense pride at her ancestor Kate's sporting prowess, admitting with a wry smile she didn't think she'd inherited her great-great-grandmother's athletic genes. However, as the NZ-based author and athlete Roger Robinson points out, "energy, pace judgment, popular appeal, and willingness to get back to full-on work soon after giving birth – there may still be some resemblances between the PM and her ancestor!".

Contacted by your author, Prime Minster Ardern was unable to contribute directly to this book due to ministerial rules surrounding endorsement and promotion. However she had already spoken publicly about how the late 19th century was an era of extraordinary women whose feats were not great just because they were 'firsts' but because they took effort, commitment and courage. She said some of the most extraordinary things in life went without fanfare, accomplished by ordinary women who were "just getting on with things". Kate Wiltshire and her contemporaries achieving the right to vote was never the destination but the start of a journey for women, said PM Ardern: "We have a history we can be proud of in Aotearoa. Every family will have a tale of a pioneering woman [like my ancestor Kate] but these women also exist today and their strength is manifest in our daily lives."

TWELVE

A FAMILY AFFAIR

Some of the British pedestriennes enjoyed a series of big paydays, but for the majority making a decent living proved a constant struggle. Travelling around plying this unusual trade could be an uncomfortable and hazardous lifestyle. This is amply illustrated by the gritty adventures of a West Midlands mother-and-daughter duo known on the circuit as Madame and Miss Richards.

The pair were active during the 1870s and early 1880s and over this period were mostly reported as being mother and daughter but occasionally as mother and niece. To add to the confusion, the stated age of the younger woman Lucy was a number that seemed to fluctuate wildly. And to make things even more vexing for the modern-day researcher, at least four different first names crop up when seemingly referring to the same two Richards women!

Maybe age and identity were matters that these two pedestriennes preferred to keep vague and flexible for reasons best known to themselves? Or perhaps the newspapers were simply guilty of accidental misreporting from time to time. It is even possible other female members of the extended Richards family were pressed into action as 'substitutes' occasionally. The full facts are hard to pin down, but the bulk of the evidence points to the main characters in this saga being 'Madame' Rebecca Richards and her daughter Miss Lucy Richards, who were both usually accompanied and managed by Rebecca's husband John. One thing is certain, the multi-day walks undertaken by the Richards women were rarely dull affairs.

STORY 16: MADAME AND MISS RICHARDS – NO STRANGERS TO CONTROVERSY

Controversy seemed to follow the Richards family everywhere they went. They would be involved in several court cases, alleged sexual assaults, a number of clashes with the Lord's Day Observance Society and accusations of extortion. On several occasions the family elders were publicly accused of exploiting the athletic talents of a young girl for money, instead of trying to earn a conventional living.

John Richards would be lambasted in both the press and the courts for trying to win bets by sending young daughter Lucy on extremely demanding walks with little apparent regard for her health and well-being. He would dispute suggestions he was forcing her to walk, and she would usually endorse this.

The family spent around ten years travelling the length and breadth of England and Wales to stage their walking feats. It was certainly not a comfortable lifestyle. Sometimes they would sleep and recuperate in what was basically a wooden shed, shunted into place beside the field being used for the performance. If the weather was warm, sometimes a tent would be used. The Richards' wooden contraption only had room for one large bed, which would generally have to meet the needs of their entire family. To make this work, we can only presume a careful schedule had to be drawn up to avoid all four or five of them needing sleep at the same time!

However, having a cosy hidey-hole positioned next to the track didn't always mean the women would be safe and sound during rest periods between their walks: during their careers the Richards women appeared in court on at least three separate occasions, claiming they had been victims of assault of a physical and sexual nature by men attending their events.

Rebecca's husband John was present for most of the walks, his task to help keep his womenfolk safe, as well as general management of affairs behind the scenes. John was no angel himself, and will have been only too well aware of the occupational hazards that faced a pedestrienne, especially after dark. The ever-present dangers could include relatively harmless drunkards wandering around the track area, or slippery characters attempting to fix the outcome of a match, plus the danger of assault, either sexual or otherwise.

John Henry Richards was born in 1841 in Dudley and had a number of different jobs, describing himself at various points over the years as a barber, a leather dealer and a poultry dealer. He could turn his hand to many things, but what he really wanted was to make a living in the world of sporting theatre. Wife Rebecca, born in 1843 and a shade over five feet tall, was initially the passport to that world, the couple then living with their young family in Flood Street, Dudley, just a few hundred yards from her birthplace in the Kate's Hill district.

The fame of the Richards women began to spread in 1873. A wakes week – an annual holiday involving organised closure of local factories – took place at Bucknall in the Potteries in the September and the centre of attraction for thousands of working-class folk were the spacious pleasure gardens beside the River Trent known as Finney Gardens. It was here Rebecca attempted her first 1,000-miles-in-1,000-hours, billing herself 'Madame Richards from the Black Country'.

The weather was good and the gardens – advertised as "a lounge for the tired artisan" – were packed with all sorts of attractions laid on by enterprising and well-established proprietor Theophilus Cartledge. Over and above the boating, skittles, quoits and swings on offer, Madame Richards found herself vying to be top attraction of the weekend with a pigeon shooting match featuring two noted shots from Sneyd Green. There were no licensed premises at the venue, meaning it was seen as a relatively safe place for women to perform. She had to complete 16 laps of a section of the gardens on each mile and was never short of vocal support. Naturally the volume of spectators would fluctuate over the course of the 42-day event, but big numbers arrived at weekends and again at the finish at the tail end of October.

The following summer, it was the turn of young Lucy Richards to take centre stage, setting off on her 1,000-miler at the gardens of the Three Blackbirds Inn, Stapleton Road, in the Horfield district of Bristol in mid-May 1874. This was a well-known local entertainments spot, active for some years, a roomy 1.5 acres with a bowling green, lawns, shrubberies and gardens, a coach house, piggery and stables with James Osborne in charge. The venue was still operating as a pub of the same name, almost 150 years later in 2020.

Lucy was reportedly a mere 15 years old at the time, and to see a female of such tender years attempting such a gruelling feat sparked major interest from the press and prompted a lively debate about exploitation – particularly when it was pointed out Lucy's father had set things up with the sole aim of winning cash bets for himself.

The Taunton Courier reported Lucy as walking consistently with "judgement and discretion" at a pace of 11 minutes per mile and said many thousands visited the gardens during late May to see her. The general fascination with proceedings was tinged with sympathy for the girl, a number of papers reporting that people had come forward to demand the authorities put a stop to Lucy's ordeal. They felt she needed protection as she was only walking due to pressure from her father who had laid a wager to win £50 if she kept going. The local magistrates considered the case and announced they wouldn't intervene, stating that Lucy was a free agent and there was no law to prevent girls walking a million miles in a million hours if they chose to, and if they lived long enough.

So the show went on and the teenager surprised many by looking as fresh as a daisy at the finish and perfectly happy with her lot. The final stages saw her normal walking routine interrupted in order that she could join a parade around Bristol with a brass band, the aim to attract extra crowds to the Blackbirds Inn for the big finale, and thus boost donations to her benefit collection.

Mr Richards duly won his £50 and a syndicated report appeared in several papers imploring him to use his winnings to buy his daughter a new bonnet and a pair of boots! However, *Bell's Life* was not quite as willing to joke about what had taken place, and was sceptical about what had been achieved. They stated: "However ungallant it may be thought, we must once more express our conviction that no one but Captain Barclay has ever [genuinely] accomplished this feat in this or any other country". *The Daily Telegraph* took a far more positive line, their lead writer commenting that most modern young women of the 1870s tended to spend their lives "lounging and sauntering" and could benefit and flourish with more fresh air and exercise, as Lucy had demonstrated. However, they reckoned five miles a day would be more suitable for most, rather than the huge task undertaken by Lucy:

"We cannot but contemplate with interest the lesson which Miss Richards teaches indirectly to her sex. Few of our modern young women walk enough; they lounge, they saunter, but they do not take the hearty constitutional which works such wonders for lungs and limbs. If we may be bold enough to say so, we will venture with the utmost confidence to assert that Miss R does not choke herself with tight ruff, or pinch herself with fashionable stays, or deform her feet with narrow high-heeled boots. She is as heaven made her, we may be sure; and it was surely the design of Providence that the natural cosmetic of female beauty should be healthy blood, and its sovereign tonics fresh air and exercise. This notable victory over Time proves that a woman can walk as well as a man; and while we congratulate the happy parent upon his winnings, and his daughter, we would urge modern young ladyhood to look at the best side of this demonstration and to try good old-fashioned walking exercise instead of physic and restoratives. It might prove a national service if Miss Richards would conveniently send her boots and walking dress up to London for exhibition. Fashion might turn pale at them; but so too would the doctors – for if every young woman did but walk five miles a day 'fair toe and heel' we would not see, as we do now, pearl powder and 'bloom of roses' plastered on pallid cheeks and the health of the next generation sacrificed to the absurd and unwholesome modes of this one."

The *Pall Mall Gazette* urged caution, acknowledging that had the local magistrates stopped this event, women everywhere would have had grounds for complaint that they should be allowed to exercise their own discretion as to the amount of walking they felt inclined to take and not be controlled by a court of law. But, they added: "It may be well for young ladies not to attempt to follow the example set by Miss Richards without the approval of their families and advisers – girls are very imitative and there is reason to fear that thousands of them will now take to walking thousands of miles in thousands of hours without pausing to consider the effect on their constitutions".

The debate bubbled along for several days and the *Edinburgh Evening News* pointed out: "A dutiful and self-sacrificing daughter would seem to be a rarity [these days]. The feat of Miss Richards, who walked 1,000 miles because her not-too-considerate parent had made a bet that she could do so, has been regarded as surprising proof that a modern young lady can endeavour to please her father. She would seem to have a more profound admirer... for a Staffordshire farmer the other day entered her room and sought, like the hero of *Sartor Resartus* [Thomas Carlyle's 1836 novel] to be made immortal by a kiss. For his laudable desire he was fined five pounds".

It was an amusing line, but the *EEN* had got its facts mixed up – for the woman who received the kiss from a farmer was actually not Miss Lucy, but Madame Richards, the more senior of the family pedestriennes. It had happened that same summer of 1874 at Mr Swift's grounds at The Mear pub, situated between the railway and the main Uttoxeter Road in Longton, Staffs. Madame Richards had been one month into a 1,000-mile walk at the time, and the kiss was part of an alleged assault leading to a court case in Longton on Wednesday 22nd July.

James Alcock, described as a gentleman farmer from Butterton, on the Staffordshire Moors near Leek, was accused of forcing his way into Madame

Richards' private bedroom within her tent while she was resting and eating dinner between walks. The court heard it was a Friday evening when he pushed his way in under pretence of delivering a message from landowner Mr Swift. Once inside he sat down and drank a bottle of apple wine which he found on a table. She ordered him out, saying no strangers were allowed in the tent, but Alcock refused to go and followed her into the adjacent bedroom. He then demanded a kiss and took hold of her, roughly ripping her jacket in attempting to kiss her. Her assistant Prudence Stacey ran for help and found two men, named Lowe and Smith, who returned with her and turfed Alcock out of the bedroom. Miss Stacey confirmed Alcock had become drunk after consuming the wine.

During cross-examination, Madame Richards was asked about a dispute between her and landowner Swift about money from admission tickets. She was non-committal over this but agreed she had at one point wanted to quit the match, but only because of the gambling and dog running being permitted in the grounds during her performance. She was accused of pressing charges against Alcock a suspiciously long time after the assault allegedly took place. She had finished her walk and gone home to Dudley where she then falsely drummed up a case against the farmer, it was suggested. She denied this, saying the delay had been because the rules of her walk didn't allow adequate time or opportunity to do anything except walk, rest and eat.

With a flourish, the defence stated: "Why, my good woman, you have not spoken a word of truth!" and added that he could provide witnesses who would verify that during her walk she sometimes slept for five or six hours at a stretch instead of the maximum 90 minutes claimed. Madame Richards batted this away, saying there had been too many dogfighters and other disorderly characters present at all hours for her to ever get much sleep at all.

The defence called Julia Dawson, barmaid at the New Town Hotel, who alleged Madame Richards stopped walking before the allotted time and had not settled up financially with Mr Swift. She said she overheard in the pub Madame Richards' husband John say: "We may as well get £50 out of Alcock as not," replying to William Viggers, an ostler, who had asked him: "If I summon Alcock do you think I could get a pound or two?"

By now it had become apparent that Madame Richards' toughest battle of summer 1874 was here in the courthouse and not on any walking track. However, after the magistrates considered all the allegations and counter-allegations, it was concluded Alcock had no right to be in her tent that Friday night, especially the bedroom area, and they believed an assault had been committed there. A fine of £3 plus £2.14d costs was imposed.

The following spring of 1875 saw the Richards entourage return to the attractive setting of Finney Gardens in the Potteries where they decided to ramp things up by having Rebecca take on a fellow walker as well as the clock, with a silver belt on offer to the winner. This experiment had the potential of creating future earnings as it might attract other women to come forward to try and wrest the belt from Madame Richards. Calling the match a 'championship' and putting up a belt to be won gave the instant impression the event had prestige and importance. Advertisements were as bold as ever, this time claiming Rebecca was the only woman in the world who could walk a mile in nine minutes. She lived up to her billing by defeating the so-called 'London champion' and reportedly completed 1,024 miles in total to do so. After accepting the impressive silver belt she issued the inevitable challenge for someone to come forward and try and win it from her. Within a few weeks she had chalked up other triumphs in the Midlands, at the Peacock Inn recreation grounds in Belgrave Road, Leicester and the grounds of the Fighting Cocks pub in Moseley, Birmingham.

By 1876 Rebecca was approaching her mid-thirties but still going strong and taking on more challenges, while her daughter Lucy, still well short of 20, was starting to make a real impact in the sport. On Whit Monday the latter completed a 1,000-miler at Stanley Park recreation grounds in Liverpool, throwing in an impressive six miles in one hour at the end to gain some extra publicity and kudos. The public responded in good numbers, paying 3d for admission to see the celebrations at the climax. Her efforts at Liverpool sparked interest down south and as summer reached its height she found herself attempting another 1,000 miles in 1,000 hours in the Oxfordshire village of South Hinksey. It would take place at a bowling green attached to the General Elliot inn, which was situated well off the beaten track although within sight of the dreaming spires of Oxford.

South Hinksey was a far more bucolic and tranquil spot than usually hosted pedestrianism in Victorian England. No dark satanic mills, grimy backstreets or polluted skies here. The General Elliot and its little bowling green was positioned at the very heart of the area which inspired Matthew Arnold to write his epic poem *Thyrsis*, from which came the phrase 'dreaming spires' in reference to Oxford. *Thyrsis* is of course nowadays recognised as one of the greatest elegies in English literature, and was written not long before

Miss Richards came here. Maybe she too was inspired by the wonderful surroundings and ambience that had captured the poet's heart.

On the bowling green at 7.45 on Tuesday morning in July, Lucy set off on her task, seemingly unhindered by the pressure of being heralded 'The Female Champion' prior to her arrival. The *Oxford Times* reported a large crowd and great cheering when she appeared, and said her age had been given as 16 – "but if this is correct she is a precocious young woman and appears to be about 25".

Dressed in the bloomer style, Lucy sported a loosely fitting blue tunic, trousers of the same hue edged with white lace, and a black beaded bodice with a belt of red leather. Her 'gipsy' hat was trimmed with white and blue feathers and ribbons and she carried a short cane in her right hand. The first mile of 22 laps was completed in 13 minutes and she followed the now conventional method of single miles either side of the hour mark and 90 minutes of rest every two hours. She was able to listen for the local church clock to strike the hour and signal the start of every other mile.

One reporter reckoned she appeared "very muscular and in good form" and impressed the spectators by finishing several of her miles in a very brisk ten minutes flat, with no signs of distress or fatigue. There was great interest among the Oxford press corps in the scientific side of things and one report went into considerable detail, suggesting the strain upon her constitution would begin to tell after about 500 miles as her lack of lengthy sleep would be felt from then onwards. Her diet during the walk was said to be mainly eggs, beef, mutton and milk, with the occasional glass of sherry.

As the first day wore on, some of the crowd began to drift away but proceedings were suddenly enlivened by the arrival of a group of well-spoken upper-class types from Oxford, who amused everybody with jolly banter, calling out in their clipped accents to ask how the betting was going and about the young lady's marital status. Pedestrianism was often regarded with grave suspicion at a new venue, but the good people of Oxford seemed to find the whole thing amusing and fascinating and their local press didn't rush to condemn the seedier side of the sport as occurred so often elsewhere. Indeed the following write-up by an *Oxford Times* columnist was more reminiscent of an academic essay than a straight sports report:

"What a halo environs happy girlhood! I recollect being at the opera when Madameoiselle Zare Thalberg, the daughter of the great pianist [Sigismond], made her debut. Her voice was sugar itself, her face and figure beautiful, her action graceful and bewitching – yet after all, what made Covent Garden re-echo as if a hailstorm had burst through the roof? It was because Madameoiselle Zare was only 17! She was beyond the embryo stage of the infant phenomenon – that disgusting piece of precocity – and yet not as amenable to severe criticism as a full grown woman. It was a similar feeling perhaps which induced people to shout and applaud Miss Lucy Richards the female pedestrian as she paraded the streets and covered the beaten track at South Hinksey. She hails from the muscular region of the mythical 'Dog and Man Fight' and who most assuredly can walk at a terrific pace. Six miles an hour, heel and toe, is enough to make one's hair stand on end to contemplate, especially as the young lady is rather short, and – not to be too graphic – her legs, though symmetrical and agile, are not long.

"Whether she did actually accomplish her 1,000 miles in 1,000 hours I have no means of judging. While I leave others to dispute the assorted facts, I can testify to her getting over three miles in less than half an hour and six miles in a little over 59 minutes. Say what you will, this is tall walking for a member of the fair sex, and although such exhibitions possess no higher value than mere sensation, still we Britons shall never cease to admire pluck and grit, especially in the sex which is constitutionally debarred from excessive athleticism".

Lucy stuck to her task resolutely despite a good number of very hot days, while each of the Mondays and Saturdays were enlivened by the presence of brass bands, at which point spectators were invited to dance. By the first Friday morning she had done her 72nd mile and didn't appear in any discomfort despite that day's intense heat. Throughout the first Tuesday and Wednesday nights it was noted that several persons were monitoring events to ensure there was no shirking, while on the Thursday two representatives of the sporting press were present to see fair play.

Conveniently, from a logistical point of view, Lucy's mother Rebecca found herself a walking engagement not far from here – a 1,000-miles challenge staged in the Marquis of Granby Inn's gardens in Reading. It was a rather more hectic venue than Lucy's, fronting the main turnpike road to London, just a mile outside Reading town centre. Madame Richards' reception was good from the working people who paid threepence to watch, but not so enthusiastic from the *Reading Observer* which suggested sniffily that pedestrian and swimming feats had become so common it was doubtful whether she would generate much interest in their town. They would be proved very wrong.

Madame Richards set off in the tiny gardens at the rear of the Marquis of Granby at 3.45pm on Saturday 12 August, circling a roped-off route that required 22 laps of 80 yards each to complete a mile. One paper pointed out that the only 'umpires' on duty at the time their reporter checked appeared to be her husband and young daughter, which if true didn't help the Richards' family claims that all walks were 100 per cent genuine. In terms of sheer entertainment there were few complaints however and large crowds attended, particularly in the closing stages when the now familiar town parade with horses and brass band was staged. She concluded her final mile soon after dark with infant daughter in her arms. She received a great ovation after stepping off the track for the final time, proceedings concluding with a grand fireworks display.

Having now performed with distinction within sight of the dreaming spires of Oxford, Lucy Richards turned to the other powerhouse of academia the following summer for her first big outing of 1877. Her task was 1,000 miles in 1,000 hours on a bowling green in the Cambridge suburb of Chesterton, close to the various colleges and student hangouts of Jesus Green and Midsummer Common. However, unlike her Oxford adventure, this time things failed to go smoothly.

After less than a week of the 42-day challenge had passed, the event was brought to a grinding halt by the county magistrates. There had been complaints from locals unimpressed by the size of the crowds that gathered, and who found the whole affair rather sordid, particularly offended by the fact it was to carry on during Sundays. As a result, Lucy's enterprising father hastily arranged for her to switch to privately owned land nearby, and she made a second start on Tuesday 8 May. This private garden just off the Chesterton Road in Church Lane was not large but proved a good move for over the period the place was packed by crowds estimated as well into the thousands. Some of these questioned the integrity of the affair, presumably due to the lack of independent officials, but one local paper generously pointed out that each occasion their reporter attended, Miss Richards was "walking gracefully and in excellent style", usually completing each 18-lap mile in under 11 minutes. On the final day she was paraded in Cambridge before completing mile number 999 and then embarked on a farewell flourish of six miles within an hour, smiling and waving to the cheers of the crowd.

A week after Cambridge Lucy was due to repeat her act in Ipswich, the nearest the Richards had been to England's east coast, while far away on the western side of the island Madame Richards was simultaneously entertaining the public at the Cwmbran Pleasure Grounds in South Wales, a highly popular summer gathering spot, before more good-sized crowds.

Following a quiet winter, Madame Richards was billed in May 1878 to appear in Swindon, but once the event got underway the walker would be identified as a young woman going under the name of Miss Selina Richards. The Richards camp put out the word that Selina was being mentored by Madame Richards, but it remained unclear whether this was actually Lucy stepping in and using another name, or whether Selina was another member of the extended family.

The teenage 'Selina' certainly looked the part and set off confidently, aiming at 1,000 miles in 1,000 hours in a paddock behind the Goddard Arms Hotel in Swindon's High Street, watched by a good crowd. The site is today better known as Lawns Park, part of 50 acres once occupied by the wealthy Goddard family. Selina started on a Saturday afternoon, circling the small track 20 times per mile and battling through awful weather, spells of heavy and lengthy rainfall, with her entire route unsheltered. The *Witney Express* pointed out: "Richards has plodded on and the manner in which she acquits herself of her self-imposed task cannot fail to dispel the prejudices which many people entertain in reference to walking as an exercise for women. For if this be not a test of physical endurance then what can said to be?".

Miss Richards reported blistered feet during her ordeal but not serious enough to cause an abandonment. *The North Wilts Herald* sympathetically reported that she was not backed by any private individual to complete the distance and consequently the performance would continue or cease according to public demand. Many who witnessed the early stages and the shocking weather were convinced she would be forced to stop, not least because of lukewarm public interest. Others, the paper pointed out, accused the whole affair of being a sell-out that was being organised solely by interested parties with no independent observers.

However, the unfavourable prognostications were defied and Selina remained on the soggy paddock long enough to complete her six-week task according to the rules, and the *NWH* admitted it had not heard of a single instance in which she failed to appear on the track at the appointed time. The paper added that as there were no stakes on the contest's outcome, the only pecuniary benefit would be from gate money: "It cannot be denied that Miss Richards has displayed remarkable pluck and stamina and whatever may be the opinion of some as to the indelicacy of the contest – though we fail to see anything indelicate in the matter – it plainly proves, to a certain extent, that the gentler sex is as capable of sustained exertion as those of the sterner type, while it is beyond doubt that the health of many fair ones would greatly benefit if they took a regular amount of walking exercise every day".

Selina finished on a Saturday morning and was carried triumphantly around Swindon by horse and carriage, the parade urging townsfolk to attend other athletic competitions later on and contribute to a benefit for the brave young walker. That evening the track pounded by Selina was used for various foot races but with such limited space it was decided only one competitor could run at a time, going against the clock rather than directly against an opponent. This killed much of the entertainment value and Miss Richards was urged to come out and do some more walking to ensure the crowd didn't dwindle too quickly. Somebody had the idea of offering a fattened pig as the prize for a baby competition. The babies had to be nine months or under to qualify and four women and one man entered, proudly carrying their offspring "to the interested gaze of laughing spectators". Mrs Gardiner and infant were judged winners and her husband was soon spotted chasing a runaway pig around the enclosure. Miss Richards reappeared at this point and completed another two miles at her usual walking pace. Later on she emerged again and did six miles within an hour with three minutes to spare. This somewhat chaotic evening was hailed a success and a good crowd remained throughout.

The south of England was proving a happy hunting ground for the Richards family despite female pedestrianism's strong association with the industrial north and Midlands. Consequently the tour of these 'uncharted waters' of the south continued with a visit to the Sussex coastal resort of Hastings earmarked for several weeks later, in the autumn of 1878. This time Selina (who, we suspect, may well have really been Lucy) would go for the bold target of 1,250 miles in 1,000 consecutive hours. The venue was a popular tea and pleasure gardens adjacent to the Kite's Nest Hotel and assembly rooms in St.Helen's Road. The proprietor Henry Phillips tempted visitors with cricket, quoits and a bowling green, and a working farm where people could buy milk, eggs, fruit and vegetables.

Extravagantly billed as the greatest sporting event of 1878 (had they forgotten the world's first floodlit football match at Bramall Lane, Sheffield?), Miss Selina's appearance commenced in early September and doing the required 1.25 miles every hour saw her hit halfway (625 miles) by the 28th, using the chimes of a local clock to indicate each restart. Saturdays and Mondays saw a brass band tune up for public dancing and the gates remained open night and day with a 3d admission charge. As had become *de rigueur*, the finish was jazzed up to include a six-mile walk in 60 minutes on Monday 21 October. That day the grounds were brightly illuminated, various sports staged with a quadrille band in attendance, and admission was doubled to sixpence.

She kept up the pace beautifully by all accounts, overcoming a degree of stiffness and discomfort in the final stages. It was a great feat, 25 per cent more mileage than the Barclay match, and eyebrows were raised when the Richards family announced Selina wanted to return to the town the following year to attempt 1,500 miles in 1,000 hours. The noisy and colourful finale was a real family affair, with Madame Richards, described as Selina's trainer, and young Angelina Richards also putting in a mile or two on the roped-off track. *The Hastings & St Leonard's Observer* pointed out that the baby show which accompanied the walk had been judged by a local gentleman who had been in the medical profession for more than 25 years, but had refused to give his name: "He did not desire to have it known that he had been mixed up with such an affair as this".

It looked like another success for the Richards family, but once again the affair was marred by controversy. While Miss Selina had been patiently circling the enclosure, a short distance away the validity of the event was being debated at length by local magistrates. This little courtroom dust-up was typical of what went on around this time, and was prompted by unhappy officials of the Lord's Day Observance Society. Complaints about the walk were aired to Sir Anchitel Ashburnham, 8th baronet of Broomham, who chaired the bench.

Sir Anchitel was told that on the second day of the six-week walk, i.e. Sunday 8th September, more than a thousand people visited the venue. This had been "most demoralising" to Sabbatarians who believed it contravened the terms of the license of the Kite's Nest Hotel. Admission money was charged and intoxicating liquor put on sale on this and subsequent Sundays. But the magistrates were reluctant to act and insisted that if specific offences were alleged and there was a case to answer, the complainants must withdraw and take the matter up with the Chief Constable of Hastings. The LDOS deputation duly stood down, looking frustrated, but no doubt glad to have at least made their point publicly.

Just a few days later the Hastings courthouse was again dealing with fall-out from Miss Selina's walk. This time the business of the day was to hear an accusation by Selina that a man had "openly and obscenely exposed himself, with intent to insult her" during the event. Defendant Thomas Curry hotly denied the crime and his solicitor accused the Richards family of fabricating the incident to extort money from his client. He said Curry had gone to great expense seeking out witnesses to prove the counter-charge of extortion, and he applied for those costs to be awarded to his client, who was "a young man of the highest respectability". The magistrates ruled they were not in a position to consider extortion as the indecent exposure charge was the only thing on their list. The solicitor then accused the Richards family of not being worth "the powder and shot" of assembling a case against them. After lengthy consultation the bench dismissed the charge of indecent exposure and awarded £5 costs.

By the end of the 1870s an increasing number of women, notably the talented Londoner Madame Ada Anderson, were finding sufficient engagements to make a living from pedestrianism. But the various women of the Richards collective, for reasons not entirely clear, faded from the limelight for several years. It wouldn't be until the summer of 1881 that Miss Lucy Richards would capture headlines again. Not for the first time, this publicity centred on outbreaks of trouble rather than her athletic prowess.

On this occasion a publican in the East Midlands found himself summoned before magistrates, accused of assaulting Lucy during her attempt to cover 750 miles in 500 hours on his land in the Thorpe Acre district of Loughborough. The exchanges that took place before the Loughborough Petty Sessions courthouse in June 1881 provide another fascinating insight into the way that pedestriennes were regarded, how they were treated and how they lived and behaved.

The court heard Lucy's complaint, which centred on an incident that occurred in the wooden shed at the ground that she used for sleeping during her event. While resting after finishing an early morning stint on Tuesday 14th June, she could hear the landlord of the premises swearing loudly at her father. She left her shed to investigate and saw the two men arguing beside the mile-checking box. The landlord then turned on her, using threatening language, and she quickly returned to her shed and secured the door. After a while, the landlord forced his way in and pulled down the curtain surrounding her bed. She told him to leave this private place and attempted to push him out, but he refused and struck her on the breast. The police were called and the landlord removed.

For three days she suffered considerable pain from the effects of the blow and needed treatment from a doctor. Cross-examined, she admitted there was only one bed in the shed, and her father, mother, she and three children all used it. She denied the landlord had complained earlier about the manner in which the family were living on his premises. The chief magistrate, Reverend Burton, asked Lucy how her father made his living: "He goes with me. I and my mother both walk in the summer time. It started when I was about 14 years of age at Whitehaven where I walked 1,000 miles."

Lucy's sister gave evidence that she saw the defendant strike Lucy and Dr. J. H. Eddowes confirmed when he arrived later that day that he found Lucy in an extremely low condition, complaining of pain at her breast and the symptoms presented could have been caused by a blow. He treated her and told her to quit the walk, but she later pressed on against his advice. Lucy's father confirmed the defendant had struck his daughter and when asked how he earned a living, said: "I am a barber." It was suggested to him that he made his money travelling around the country and walking his daughter in public against the clock. "No, I have plenty to live on. She does it at her own option." Lucy agreed: "I should not do it if I did not want to."

The landlord's solicitor told the bench he believed no assault was committed and furthermore Lucy's parents were earning a living by their daughter's exertions which he described as "most infamous". He posed the question: "Is not a walk of 750 miles in 500 hours likely to produce permanent injury to a girl like this if persisted in month after month?" The Bench sided with him and dismissed the case with no costs awarded, but indicated their disapproval of the landlord's conduct in letting his ground to such a discreditable affair. Furthermore, the Rev Burton said, the general conduct of the father and mother had been "most disgraceful and discreditable". He didn't believe the evidence put forward that the family did not make a living from their daughter's walks. He added that if Mr Richards had heard and understood the medical evidence relating to Lucy's injury he would surely now give up trading upon "the almost superhuman efforts of this girl".

Perhaps the regular court appearances and the advice of the Reverend Burton had an effect, for little would be heard of Lucy for a year or two. Then in 1884 she would return in dramatic style, enjoying her finest hour as a walker and national recognition in an unprecedented event staged in Birmingham's Bingley Hall (covered fully in Chapter 17).

THIRTEEN

THE CATTLE MARKET SYNDROME

The subliminal message to British pedestriennes in the mid-1870s was stark: if they objected to having their bust, loins, hips and thighs scrutinised and discussed in public – like a prize animal at an agricultural show – they should quit pedestrianism and keep their exercising habits private!

Far from being encouraged to develop an interest in sport and exercise, the British female peds continued to find themselves accused of lacking decency and dignity by venturing out and allowing their bodies to become matters of public discussion. To drive home the point, the influential *Bell's Life in London*, a 12-page weekly broadsheet, quoted some examples of the explicit coverage of a high-profile match in early 1876 between USA walkers Mary Marshall and Bertha von Hillern. One of these reports stated:

"Mrs Marshall has a fine pectoral development, but she is slack about the loins, and as she does not swing out her legs clear from the hips, she cannot expect to hold her own with Miss Von Hillern, who is very deep chested, has the powerful loins and a rare stride that reminds us of that illustrious ped Dan [O'Leary]; if she would but take down some of the superfluous flesh about her shoulders and back, she would make as fast time as any of our flyers".

There was more grist for the *Bell's Life* mill in 1877 when a number of other papers ran a profile of plucky newcomer Kate Lawrence, a 30-year-old who had quit dressmaking to take up professional walking. But instead of focussing on her athletic prowess, the coverage gave Lawrence a thorough physical examination, describing her thus: "A petite figure, built for endurance, five feet two inches in height – shoulders higher and squarer than those generally seen on a woman – a well-formed bust, hips not as broad as usual – a head large and well formed, with a clear, colourless complexion and a face not especially attractive to a casual observer, but to one who studies it, alive with marked character and strong will; eyes bluish grey, hair dark brown – features marked, especially as to the mouth and lower jaw".

This type of comment about bodily features – already commonplace in relation to male athletes – was now being applied to British female competitors, and *Bell's Life* said this begged the question: "Would we like our female friends and relatives to be exposed to such?". As well as their physiology, women walkers' choice of clothing and their 'attractiveness' or otherwise had become matters of discussion. *Bell's Life* pointed out that if women continued to perform in public they would have to learn to "leave blushes behind them" and be nonchalant when they were remarked upon as if they were being exhibited in a cattle show. Comment about a male competitor's body shape, build, gait and general appearance had always been seen as fair game for sporting reasons – but now women must accept this scrutiny too, however intrusive or humiliating it might feel.

By now many years had passed since pedestriennes first braved the roads, tracks and music halls of Britain. Nevertheless, the air of strong moral disapproval still hung over their sport and attitudes towards them had in some ways hardened rather than mellowed. A woman's place was supposed to be at home and these walkers were only being naïve to believe the passing of time would see their branch of athletics become an acceptable and a safe environment or so it seemed.

In February 1876, when the celebrated male pedestrian Daniel O'Leary stood up for his female counterparts by agreeing to help organise a match between Mesdames Von Hillern and Marshall in Chicago, he ignited a debate over whether women's contests ought to be given such seals of approval. *Bell's Life* chimed in again: "That [they] can both walk well we have no doubt, for there are many women who could walk clean away from our average city-bred man. We have the greatest satisfaction in knowing women can walk, and do take care to keep perfect the divine form they have been endowed with. But we think that a woman's place is at home; that her athletic and physical culture should be her own private concern, and that her proficiency in this should not be made public. How do these ladies propose to walk? If in petticoats they will soon tire, if in bloomer costume they will not make very extraordinary time, but if they strip to tights and trunks, and go for putting on a record, they will expose themselves to criticism".

The social mores and attitudes of the day were holding back female pedestrianism in Britain, and women's participation in sport generally, particularly compared to the USA where significant change was underway. By actively supporting the Marshall-Von Hillern match, O'Leary gave women's walking a significant boost. He wrote: "I shall be glad to do anything in my power to aid in the promotion of the walk and will at all times be [of] service in carrying out the arrangements necessary to bring to a successful issue a sporting event at once novel and interesting".

During the 1870s, solo walking outdoors by American females largely gave way to indoor matches against other competitors, sometimes pitting them against men. Initially women could expect generous handicaps in a mixed-sex contest, but this wasn't necessarily the case after Mary Marshall sensationally beat Peter Van Ness twice in New York in 1876 in a series of three 20-mile contests. Mary wasn't the first example of a professional foot racing victory by woman over man. A year earlier at Barnum's Hippodrome in New York, William E. Harding challenged 'Madameoiselle Lola' that she could not complete 30 miles before he managed 50. Averaging a mile every 13 minutes, Lola won the bet, completing her task 19 minutes faster. These previously unthinkable female victories were not isolated instances – in early 1882 'Madame Dupree' had won a six-day heel-and-toe walking match at Tucson against a relay team of male soldiers. The male opposition fielded a fresh infantryman every 24 hours but Dupree won the 500-dollar stake by chalking up a total of 456 miles to win comfortably by 31 miles.

Recently arrived from her native Germany, Bertha von Hillern championed the women's cause in great style in the USA, performing at least 25 events in 13 different cities between 1876 and 1878. Her appearances were billed as a symbol of physical culture for women and New England suffragists supported and profited from her exhibitions. The leading suffrage newspaper *Woman's Journal* promoted Von Hillern's efforts with regular articles and praised her for refuting the Victorian beliefs and medical claims that women were too frail to be full citizens.

While female walking was showing signs of really taking off in the States, back in Britain the sport remained the domain of a limited number of regular and consistent performers. Mesdames Willetts, Englo, D'Omer, Elven were among the best known on this side of the Atlantic during the 1870s and 1880s, but it remained to be seen if any of them possessed the talent and enterprise needed to take things forward over here. Perhaps what the British pedestrienne scene needed at this point was more charisma and colour. Maybe more performers such as Madame D'Omer, who combined her feats of athleticism with other novelty acts, gaining herself a reputation as a fine all-round entertainer. D'Omer performed regularly in Britain for a number of years, although French by birth. She was an altogether different type of pedestrienne to those who had achieved some success in Britain thus far.

Plodding along for hours to achieve great feats of stamina was not D'Omer's *raison d'etre*. She found fame for performing in a range of styles, often in music hall settings, and her repertoire even included boxing. D'Omer could walk a mile very briskly and did so many times on British music hall stages in the 1870s, but her pedestrianism often took a back seat to other entertainments put on alongside her husband. One speciality was to recline and have a lemon placed on the nape of her neck – Monsieur D'Omer would then cut the small piece of fruit clean in two with a downward sweep of his sword, without so much as a mark left on his wife's neck! Commendable though her 7.5-minute mile was at the climax of the performance, the trick with the lemon tended to generate most excitement. The pair also performed a William Tell-style feat of him shooting an arrow through an apple perched on her head with a blowgun. This type of show delighted audiences and stage managers would often present her with a medallion or other jewellery as a token of esteem.

The D'Omer couple would sometimes end their shows with an exhibition of "the manly art of self-defence" for which boxing gloves were donned. Modern-day boxing writer Malissa Smith says Madame D'Omer had by now become a very versatile all-round athlete and a skilful boxer who could land telling blows upon the head and face of opponents and then parry counter-attacks with grace and agility. Her promoters always promised no 'objectionable' features to her bouts of boxing (i.e. no blood nor injury) to ensure the event would be suitable for other women to attend without having their sensibilities shocked. One contemporaneous report noted that D'Omer had an excellent temperament and was even seen to laugh when receiving blows as well as when dishing them out. On one occasion she pummelled her husband so forcibly he called a halt, bowed politely and told the audience this had been his first defeat in a while, and his wife left the stage to great cheers with a face crimson from the blows she had taken. She is said to have won a studded silver belt as female boxing champion of England although her success in the USA meant by the mid-1880s she had waved goodbye to Europe to settle in Rochester, New York.

With all the outrageous hyperbole of the time, she would be advertised around the British music hall circuit as the country's champion pedestrian, performing "a feat that has never been done by any lady in the world – walking a mile around the stage in under ten minutes!". And if that wasn't enough, screamed the adverts, "tonight Monsieur and Madame D'Omer will set to with the boxing gloves!".

A typical early display came in the summer of 1872 on a good-sized track at the soon-to-be-closed Gateshead Borough Gardens. Top of the bill was the walking match in which Madame D'Omer, at the time doing a short residency at the Oxford Music Hall in Newcastle, undertook to walk a 'heel and toe' mile in under eight minutes. It was announced: "The backer of time, a well-known gentleman connected with the turf, is staking £30 to £25". As D'Omer was said to have only attempted the feat three times in her career, successful on each occasion, it seems few punters came forward to bet against her. The Geordie home crowd found it a marvellous spectacle. She appeared at trackside to encouraging cheers, attired in a white shirt, dark pantaloons and a white jockey's cap, her stature reported as "diminutive but compactly built".

Her task was to complete just under three laps of 510 yards each, and arrive in front of the well-filled main stand in less than eight minutes. She set off so quickly there was much discussion over whether she was trotting rather than walking, but officials ruled her short-striding brisk style did constitute a fair display of 'heel and toe' walking. The first lap was completed in 2 mins 24 secs, the second in 2:48 and the slightly shorter final circuit in 2:29, giving her a final clocking of 7:41, well inside target. She would go on to improve this to 7:30 later, but longer distances gave her more trouble, one example the valiant failure in 1874 to complete two miles in 16 minutes, despite wearing spiked shoes to cope with the mud in Hyde Park, Sheffield.

STORY 17: JOSIE WILLETTS – GRIM DETERMINATION

Probably the most tenacious character among the British pedestriennes during the 1870s was a 34-year-old mum from Worcestershire called Josie Willetts. She followed the trend set by fellow walkers by styling herself 'Madame' Willetts and was known particularly for her determined posture and gait. Her career started badly but she displayed tremendous spirit by overcoming failures to become a star of the sport.

Josie failed twice in attempting 1,000-miles-in-1,000-hours at the Prince Arthur grounds in Linthorpe Road, Middlesbrough during 1875, but bounced back to complete this task the following year in Brighton, Durham (twice) and Portsmouth. Madame Willetts was around 5ft 4 ins tall, weighed between eight and nine stones and was described rather unkindly by one report to be "of masculine appearance" and a walker who proceeded "very firmly" with a forward-leaning posture. She generally turned out in a bright orange bloomer costume, trimmed with black lace and velvet, black leather boots, straw hat with white feather, three rows of white beads as a necklace, blue ribbons flowing at her back, and a metal waistband. Like many other pedestriennes she adopted the habit of wielding a small riding whip with one hand to keep children and troublemakers from getting too close, while in her other hand carried metal chocks, one of which would be deposited at the feet of a timekeeper at the end of each lap.

Despite having given birth barely a month earlier, she put her Middlesbrough failures behind her to set off remarkably briskly on her third attempt at the Barclay feat in Brighton, early on the morning of Wednesday 26th April 1876. The event was staged on a track laid out at the recreation ground and gardens behind the Allen Arms (later known as The White Crow) on the Lewes Road. She had completed her first mile before the clocks had even struck 6am. Her efforts caught the imagination of the locals and attendance was well into the hundreds both day and night throughout. Josie was a stranger in this part of the country and she was taking no chances – it was noted she walked with a brass girdle tied around her waist containing a pistol.

There are no reports of the pistol being pressed into action and Josie was able to finish the job on Saturday 6th June as scheduled. But there was precious little time to rest and recuperate for a repeat performance had been booked just a few days later further along the coast in the gardens of the Crystal Palace pub on Fawcett Road, Southsea. Here she had to cope with a small track that required circling 21 times every mile (in total 21,000 laps of around 83 yards each). Proprietor John Sheppard charged the public threepence each for admission and although attendances were described as good, they were somewhat smaller in volume than at Brighton. The track in the early days of the event was a nicely yielding soft sand and sawdust, but by the end resembled hard gravel and was less forgiving to Josie's sore feet. One of the garden booths was fitted out as a restroom where she was attended by two female helpers. There had been hostile weather at the start but conditions warmed up considerably and it often proved a little too hot for comfort, but Madame Willetts grimly kept at her task. She was cheered home, by now showing a pronounced limp, on the evening of Monday 22nd July. In the now time-honoured style she carried her four-month-old baby as she covered the final miles, and a brass band performed in the background.

Illustrated Sporting and Dramatic News reported that on Monday 16th April 1877 an 'extraordinary application' relating to Madame Willetts was considered by the bench at the West Hartlepool Petty sessions court. At this point she was in the process of walking 1,000 miles in 1,000 hours at the nearby Stranton Recreation grounds and the court was told the venue had opened on successive Sundays with people paying for admission, which was illegal. Chairman of the bench Mr Gray said the matter was being referred to Police Superintendent Marley who would be at liberty to apply for a summons against any suspected offenders. He said it would now be at people's own risk if they chose to attend on a Sunday and continue breaking the law of the land. The applicant thanked the bench and chose not to proceed further for the time being.

Josie Willletts' career appears to have peaked around now, although she continued to appear from time to time in various locations in subsequent years. There was an attempt at another 1,000-miler at the grounds of the Pyewipe Inn on the edge of Lincoln. This event in summer 1878 pulled in sizeable crowds to see her perform at a picturesque canal-side location. Later, in the spring of 1881, she travelled down to Hampshire to try for 1,500 miles in 1,000 hours to win a wager of £100 (equivalent to roughly £8,500 in 2020 terms) at the Cliff Hotel's pleasure grounds, just across the River Itchen from Southampton. Despite the gambling aspect, this event benefitted from an air of respectability for it had been organised by a large committee of 'reputable gentlemen' from the Southampton and Woolston district. With little fuss and apparent economy of effort Madame Willetts completed the task in early June, her confidence illustrated by the challenge she issued just before finishing, aimed at Madame Blanche Victor of London, inviting her to battle it out over 2,000 miles or more. The pair would subsequently meet several times, although not over such a distance.

A few weeks further on in 1881, in North Yorkshire, Madame Willetts was again the centre of attention, this time at the Royal Oak Running Grounds in Old Malton, a popular place of entertainment and refreshment for millworkers. Here she performed a feat that fully deserved its billing of "extraordinary" –

an often overused term at the time – when she took up a challenge to walk a quarter mile every 10 minutes, non-stop for 88 hours. This involved starting at midday on a Wednesday in June 1881 and not stopping until 10pm the following Saturday evening. She therefore carried out walks of 440 yards a total of 528 times within 528 consecutive periods of ten minutes. These statistics might have been difficult to absorb for some of the noisy audience, but they were not slow to show their appreciation regardless!

During her career Josie Willetts provided ample evidence she was one of the stronger multi-day performers. Her appearances came during the period between 1870 and 1885 in which it has been estimated more than 50 organised ultra-walks by around a dozen identifiable pedestriennes took place across Britain. That list also includes 'Madame Stephenson', who in early summer 1876 made her mark over 1,000 miles while based at the Fox & Hounds Pleasure Grounds, in Prestbury Road, Cheltenham. The proprietor George Holland boldly advertised her efforts as 'unparalleled' and many attended, paying threepence for admission.

During that summer of 1876, Prime Minister Benjamin Disraeli pushed the Royal Titles Act through Parliament and successfully persuaded Queen Victoria she should become the first Empress of India. A short distance down river, the working people of London found their own 'empress' in the shape of 23-year-old walker Miss Bella St Clair, who entertained them royally for 40 glorious days of July and August on the banks of the River Thames. Miss St Clair regally completed a very well-publicised 1,000 miles well inside 1,000 hours at North Woolwich Gardens before huge, adoring crowds.

She managed to complete the journey two full days ahead of schedule, taking 950 hours to finish late on the last day of August 1876. This would win her a place in Andy Milroy's *Long Distance Record*

Miss Bella St Clair entertained huge crowds with her 1,000-mile walk at Woolwich on the banks of the Thames.

Book, published more than 100 years later. Her achievement was deemed worthy of coverage in respectable newspapers such as *The Times of London,* which featured a cartoon image of her in action. According to *Lloyds Weekly,* "Miss St.Clair steps out in a manner that bespeaks confidence in her powers". Venue manager J.R.Carter made the most of Bella's tremendous success by announcing a 'Monstre Benefit' event as soon as the walk was over: here the versatile Bella posed as 'a representation of Grecian statues' for the admiring crowds, appearing alongside the Surrey Theatre Company, Tom Lovell's Great Ballet Troupe and tightrope walker Young Blondin. Admission was sixpence per person, or a shilling if you wanted a return rail ticket from Central London thrown in.

Triumph though it was, this event didn't prevent the proprietor William Holland having to file for bankruptcy a few months later, estimating he had debts at £14,000 and assets less than one-tenth of that sum. Nevertheless the North Woolwich Gardens remained in business and in August 1878 popular Miss St Clair was back, attempting to walk 50 miles in 12 hours. This occasion was billed as a benefit event for the flamboyantly moustachioed Holland, who liked to brand himself "the people's caterer" and would later be widely regarded as the man who invented the idea of the beer festival. Holland made Miss St Clair part of a top-notch line-up of entertainments for Londoners and visitors that week – there was theatre, music, the Channel swimmer Captain Webb demonstrating his art, and Baker the diver, who demonstrated diving from a height representing London Bridge at low water, the whole thing climaxing with a grand fancy dress ball.

STORY 18: MADAME BLANCHE VICTOR – DELIGHTING THE DEVONIANS

By the mid- to late 1870s, women's pedestrianism had shed its reputation as a pursuit confined to the backyards of pubs in grimy northern industrial towns. As well as the excitement of Bella St Clair's exploits in London, many other events took place in the south, not all of which were low-mileage affairs attached to music hall shows. As far afield as the county of Devon, country folk could now come and marvel at modern versions of the great Barclay match.

In the autumn of 1878 in Plymouth's Albert Hall a relatively unknown walker from London, Madame Blanche Victor, lay claim to one of the longest single walks of the era, completing a challenge of 1,500 miles in 1,000 hours. It was not an entirely trouble-free affair, but the locals cheered her home heartily on her final mile, full of admiration for her staying power and amazed to find no signs of serious fatigue on the final day. There was one dissenting voice however: the correspondent working for the *Exeter and Plymouth Gazette* had left the arena with a very bitter taste in his mouth well before the finish. He wrote:

"The track was fringed by a gathering of extremely dingy-looking persons, and the atmosphere was heavy with the depressing fumes of tobacco. Upon a raised platform was a band, consisting of two fiddles and a cornet. Madame Victor was, of course, the cynosure of all eyes, but her appearance was far from cheering. Some miscreant had, on a previous evening, placed a piece of broken glass upon the track and upon this went Madame's heel, so when I saw her she was limping in evident pain, her foot in a shapeless slipper and a damp moisture over her face. When the woman entered upon this feat she was of comely appearance, bright of face and shapely of limb. She is now a wreck, thin to the point of emancipation, with despair in her eyes and the complexion of the grave. Permit me to ask: what is the virtue of this sort of thing? Where is the 'public amusement'? I cannot see that any useful purpose whatever is served by this struggle against nature... comparatively few persons will have seen the wretched woman in the performance of her bootless undertaking, while the majority of mankind will pronounce the whole achievement 'rot'".

Her achievement was not 'rot' as far as Madame Victor was concerned. The income gained meant she could supplement her husband's meagre wages and put food on the table for her small children. Still in her twenties, she had first gained widespread attention earlier in 1878 after an unusual performance at Dewsbury and Batley Skating Rink in Batley Carr, Yorkshire. Here she courageously chalked up 1,000 quarter miles in 1,000 consecutive periods of 10 minutes. Roller skating continued alongside her walking and there was at least one painful collision between Madame Victor and a skater. The rink was an all-wooden building, highly popular since opening in 1875, but would soon be forced to close after a balcony collapsed during a packed political gathering, killing four people and seriously injuring 45. The tragedy occurred just a few months after Madame Victor appeared here.

Churning out six separate quarter miles every hour for 166 hours meant very short rest periods and a severe lack of sleep. This took its toll on Madame Victor who suffered severe back pains that nearly forced her to quit. Such a challenge, said to have never been attempted before by a female, lasted a full week and she was helped and encouraged at trackside by the sport's rising star

Madame Ada Anderson. The latter was also signed up to perform at the Rink but she quickly cancelled when word got out that Madame Victor had not been properly remunerated for her efforts. Even though women's pedestrianism was now better accepted by the world at large, it was evidently still rare for an event to end with everybody happy.

Fully paid up or not, Madame Victor returned to the same roller skating rink just a few weeks later – this time attempting a half mile every 20 minutes for five continuous days and nights. Her helpers were confident and denied gossip suggesting she had suffered badly on her previous walk, needing the attention of doctors in the aftermath. Her appearance at the start caused a frisson of excitement, for her chosen costume was spectacular, described as a princess robe made of blue llama, incorporating a large number of tiny bells. Prominent on her chest were the gold and silver medals presented on her previous visit. As she set off the tinkling of her bells could be heard, accompanied by a series of piano pieces played by Miss Josephine Thomas. For most of the event Madame Victor averaged six and a half minutes for each half mile and the only reported trouble emanated from a painful toe – caused by the nail dropping off, having been crushed on her previous visit when a skater ran over her foot.

Blanche Victor was certainly a doughty performer at the ultra-long distances, and was willing to try different formats. Starting in the summer of 1880 she returned to Devon to take on the ambitious job of covering 2,500 miles in 1,000 hours by way of walking from 8am to midnight every day except Sundays. It took place at St Andrew's Hall Skating Rink in Plymouth and required her to complete around 42 miles every day for roughly ten weeks. It was a format that allowed her a regular eight hours' daily sleep, but meant she had to work very hard the rest of the time and of course the cumulative effect would be massive. It was advertised in the papers as "the most difficult walking feat on record – arduous and unparalleled" and for once the promoter could be excused the hyperbole. Although no record can be found to confirm she completed the task, one local paper did report that with a mere five days left she was now starting an hour earlier each day and was on course to hit 2,500 miles on the evening of Tuesday 5th October. Slowly Victor's fame increased and before long she was taking on and beating the likes of Madame Englo, who was generally regarded the best of the women walkers at this time.

Madame Victor reached the height of her powers at a time when professional female pedestrianism was beginning to fade, and opportunities for her to grow her fame and fortune were limited. Even so, by the early 1880s, the few events still being staged were nevertheless mostly well supported by the public. One good example was that held at Whitsuntide 1883 at the very muddy Bassett Grounds in Southampton. Here a noisy crowd saw Madame Victor steadfastly refuse to change her style from 'heel and toe' walking, even though the five-mile event was a 'go-as-you-please' race. The lesser-known Miss Amy Monte from Lancashire was given a 50-yard start and made the most of the situation, using a mixture of walking, trotting and running to stay ahead of a grim-faced Victor, who had clearly decided running was not for her. Miss Monte was one of a number of promising talents emerging from Lancashire – others included Madame Flora Lee and the Misses Ann Booth and Minnie Lewis – who all appeared eager for competition but unable to find many lucrative opportunities.

FOURTEEN

COURAGE AND INSENSIBILITY

Perhaps more so than any other British walker, a short, muscular woman called Ada Anderson provided the compelling evidence that Captain Barclay's famous trek of 1,000 miles in 1809 wasn't quite the incredible feat it had been cracked up to be. 'Madame Anderson' was the first woman to convincingly wipe the floor with Barclay's record, making a nonsense of the old idea his achievement would never be repeated by walkers of either sex.

Ada, a charismatic Londoner in her late thirties, laid claim over a three-year period to the title of the greatest of all British pedestriennes. She emerged just as the female side of her sport had been sliding into serious decline. Among her triumphs would be walks of 1,250 miles in 1,000 consecutive hours – performances that bolster the view the noble Captain's long-lasting celebrity had been somewhat overcooked.

Author and athletics historian Peter Lovesey points out that for years the journal *Bell's Life* rubbished many multi-day performances on the grounds of cheating, while setting aside the possibility that Barclay himself may have cheated. *Bell's Life* rejected the rumour that Barclay's younger brother James had sometimes been secretly substituted for the Captain back in 1809, but they regularly implied that more recent walks did involve cheating.

STORY 19: MADAME ANDERSON – A BORN ENTERTAINER

Nothing about feisty Ada Anderson suggested she might be a fraud. She was born in February 1841, more than 30 years after Captain Barclay's glory days, entering the world as Ada Louisa Nymand, daughter of Gustavus, a German-Jewish hat and cap manufacturer, and his English wife. Gustavus earned roughly 28–30 shillings a week as a milliner, well above the poverty level of the time. Ada would grow up to be an articulate and outspoken woman, who liked to tell people she had inherited courage from one parent and insensibility from the other, both valuable traits for a pedestrienne. Home was on Blackfriars Road, just south of the Thames in London, close to popular nightspots like Astley's Amphitheatre and the Surrey Theatre, which sparked her ambition of making a living on stage.

She left home in her mid-teens to pursue this dream, spending at least 15 years travelling and performing with provincial shows. She could turn her hand to acting and singing, had a fine contralto voice, and was one of the first female circus clowns – but she found fame and fortune elusive in a business where a woman's appearance and looks were closely scrutinised. Ada was not a classic beauty and even had to put up with being labelled "masculine" by some newspaper reports, one of which described her as having "a stocky body, square jaw and wide nose that set her eyes too far apart". She was just an inch over five feet tall but weighed 150 pounds, with bright and expressive eyes, broad shoulders and stout muscular legs.

The 1871 census lists her as a dancer, born in Lambeth, who, along with fellow performer Elizabeth Sparrow, was at the time lodging in Free School Street, Northampton, presumably on tour at the time. Soon after this Ada married a theatre manager called Anderson, temporarily giving up performing to help run a Cardiff theatre with him. Sadly within just a month or two her new husband died. Making a living proved immensely difficult over this period, particularly after Ada was widowed.

But life would take a dramatic turn for the better in the summer of 1877 when Ada witnessed a performance by well-known male pedestrian William Gale which inspired her to have a crack at the sport herself. It is said that Gale, based not far away in Penarth, was impressed by her keenness and helped coach her for a month or two. He was a big name in the sport, a former bookbinder who had taken up walking as a teenager, becoming a big star of the 1850s and 60s. He initially retired at the top of his game in 1870 after performing a magnificent 2,000 quarter miles in 2,000 successive quarter hours at the Canton Gardens in Cardiff. But he had made a surprise return to the sport in summer 1877 at the same venue, aiming to cover 4,000 quarter miles in 4,000 consecutive periods of ten minutes. Or, to put it another way, six separate walks of 440 yards every hour, for roughly a month! This astonishing comeback performance was said to have been inspired by a desire to strike back for England after the achievements of American pedestrians such as O'Leary and Weston. It completely captivated the watching Ada Anderson, who within a month or two would make her own debut at long-distance walking in Cwmbran.

No wonder Ada was inspired by what she saw. Gale's remarkable display had gone smoothly until, with just a few days remaining, he collapsed three times in one week. The first was said by doctors to be due to "delirium", the second to "physical weakness" and the third to "mental and physical stress". Each time Gale managed to struggle back to his feet within a few minutes, thus avoiding any controversy over being assisted. He had started at 1am on Thursday 28th June and chalked up a quarter mile during every single 10-minute period until 7.34pm on Wednesday 25th July, some 1,000 hours later. Amazing scenes surrounded the climax of his walk, the final quarter mile greeted by a huge ovation from a crowd who mobbed him at trackside when he stopped. It was widely reported as the greatest feat of pedestrianism ever recorded and Gale had certainly restored British sporting pride.

Ada looked on and decided she could aspire to something similar. She felt multi-day walking was something she could excel at. Feeling unfulfilled as a stage performer, she was convinced her natural instincts as an entertainer and her strong desire to be admired by the world at large would serve her well as a pedestrienne. It was time to make some plans. She followed the fashion of calling herself 'Madame' and retained Anderson as her stage name. She signed up for a three-week outdoor challenge involving 1,000 half miles in 1,000 half hours, to be staged a few miles to the east of home in the town of Cwmbran starting on Saturday 1st September 1877. It was a very tall order for a first serious walk – with unfamiliar sleep deprivation the biggest hurdle to overcome.

As he lived nearby, she was able to spend time with William Gale, listening attentively to his advice as she prepared diligently during August. He could see she was taking her task seriously and approved of her walking form, which was strong and dignified. She held her head erect, her shoulders well squared and chest expanded as she strode. She swung her arms deliberately with toes pointed out in harmony with the motion of her legs. Her gait and posture was that of somebody who meant business.

When the big day in Cwmbran arrived, to Ada's dismay the weather proved extremely unhelpful. Working to a schedule that involved no rest periods of more than 20 minutes for three weeks solid, she had to endure many downpours, forcing her to walk in oilskins, carrying an umbrella and a lamp. But her grim determination to keep going was clear and she lived up to her billing as "a startling novelty" at the tail end of summer-long popular attractions staged at the town's Pleasure Gardens. She went on to finish the job without major incident and the impressed *Star of Gwent* newspaper verified that the lap counter's official logbook indicated her effort had been genuine. Ada's two female attendants had both been fully occupied looking after her, and she looked jaded rather than triumphant at the end, badly in need of sleep. It had been a steep learning curve, but she was ready for more.

Earlier the same summer the Eagle Tavern in Exeter's Howell Street (known in modern times as *The Rusty Bike*) staged a 1,000-miles-in-1,000-hours walk by a young unknown who identified herself as 'Mademoiselle Price'. She was reportedly aged around 20 and completed her task having to wear a slipper on one foot instead of a boot, to protect bad blistering. One account of this walk suggests Mademoiselle Price was in fact a pseudonym used by Ada Anderson, but the big difference in age puts this in doubt. What is certain is that the woman involved faced some tricky weather conditions, but nothing compared to those which fellow rookie Anderson encountered at the same Exeter venue in the autumn of 1877.

The gales of mid-October 1877 were severe, the worst seen locally for many years, with loss of life at sea and south-western England badly hit. In Exeter huge elm trees were uprooted and Cathedral Green was a scene of devastation with the building itself sustaining damage. The streets were a very unsafe place to be with shutters ripped off shopfronts and chimney pots and roof tiles flying around. This hostile weather struck around the halfway point of this second major walk of Ada's new career which was an ambitious attempt at 1,250 half miles in 1,000 half hours – billed on the posters as a bid to outdo Captain Barclay's famous feat. Not only was it rudely interrupted by the storms but a day or two later by a police court summons issued against Ada.

She was forced to leave the track to appear before Exeter magistrates to answer three charges: assaulting Harriet Lethaby, landlady of the Eagle Tavern in Barrack Road; assaulting landlord Richard Lethaby; criminal damage of two teacups and saucers, three tumblers, a pint cup and an earthenware teapot. Ada asked for the hearing to be delayed until her representative Mr Fryer could attend to defend her, but the bench refused and ordered matters to proceed. Mr Toy, representing the Lethabys, said Ada had been professing to walk 1,250 half miles in 1,000 consecutive hours at the Recreation Ground adjoining the Eagle Tavern, having been engaged to do so by John Martin, proprietor of the Northernhay Skating Rink. She had been there about a fortnight when allegations were made that she was not carrying out the task according to the rules, and consequently landlord Lethaby called a halt to the walk, keen to maintain the good reputation of his inn.

Lethaby had sent his wife out to the trackside cabin where Ada rested, to make his decision known and to present her with a bill for items she had borrowed from the pub (bed, bedding, table, chairs, cups and teapots). The court was told Ada responded by refusing to pay for these items and reacting violently when told the walk must stop immediately. When Mrs Lethaby collected up the tray of cups and teapots, Ada was said to have lashed out with her fist, screaming, "Take that, you vile wretch," smashing items on the tray which then hit Mrs Lethaby in the face. The landlady was cut badly and bled profusely. In her defence Ada admitted upsetting the tray with the intention of breaking the articles, but claimed the sum total of damage she caused would have been around 1s6d and not the £5 being claimed against her.

The landlord stated he arrived at the scene and calmly told Ada the walk must end or the police would remove her. He said Ada had been in the habit of walking with a riding whip, and she brandished this at him. He told her not to leave until the police arrived. While they waited she allegedly "amused herself" by striking him with the whip several times, over the shoulders, arms and back, but carefully avoiding disfiguring his face, and saying he had acted like "anything but a gentleman". This prompted laughter in the court. Robert Savery, employed by promoter Martin to collect admission money at the ground, confirmed Ada was violent towards the landlord, calling him "scum" and "a villain". Ada's attendant Elizabeth Sparrow was called and conceded that her employer had upset the tray, but said Mrs. Lethaby attempted to strike Ada, and together with her husband had violently taken hold of her. Elizabeth said she placed herself between the warring factions and the landlord shouted he would kill Ada rather than allow her out walking again. He blocked her exit from the cabin and she struck him once with the whip – but it was only a sixpenny toy riding whip and not a dangerous weapon, said Miss Sparrow. Later the Lethabys removed the furniture from Ada's cabin, and she had to sleep on bare floorboards the following night.

In her defence, Ada strongly denied her walking feat was a swindle. She said the only time she had not performed to schedule was on the Sunday when the severe gales struck between midnight and 4.40am. Roof slates had come down and narrowly missed her and the storm had brought down two bowers next to the track and wrenched the gates from their hinges. Otherwise her walking had been exactly as planned. She admitted being so upset she had struck the tea tray and been abusive to the landlady. For each of the two assault charges the magistrates inflicted fines of 10 shillings plus damages. Faced with a prison sentence if she refused to pay, Ada coughed up the total of £2.3s.6d.

It is assumed the walk was abandoned at this point, but, undeterred, Ada would remain in Devon, and just a few days later was engaged to appear at the Royal Albert Hall in Plymouth. This would be another attempt at the highly ambitious target of 1,250 miles in 1,000 hours – walking 1.25 miles every hour for six weeks. The hall was a sizeable concert venue with a skating rink and the potential to pull in large crowds. To assuage the inevitable doubters a £10 reward was put up for anyone who could prove she didn't stick to the schedule. This time things went remarkably well and by the end of November she had completed around 900 miles and, desperate to keep accusations of a swindle at bay, announced via the local press she would be happy to spend some of her rest periods answering questions from audience members who might think the walk was not genuine. Coverage in the papers was very limited but it appears she finished the job in the allotted time in early to mid-December. It meant after just two and a half events in her new career she had effectively reached 'elite' level, having trounced the old Barclay benchmark. Only William Gale was widely acknowledged to have achieved a distance longer than Ada's 1,250 miles in a 1,000-hour period – his 1,500 miles at Lillie Bridge in West London having come just a short while earlier.

In terms of public acclaim, Gale's concurrent exploits in London had the effect of overshadowing Madame Anderson. The day after finishing at Lillie Bridge, instead of resting he caused a fuss by heading out for a training spin, and then within a few more days was in action at the Agricultural Hall in Islington. Here he chalked up 4,000 quarter miles in 4,000 consecutive periods of 10 minutes. The world of pedestrianism was amazed and Gale's heroics were celebrated in the London sporting press to a far greater extent than those of Ada Anderson in faraway Plymouth. She wasn't yet a big name nationwide, but her efforts did gain enough attention to make it worthwhile staying put in the area for a few more weeks. She agreed to appear as part of a local circus where she would start walking at 6pm on Christmas Day 1877 and attempt to clock up 100 miles by 10pm on Boxing Day (28 hours).

This was another new format to test her stamina and judgement, but proved too much too soon. Ada reportedly collapsed and fainted twice, first at 60 miles then at 87. The doctors who came to her aid didn't approve of the ordeal she was putting herself through and later spoke publicly of being amazed she hadn't perished altogether. The circus arena featured a very small ring and the continual circling made her task psychologically difficult. When she got within a few minutes of the 10pm cut-off time it was announced she had completed 96 of the 100 miles. Her helpers and the sympathetic audience could see she was thoroughly exhausted and wouldn't achieve her target, and they successfully persuaded her to stop immediately and not attempt the final four miles.

Ada and her small entourage were in accommodation on Eldad Hill in Plymouth and here they remained while she rested and recovered. They placed advertisements offering further appearances – "At home or abroad in halls, circuses or skating rinks". They occupied rooms at The No Place Inn, a small hotel whose unusual name had been chosen because of a strange episode nearly 40 years earlier. Back then the three towns of Plymouth, Devonport and Stonehouse were embroiled in a dispute over where to build a railway terminus to serve the region. Called upon to make the final decision, the famous engineer Isambard Kingdom Brunel controversially chose this site at the top of Eldad Hill. Opponents called this madness and insisted the hilly location was "no place to build a railway station". Brunel's choice was subsequently overturned and the station built at Millbay instead, allowing the building left behind to become a pub called the 'No Place' as a reminder of what had happened!

A booking was secured for Ada to appear on Wednesday 23rd January 1878 at Plymouth's Royal Albert Hall for a second time, this one billed as a Grand Challenge Match for £100 against a male pedestrian by the name of J. H. Lake. The idea of pitting a man against a woman sounded straightforward enough, but the format of the contest turned out to be anything but! Ada's task would be to complete 1,344 quarter miles in as many quarter hours, a challenge that would last 14 days and nights, while Lake would be doing 672 miles in 336 hours over exactly the same period. Put simply, Lake had to complete two miles within every hour, Ada 0.25 of a mile every 15 minutes, both of them toiling for an uninterrupted fortnight.

Lake was no novice, having completed 115 miles in 24 hours recently, but having to cover twice as much ground in half as many appearances on the track as Ada, would be a fearsome challenge for him. The promoters reckoned it would be a close thing as to who finished first and that having a man and woman in action together would be something new and thrilling for the paying public to witness. Sports fans not based in the Plymouth region had to wait many days for news of this groundbreaking contest. *Bell's Life* eventually confirmed to the world during February that Madame Anderson had finished her gargantuan challenge in the allotted time – adding that she finished with flourish, her 1,344th and final quarter mile a crowd-pleasingly swift perambulation of only 155 seconds. But there was no mention of Lake's fate, which suggests he quit early.

Ada had made herself a star in Plymouth, and the possibility of further engagements in this busy port was discussed. But now that her name was clearly becoming known more widely, the time seemed right to hit the road again in search of new opportunities and audiences. A long train journey of more than 300 miles up to Lincolnshire to perform in the small port and market town of Boston would be her next adventure. Another attempt to outperform Captain Barclay was on the cards, Madame Anderson lined up to attempt 1,000 miles in 672 consecutive hours (28 days), which would mean finishing 328 hours quicker than the Newmarket hero of 1809. As well as the walk itself, Ada also had to fulfil an appointment at Boston's police court where she had to convince the local authorities that this show at their Corn Exchange building was 'genuine' and above board.

She reassured the Mayor of Boston that the proprieties of life would not be outraged by her performance and that the effect on the youth of the town would not be demoralising. Speaking to the court represented an important mission for Ada, for as the *Illustrated and Sporting and Dramatic News* had reported: "The Boston magistrates appear to think that what is called a pedestrian entertainment is calculated to corrupt the morals of the inhabitants of that most respectable town". But Ada was having none of that, and confidently told the bench: "The way in which I conduct my business is entirely different from that pursued by other pedestrians. I have been on the stage a great many years and profess to be master of my audience. I do not allow anything objectionable to be carried on and providing there is, I halt in my course and put a stop to it. I have been performing in Plymouth and several other large places and the superintendents of police in these places can testify as to the manner in which the performances were conducted."

If he was impressed, the mayor didn't show it. He responded: "We wish to observe that Boston differs widely from a town like Plymouth. We try here as far as possible to protect the morals of the people, and we think this entertainment will be the means of bringing together the lowest scum of the town. There is a certain class, not merely in Boston alone, but in other towns who gloat over sensational exhibitions, and especially when the agents are females."

Once her walk at the Corn Exchange had got underway, Ada was visited by a representative of the *Boston Guardian*, who wrote: "The bearing of Madame Anderson and the conduct of everybody connected with her are as exemplary as the most fastidious could desire. In every case where she has walked the authorities say that the performance was conducted in an orderly manner and there was nothing whatever to complain of on the score of propriety. As a pedestrian [she] is a marvel, she walks in splendid form and is worth seeing. There is nothing in the performance to offend the taste or shock the sensibilities of anyone… but those magistrates! Naturally Boston differs from a town like Plymouth, but the difference is probably more in the direction of narrowness than width! Boston is fortunate in its mayor – just as that workhouse immortalised in *Oliver Twist* was blessed in its Bumble".

The event was recognised as an entertainment of a kind never before seen in this part of the Lincolnshire Fens, creating unprecedented excitement which sparked the interest of both sexes and all classes. Good crowds were reported on the midweek days and a tightly packed hall at the weekends. Ada was routinely attended by Dr Arthur Tuxford to check her condition – and one of his reports stated: "Not the slightest irregularity in the heart's action or any other indication of constitutional disturbances. She undoubtedly has a fine physique, great energy, pluck and endurance rarely equalled in any woman". Nevertheless, onlookers noted that fairly early in proceedings Ada looked white as a sheet, jaded and fatigued, although her leg speed was apparently not affected. She evidently overcame this sticky patch and swept past the 250-mile point looking fine. The *Boston Guardian* reported that her attendants were kept busy looking after her, ensuring she took a cold bath twice a day and they washed her feet up to eight times daily. They marvelled at her ability to sleep readily, sometimes leaving the track to collapse on her bed and falling asleep instantly, not even stirring when an assistant unlaced her shoes and washed and dressed her feet.

The anxious Mayor of Boston contacted the police, requesting they keep an eye on events on the track and was reassured to hear that Superintendent Bellamy had visited the Corn Exchange during the busy Saturday night session. Bellamy had encountered a very respectable gathering of well-behaved people who were highly appreciative of the entertainment, which he felt was carried out in a legitimate and straightforward manner. No drink was being sold to spectators, he added. All this would have been music to the ears of Madame Anderson, as gaining the respect and approval of the authorities had eluded most of her pedestrienne predecessors, meaning their careers had often been troubled and short-lived as a result.

The good behaviour of spectators and positive atmosphere in the hall was endorsed by a number of sources, including the reader's letters column in the *Boston Guardian*, where it was observed: "Madame Anderson seemed to electrify her audience with her ever-welcome smile as she tripped lightly round the hall [de]void of all vulgarity and rudeness, something which every other artist should copy. I hope she will meet with the patronage she deserves". Despite all the approval and support, Ada found this trek more punishing than usual for her feet, and during rest periods her helpers took to swathing them in turpentine and flannel, and sometimes used raw chunks of beef to reduce the painful swelling. She had the services of a footman, a page and three female attendants to deal with her problems, and responded by ploughing on regardless. She appeared acutely aware this feat of 1.5 miles every hour for 28 days non-stop had never been accomplished by a woman and wanted to be the first, no matter what.

The track marked out around the hall was 100 yards long, requiring 26 laps for every 1.5-mile session, and promoter Charles Thorpe, who leased the hall, had decorated the building superbly with the arches covered in a profusion of flowers, evergreen plants and flags. Ada benefited from a constant stream of visitors, many of them farmers who had brought along their wives and daughters, most of whom were so fascinated by proceedings that they stayed for long periods despite the repetitive nature of the action. Ada, of course, was an experienced entertainer and knew what to do to keep interest levels high… on one occasion she allowed a young girl to accompany her on the track for a spell, the pair of them amusing the crowd greatly by mischievously creeping up to startle audience members that were not paying full attention. It all helped a few more laps go by and kept the punters happy.

The 28th and final day – Wednesday 13th March – arrived and a beaming Ada finished the ordeal to a wonderful ovation and scenes of celebration rarely witnessed before in Boston. Even her trusty attendant Miss Sparrow was close to tears as she reflected on what happened: "The whole town turned out and the parish bells were rung when she was finishing." Ada herself could hardly believe it: "The cheers and warmth of the crowds here were so overpowering that my heart seemed to come up in my throat and nearly choked me for a while! It was the proudest moment of my life."

Far from the disapproval garnered by Ada's pedestrienne predecessors in many a northern town, this was an occasion when everybody seemed deliriously happy and delighted by what they had witnessed. Henry Farrow, proprietor of the *Lincs Herald* called it "astonishing walking" and wrote that the Boston public had greeted her finish in such a frenzy that officials and police struggled to keep them from storming the track *en masse*. The Corn Exchange management were so happy with the outcome they allowed two concerts to be staged later in the month as benefit events for Ada. Hugely encouraged, Ada's entourage wasted no time in announcing her availability for more action from the end of March onwards, urging interested parties to contact her via the Boston Station Hotel, or alternatively an address in South Norwood, SE London.

Ada Anderson, a formidable and talented woman who didn't suffer fools gladly.

Ada's success over February and March 1878 represented big news in Boston and, somewhat inevitably, the town's police and magistrates would become part of the story. Rarely did a major walk go off without somebody or other being summoned to the local police court in connection with it – and Boston proved to be no exception. This time the man facing a criminal charge was the entrepreneur who hired the building, Mr Charles Thorpe. A carpenter employed by him to decorate the hall for the walk, James Lovell, had accused Thorpe of assault after they had a disagreement over payment. Madame Anderson was called to give evidence and confirmed Lovell had created a disturbance and two policemen were needed to throw him out. The magistrates were unable to reach a decision and adjourned the case, but within a few days the warring parties came to an out-of-court settlement.

In the wake of Boston another booking was soon secured for Ada, setting her up at the Olympian grounds in Woodhouse Lane, Leeds, in April, for an attempt at the age of 37 to be the first woman to walk 1,500 miles in 1,000 hours – and in doing so emulate William Gale's recent great effort over the same schedule. Recent weather had been appalling across the British Isles with snow showers, gales and temperatures barely above freezing point, but things had improved a little by the time the walk got underway on Monday 8th April 1878. However, before nightfall Ada and the spectators complained about the poorly lit nature of the grounds, an issue that was resolved on the third day when some gas lamps were brought in. Ada was in the form of her life and completed the massive feat on Monday 20th May with strength and energy to spare. She completed her last official mile in the morning in a brisk 14:30 but then continued to do a gentle quarter mile every hour to prolong the show a little longer into the evening.

While all this was happening, ten miles up the road in Dewsbury at the Batley Carr Road skating rink, Madame Blanche Victor – by now regarded as a protege of Ada – was working hard to complete 1,000 quarter miles in 1,000 consecutive periods of 10 minutes on a 62-yard narrow track of bark chippings, a feat that would take a full week. Once Ada had finished her Leeds walk she made a number of visits to the Dewsbury rink to give support and even accompanied Victor on the track for several spells.

During the week after the Leeds walk, as well as recovering from her own efforts and cheering on Madame Victor, Ada found time for a further important appointment when marrying Boston man William Paley, a farmer's son who was by now acting as her personal manager. The marriage was solemnised at St Matthew's Church in Leeds by curate Fred Kapellenberg and witnesses to the ceremony included her long-time assistant Elizabeth Sparrow. The couple tied the knot a few days before setting off eastwards for her next walking engagement in Lincolnshire.

During that summer of 1878 newly-wed Ada would manage four more walks – in Skegness, King's Lynn (twice) and Peterborough. In summary, from September 1877 to September 1888, her first year as a professional pedestrienne, she would record a remarkable tally of at least eight successful multi-week walks, which almost certainly surpasses anything any woman had done before. At this point it appeared there were no women around to provide serious competition in the UK, so inevitably the idea of Ada heading over to the USA was discussed.

Meanwhile, on Whit Monday, June 10th she set off for some bracing sea air at Skegness where, at the new cricket ground in Richmond Drive, she would cover 1.5 miles every hour for 28 days. On Monday 24th June she reached the halfway point looking in good shape and full of confidence, the number of visitors reportedly increasing to see her as days went by. Other attractions included a handicap race on the Saturday evening of three hours for various locals, and a tug of war involving 20 local men against two horses, which the humans would win. Despite appearances to the contrary, the *Boston Guardian* reported that after finishing her task she found her visit had not been profitable, having to leave town "with only a miserable pound or two" to show for all the work. "Who would choose pedestrianism as a profession after this?" the paper mused.

Word was spreading about the splendid entertainment put on by the indefatigable little woman from London, and within days of finishing at Skegness her contingent headed the relatively short distance around The Wash and over the border into Norfolk for an engagement at the King's Lynn Athenaeum Music Hall. This impressive building on Baxter's Plain (where the Old Post Office now stands) had opened 34 years earlier with the aim of uniting the town's literary, artistic and scientific societies under a single roof. Unfortunately it was by now struggling to break even and high hopes were pinned on Madame Anderson's show providing a boost for the coffers. There would be great interest stirred in 'Lynn' by the visiting walker, but this would just be temporary respite, for the Athenaeum would subsequently close after being declared a commercial failure five years later.

On the evening of Tuesday 16th July, at 9 o'clock precisely, Madame Anderson – unashamedly billed 'Champion Walker of the World' – set off on a trek that would see her tot up 1,008 miles, by way of 1.5 miles being completed within 672 consecutive hours (28 days). Measured by Mr Thomas Burton, each mile and a half would involve 45 laps of the little track marked off around the interior of the King's Lynn hall. On the four Sundays covered by the schedule the public was not admitted, leaving just a handful of police, press and officials to keep an eye on things. On frequent evenings, by way of a change, spectators were treated to three-mile walks undertaken by local schoolboy Walter Cooke who regularly achieved this inside 28 minutes and was cheered heartily and hailed a real local talent. Additionally the crowd was entertained by turns from soprano Miss Lizzie Gasson and pianist Harry Stewart. Things went well for a fortnight but Ada was hampered in the third week by a nasty blister which formed on one of her heels. This was regularly treated and she promised she would "walk it off". Later it was declared a painful abscess had formed and it was feared she might have to quit, but after limping through several grim days she recovered. Young Walter, being coached by Ada, walked several times alongside her and took on bigger challenges including a stint of 50 miles in 12 hours.

The final 1.5-mile walk of the 1,008 took Ada 15 minutes and won her a huge ovation, after which she climbed on stage to speak. Addressing herself specifically to the women present, she assured them she had not endangered her health and would never have tried to perform a task she was unable to accomplish, and for which she had not the strength. She was aware some onlookers had called out "poor woman, look what she has to endure!" but dismissed their sympathy, even though it was well meant. She said she was well aware what real suffering was, having a few years earlier watched at close hand seamstresses at work in London – as so graphically described in Thomas Hood's 1843 poem *Song of the Shirt*. Their life often involved working through the night with a small piece of candle and only bread and butter to eat. She conceded her own work meant she was deprived of sleep, but, unlike the seamstresses she was always well fed and taken care of. Ada then launched into some unfavourable remarks towards the promoter who had engaged her (Mr Bullock) which suggested a dispute about payment might have arisen. This sparked a few jeers and catcalls from the audience, some shouting they had heard enough of her grievances. She then swiftly concluded matters by demonstrating her excellent singing ability, which seemed to catch a good proportion of the audience by surprise.

Ada now had less than a week of rest before another event was lined up in King's Lynn for her. During this spell she was kept mostly indoors by several major storms with torrential rain and thunder and lightning, causing much local damage and a fire. Luckily better weather had returned by Monday 19th August, encouraging locals out to see her take on the unusual task of walking a quarter of a mile every five minutes between midday to midnight – for six consecutive days. The grand total would be 864 quarter miles, mostly achieved in about 3.5 minutes each, meaning she only had 90 seconds or so to recover before the next one. The schedule meant she had precious little rest over the six 12-hour stints, but the saving grace was the lengthy spells available for a proper night's sleep in between. It still needed an almighty effort of course, but Madame Anderson coped superbly and concluded the task in style on Saturday 23rd August.

Over her first 12 months as a professional, Ada had displayed serious athletic credentials, performance skills and natural 'stage presence' and was thus perfectly placed to develop her career when the idea arose to decamp to

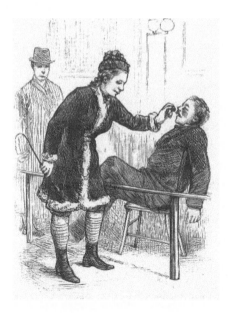

One of Ada Anderson's favourite tricks was to chalk the face of anybody who had the cheek to fall asleep during her performances.

America. She and husband/manager William had no young family to restrict them, so the way was open to head west. The sport was looking unlikely to prosper for much longer in her homeland, and there was the prospect of becoming a pioneer in the land of opportunity. Pedestrianism across the Atlantic was booming and Uncle Sam beckoned. She had established a reputation as a versatile performer with more strings to her bow than simply an ability to circle a track for weeks on end. Americans would surely love to watch a woman performing thousands of miles from home as an athlete, singer and an articulate orator with an English accent. The potential to earn a fortune could not be ignored and so a plan was duly hatched in late summer 1878 while Ada's final engagements in Eastern England were being completed.

She agreed to fit in one more 14-day performance in her homeland to earn enough funds to tide them over for a month or two. Handily situated just 35 miles from her temporary base at King's Lynn, the venue for this farewell performance would be Peterborough, a market town currently transitioning into a vibrant and growing industrial centre since the arrival of the railways. Starting Saturday 7th September 1878 her show here would involve 1,344 quarter miles being walked in the same number of consecutive quarter hours over the allocated fortnight. A large wooden pavilion was erected specifically for the show at a spot beside the Lincoln Road.

The audience was a good mix of male and female, young and old, and a fair number got the chance to walk alongside the famous pedestrienne at various points. Walter Cooke, the young prodigy who appeared at King's Lynn, participated again and there were also various music hall acts laid on. The list of attractions included a "Miss Ada Louise the impersonator", which was presumably Ada herself. The course was laid with tan bark and needed six laps to complete one mile and in the middle of the pavilion the stage was again occupied by soprano Lizzie Gasson and pianist Harry Stewart. The Great Northern Locomotive Department band also did a turn as did the Wilkinson brothers (comedians) and the Claremont sisters (burlesque). Local men Mr Ross and Mr Thomas English were timekeepers. As before, Ada also sang for the crowd on a number of occasions herself.

While Ada walked there were other shorter walking contests involving local people on a separate track within the same arena. The popularity of these contests between local unknowns prompted the *Peterborough Standard* to warn its readers that if they intended to take up pedestrianism as a result of what they'd seen, they must remember to take things carefully and prepare properly and change their habits and diet carefully. The paper listed all manner of foods and drinks that would and would not be suitable (draught beer at lunchtime was highly recommended) and gave warnings about the dangers of heart trouble and other possible ailments.

During the walk, Madame Anderson felt ill late one night and had to be examined by local physician Dr. J. Martin-Kennedy. He immediately recommended she rest for several hours. This was a worrying episode as Peterborough was currently in the grip of a typhoid epidemic, with at least 60 known cases in the town at that point. Sure enough the certificate written out by the doctor stated: "I certify that Madame Anderson had a severe attack of English cholera, which compelled her to desist walking from 12.30 to 7am".

The rest seemed to work and Ada was able to continue early the next morning, making up for lost time by adding a few laps to her remaining quarter miles. This was good news, but sadly the final gala night of the show would be marred by tragedy. A 67-year-old spectator – Susan Adams, a widow and mother of 12 – collapsed and died of heart failure. An inquest would later be told Mrs Adams had become highly excited by the sight of an ordinary woman – possibly an acquaintance of hers – walking alongside the famous Madame Anderson. Mrs Adams was from a family with a history of heart trouble and it was her first visit to any public entertainment for many years. Her daughter said she tried to prevent her mother attending for fear it would be too much for her, but had failed. Fellow spectators rushed to Mrs Adams' aid, applying water and vinegar to her face after she collapsed and a little brandy was encouraged down her throat before she was moved from trackside to the front of the pavilion and placed in a chair. A doctor arrived but she died within minutes.

Ada finished on time on the evening of Saturday 21ˢᵗ September, in front of a good crowd of at least 1,000. Amid the usual mayhem at the end, she climbed on stage to address the audience and – delighted with their reaction and general support – promised she would put on an extra performance for them in Peterborough within a few days, before taking off for the States. It would be a repeat of the King's Lynn event in which she walked a quarter mile every five minutes, between noon and midday on six successive days. It would turn out to be her last known public appearance in the UK.

As Ada prepared to quit these shores, William Gale was involved in discussions about joining her, but ultimately decided not to extend his long and celebrated career with further appearances in America. It was therefore a party of just four that boarded the transatlantic steamship *Ethiopia* on Wednesday 9ᵗʰ October at Broomielaw docks on Glasgow's River Clyde. Clutching a one-way ticket, Ada was accompanied by her agent J.H. Webb, her long-time assistant Elizabeth Sparrow and her relatively new husband William Paley, whose knowledge and experience as a theatre man would prove useful. Paley was ten years her junior, but couldn't match his wife for fitness – he was described as a large, rotund man with sallow complexion.

With Ada and William hunkered down in a 16-guinea saloon cabin, the ship steamed out of Glasgow, stopping at Lough Foyle in Ireland where a number of passengers and despatches were dropped at Moville, before heading away for New York at breakfast time on Friday 11ᵗʰ October, arriving eleven days later.

The quartet must have been optimistic about their chances of success in the USA. As academic and ultra-runner Dahn Shaulis notes, by now Ada Anderson had become established as a rising celebrity with a strong, confident voice and strong character. She had used her sweet contralto voice and her musical and theatrical talents throughout her year or so performing in England, and demonstrated she would not hesitate to speak her mind about issues that troubled her, such as poverty and exploitation of women. She didn't mince words about incompetent management at her events and always had kind words for the women and children who came to watch her. People loved her sense of humour and sense of mischief, which she managed to incorporate into her performances. She was a born performer.

On arrival in New York, Ada's party wasted no time getting down to business, and decided to aim high. They wanted her debut to be a unique and huge achievement in surroundings to match. There would be no gentle warm-ups, they wanted to make an instant impact to maximise her earning potential. They approached multi-millionaire industrialist William Vanderbilt with a request to rent his prestigious Gilmore's Garden (soon to be renamed Madison Square Garden) but he turned them down. Instead they had to settle for the more humble Mozart Garden in Brooklyn, an unfussy, plain theatre building on Fulton Street which offered enough room for several hundred spectators, a small oval track and a stage for a band.

If Ada felt any disappointment at having to settle for Fulton Street instead of glamorous midtown Manhattan, no doubt she was comforted by the fact that a purse of 8,000 US dollars was up for grabs. She was generally more comfortable walking in the fresh air at outdoor venues and must have had concerns about the claustrophobic and smoke-filled surroundings that now faced her. Ada's schedule was to cover 2,700 quarter miles in the same number of quarter hours, a continuous trek of four weeks (675 miles), giving a maximum of roughly ten minutes rest time after each quarter mile. She had tried this 15-minute format with success at Peterborough just two months earlier, but that had been a much shorter event than here in New York.

The tan-bark track was just 63 yards long and three feet wide, arranged around a sawdust-covered oval, meaning she would have to walk a dizzying total of nearly 700 laps on each of the 28 days. The track was separated from the rest of the flooring by a narrow railing about 18 inches high and within the small ring, several hundred chairs were squeezed in for spectators. To cap all this, the arena was lit by gas lamps, some of which gave off choking fumes, and many spectators were likely to ignore the 'no smoking' signs. Although her dressing room (a tent measuring 28 by 12 feet) was positioned just a few feet from the track, the sleep deprivation factor would be mind-boggling.

In charge of proceedings was Captain Alexander R. Samuells, known widely by his initials 'A.R.', manager of Mozart Garden at the time, who before the end of the walk would sign a one-year deal to become Ada's business manager. His meticulous organisation included the creation of separate access arrangements for spectators – respectable people were directed in via a door on Smith Street, while an alleyway on Fulton Street was set aside for the gamblers and prostitutes who would inevitably gravitate to the building. Ada approved of this 'safe' environment and actively encouraged gentlemen to bring their female relatives with them. Samuells' team of officials was headed by Brooklyn sports promoter Mike Henry, whose respected name and immense physical presence brought much-needed credibility to the event. Fred Coles was recruited as the race starter with timekeepers Charles Hazelton and George Force. Every quarter mile walked would be recorded and verified in logbooks. Three prominent local press representatives agreed to rotate shifts to monitor the walk, thus providing another source of verification as to the event's integrity.

New York was evidently intrigued by the remarkable little woman from London. The *Brooklyn Daily Eagle* reported attendance from the start by many prominent Brooklynites, a large contingent of women, plus gamblers with a stake in the result. The Garden's stage was decorated to resemble an open-air landscape, with a brass band playing regularly until midnight. They described Madame Anderson, reportedly now 36 years old, as looking "robust, rosy and hearty" with a bright and prepossessing face though of a "slightly masculine" type. She emerged into the arena in black velvet knee breeches, and a loose flowing robe of blue and scarlet cloth, embroidered in white. On her feet were stout but loose leather shoes topped by scarlet stockings below silver tights. This milliner's daughter chose a blue and scarlet cloth cap ornamented with a white braid and snowy feather. She was introduced and spoke to the spectators, assuring them she'd give "all my strength and nervous force" towards completing the huge task. Unexpectedly, she then admitted it was possible her brain, heart or circulatory system might break down at any time due to the stress caused by lack of sleep. Such honesty and vulnerability only endeared her further to the crowd.

It was dark and wintry outside on Monday 16th December 1878 as she set off, a spring in her step, and it wouldn't be long before she got the chance to ensure the crowd was truly on her side. In the sixth quarter mile a Hoboken man suddenly jumped over the small railing and joined her on the track. Nobody blocked his path so it may have all been pre-arranged, but Ada had to call on her theatrical skills to make the most of the situation. The fellow clearly fancied his chances of impressing the crowd by walking faster than the star of the show, but without any difficulty Ada lengthened her stride, put her head down and pumped her arms purposefully. He had no chance. She even slowed to offer him a second and third chance to catch up, but to the delight of the crowd, accelerated away every time he got close. The elderly former boxing champion Bill Tovec also joined her on another occasion. It was all good-natured fun and ensured the crowd didn't get bored with proceedings, an important aspect at this early stage.

On she went as Christmas approached, enjoying some good coverage in the local press, with the notable exception of the influential *New York Times*, which consistently derided the spectacle as absurd and tawdry. The paper also suggested Madame Anderson was talentless in comparison with other skilled entertainers performing in local theatres. The public seemed to disagree, for on Christmas Eve the building was packed to the rafters with an audience that included many rich and famous figures from New York's political and entertainment worlds, among them the tiny and highly popular circus performer Tom Thumb. The little man even did a stint on the track, putting on a great show as he stopped to shake hands with spectators and then sprinted on his tiny legs to catch Madame Anderson up again.

Ada rose to the occasion time and again, sprinkling her performance with some humorous moments that had the audience in stitches. Her favourite trick would be to home in on anybody in the front row who had the temerity to fall asleep during her performance; on one occasion she suddenly produced a three-foot long tin horn which she placed near the dozing victim's ear before giving a loud blast. According to the *Brooklyn Daily Eagle*: "The young fellow we saw served in this manner looked as if he thought Gabriel had blown his horn indeed!".

Over the Christmas and New Year period the crowds turned up in great numbers, much to the delight of Ada and her management. On Christmas Day morning she gave an interview to the *New York Herald*, reeling off a list of the food she was eating to keep her strength up: chops, beefsteaks, poultry, fish, oysters, cabbage, potatoes, beef tea, light puddings, cakes, grapes, tea, port wine and champagne. *Turf, Field & Farm* marvelled at how well the event was going: "On December 30th, between 7pm and 11pm, 4,000 people had gone in and out of the Garden. The seats in the centre of the circle were filled, and so too was nearly every available piece of ground on which a spectator could stand. People hung around at all hours of the day, with some crowds at the early hour of 3am reportedly as large as 300 people. As much as to wake herself up as to entertain the crowd, Madame Anderson would occasionally take to the stage following a quarter mile and belt out an aria from Verdi, graciously accept challenges from pedestrian wannabes and then vanquish them, or disappear into her dressing room after a few laps only to reappear in some new brown and silver trimmed velvet costume. Many doubted her capabilities but she proved them wrong".

The press attention was relentless and when one reporter asked Ada towards the end of her journey if she was still confident she could complete the job, she responded in spirited fashion despite her obvious tiredness: "Well, if I can stand the attention of 12 physicians, and having my dresses changed six times in 12 hours, I can certainly go on with my little walks!"

Occasionally if there were no celebrities around she would be accompanied on the track by her husband, despite his decidedly non-athletic body shape, and by Captain Samuells. Their appearance would help break the tedium for both Ada and the spectators, especially during the quieter periods when the band had been stood down. On more than one occasion Ada gave up her rest period to take the stage and sing and play piano between walks, something that always went down well with those watching. One aspect always of great interest would be Ada's choice of clothing, something she paid a lot of attention to, and which fascinated the female element of the audience. These women were also treated occasionally to little speeches by Ada, exhorting the feeling of well-being and freedom that walking and exercise could bring to any woman. There would be gasps when a new outfit appeared; on one evening Ada emerged from her tent in a flame-coloured silk dress that reached her knees but hung loose at the waist to make it both fashionable and functional. It had a square-cut neck decorated with a collar elaborately embroidered with a gold braid.

The American audiences seemed in awe of Ada's ability to plough on through all the discomfort and loved the polite English way she apologised to them about the aches and pains she was suffering while entertaining them. It was reported pain in her hips was coming and going at regular intervals, and she was having to cope with severely blistered feet. But it was clear the lack of sleep was top of her list of problems. She suffered occasional bouts of serious drowsiness and would totter around dangerously – a spectacle greeted with disdain by the *New York Times*: "Even babies don't break their sleep into such small increments [as Ada does]. Such tests are… useless and unattractive", they insisted. It was clear nobody in the USA – not even the top performers like Mary Marshall, Bertha Von Hallern and the undefeated Dan O'Leary – had ever attempted such a sleep-depriving endurance test as this. By now some of the unofficial 'bookies' were said to be offering 100-1 against her finishing. It was even reported a qualified physician couldn't resist putting 100 dollars on her not finishing, as he was convinced it wasn't possible.

Ada made great efforts to disguise her various discomforts, admitting to the crowd on one occasion: "I don't want to make you suffer as well as myself, so I try to hide my pain as well as I can." She added later: "I have fits of sleepiness which are very severe. While I sleep I suffer. Sometimes I wish I could never sleep, for it is so painful to wake up." On one occasion Ada managed to inflict pain on her assistant Elizabeth Sparrow – but it was purely unintentional: she was startled and embarrassed when told afterwards how she'd been semi-comatose due to lack of sleep and had lashed out when Miss Sparrow tried to wake her for the next quarter-mile walk. Poor Sparrow keeled over with blood pouring from a badly cut mouth that would need medical attention. Ada had been in a complete daze and lashing out had been an automatic reflex action.

By the second week of January with the task more than two-thirds complete, the inevitable whispers were heard about skulduggery being afoot, generated by shady characters who wanted to prevent her victorious finish. Bent pins and other small potentially dangerous objects were reportedly found on the track, almost certainly the work of someone with money riding on a non-finish. Other vexatious episodes were perpetrated by the rumour mill – one allegation suggested Ada had a 'body double' who would quietly replace her for a few miles during the quieter late-night periods while she got some sleep. Maybe she had a sister, or even a twin, who could be carrying out this task, it was suggested. This sort of story had gained some traction due to the way she would sometimes emerge from her tent full of bounce and energy, having only an hour or two earlier looked to be exhausted beyond repair. Another rumour circulated that one or two of the many bouquets of flowers she received had been secretly dosed with chloroform by somebody working for the gamblers.

Much of the gossip appears to have been without much foundation, but served a useful purpose for the press, who had columns to fill. Mike Henry, supervising the walk, was among those furious to hear the fraud allegations: "I've been out here since the beginning, put in 20 hours a day, strained my knee, and you're asking me is this a fraud? What kind of person would do that to himself for a fake?" Henry, whose duties saw him walk almost as many miles as Madame Anderson, actually collapsed later on and needed hospital treatment, but heroically reappeared near the end of the event.

Added to the fraud allegations, there came complaints from the Women's Christian Temperance Union about gambling and consumption of alcohol at the venue during the show: "We claim that the opening on the Sabbath of all stores, exhibitions, etc, to which an admission fee is charged, is illegal, and in this particular instance the illegality is heightened by the amount of Sunday liquor selling which is an inevitable accompaniment, and also we, as women, enter our protest against this pitiful display of womanhood as contrary to the dictates of humanity and God".

Ada brushed it all aside and ploughed on regardless. Her management quietened many of the complainers when they honourably paid out the advertised 'reward' to someone who had reported Ada arriving late at the start line during one particular evening. It transpired she had been enjoying a relaxing bath for slightly too long, and had misjudged her return to the start line, but only by a matter of seconds. As a show of goodwill they paid up anyway.

The smoky polluted air in the theatre was a bugbear throughout, although by New Year's Eve officials had done something about this, opening doors to let in fresh air and supplying her with a warm ulster [a Victorian working daytime overcoat, with cape and sleeves] which meant the cooler, more draughty atmosphere didn't become a problem. As the end drew ever nearer she had to overcome a number of minor problems, such as stumbling into railings and a wall, due to immense tiredness. On top of the physical strain her mental resolve was severely tested by a wizened old woman who would lean menacingly towards her every time she passed, apparently accusing her of fielding a 'body double' for some laps. Ada was quoted later: "Every time I pass her she shoves out her head and peers into my face as if to say, 'I'm bound to find out if you are the same woman every time.' I'm afraid I shall snap her head off if she keeps it up."

On the final day an estimated 4,000 paid a dollar each to watch the grand conclusion. The roads outside were blocked by hundreds of people unable to get in. The band played louder than ever but the noise of the crowd meant they could barely be heard. Remarkably, Ada sacrificed several rest periods to sing and talk to the crowds, including a few bars of *Nil Desperandum* before steeling herself for the final strides. As the final quarter mile of the 28-day event began, the crowd erupted with a deafening roar, and Mike Henry set off ahead to clear a path for a beaming Madame Anderson, who was on the crest of a wave, adrenaline pumping through her previously exhausted body. Incredibly this 2,700[th] walk would prove her fastest of the lot – a time of 2 mins 37 secs entered into the logbook.

It was suggested this completion of 2,700 quarter miles in successive quarter hours was surely the greatest pedestrian feat by any woman. It was surely deserving of a place in the record books, but a number of publications pointed out that although it had been "wonderfully plucky" it was not something that could be regarded as an athletic record and *Bell's Life* sniffed, "The performance has little merit as a purely pedestrian feat". Nevertheless

New Yorkers who witnessed the walk's climax thought she was a marvel and her performance without equal.

There was mayhem as she crumpled to her knees at the end, a real crush to get near her. Some women spectators fainted amid the excitement, but enough people retained sufficient control to stand on their rickety wooden chairs waving handkerchiefs and hats in the air and cheering loudly. In her exhausted but jubilant state, Ada was a mixture of tears and smiles. She was examined by physicians who pronounced her in sound health even though throughout those final days she'd been periodically overcome by drowsiness and often looked pale and glassy-eyed.

She was eventually carried away wrapped in blankets to a carriage outside. A coach awaited at the stage door and large bouquets of flowers handed over as she was carried off, and a basket of champagne bottles hoisted onto the coach's roof. As it began to pull away, those at close quarters could see she was thoroughly exhausted despite her big smiles, and called out to advise her to head straight to Dr. Shepard's Turkish baths at Columbia Heights to recover properly.

After a period of recuperation in a local hotel Ada reappeared at the Mozart Garden for a special reception at which she was showered with gifts and praise, and the all-important cash reward of 8,000 dollars. This represented almost a quarter of the total revenue from the show. It was the reward of a lifetime for her, considering the average annual household income of the time was roughly 500 dollars. The equivalent prize money value in 2020 would be around 200,000 dollars. US author Harry Hall points out that with one performance, albeit a month in duration, she had enthused many Americans and infused life into a sport that desperately needed a boost. Ada sensed her new public had warmed to her, and used the opportunity to beg the women of America to take up walking more and to use horse-cars less. She pleaded with the ultra-religious womenfolk who had refused to attend her events because she walked on Sundays to reconsider their position; after all, when they used horse-car drivers to get to church, were they not compelling others to work on Sundays when it was often perfectly possible for them to walk?

Over the next few weeks any empty building or space large enough for a track in New York City would play host to a woman's walking event. Many were poorly organised amateur affairs, but for a while the public couldn't get enough. One magazine publisher commented that if he printed a new essay by the philosopher and poet Ralph Waldo Emerson he'd sell an extra 500 copies, but if he ran a story about Madame Anderson's walking match it would be

25,000. Over the early weeks and months of 1879 the sport in America would experience something of a renaissance, with Madame Anderson's efforts prompting a wave of adverts for pedestrian merchandise in the New York papers, including pedometers for women (five dollars apiece) and souvenir photographs of herself and other walkers.

There was excited newspaper talk of a repeat performance by the amazing Englishwoman being lined up for Boston at which a bumper 15,000 US dollars would be on offer – nearly twice what she is reputed to have pocketed from Mozart Garden – but it seems this plan came to nothing. Ada had indicated she wanted another year in the sport before retirement, and subsequent events were arranged around the country, although none would be quite as successful and attention-grabbing as her American debut in Brooklyn.

The first came towards the end of January 1879 in Pittsburgh, where she tackled 1,350 quarter miles in as many quarter hours. This created conflict with powerful local industrialist William Park Jr and the First Presbyterian church, who objected to her performing on Sundays. The Pittsburgh mayor said he had no authority to close the walk for this reason but did agree to impose fines – Ada's husband Paley and manager Samuells were both charged with violating the ancient Sunday law of 1794 and ordered to pay a total of 85 dollars and 30 cents. Attendance was generally good although she faced competition from Buffalo Bill's popular Wild West show. She finished the task in front of a thrilled crowd of 2,000 and moved on to Chicago.

In the first week of March at Chicago's Exposition Center a two-week affair involving 2,064 quarter miles in consecutive quarter hours pulled in a series of sizeable crowds, among them the civil war hero General Philip Sheridan. However, once again there was evidence of a growing tide of opinion against exhibitions like this, protestors claiming they were immoral, brutal and exploitative. The Philadelphia Medical Society was among those calling for a ban on the grounds of cruelty. After city officials publicly called these walks barbarous and inhumane, some spectators, who had presumably paid to get in, now decided to turn against Ada – only to find the feisty Englishwoman quick to confront them and argue her case. Event officials and police were forced to step in and the atmosphere became toxic. She was accused of sleeping through a number of scheduled laps and in the wake of all this, decided not to participate in an international six-day walking championship for women in New York staged in late March. It would prove a wise move for that event turned into something of a fiasco.

Things went from bad to worse the following month at the Highland House building in Cincinnati. Chasing a target of 804 miles to be walked in 536 consecutive hours, Ada again pulled in some very good crowds but towards the end her reputation took a dive when reports suggested she was walking while drunk. Months earlier she had made no secret of the fact that her sustenance for walking included alcohol, and back in New York the papers had revealed the startling fact that during one day she had downed more than 40 glasses of sherry to keep herself moving. Things deteriorated further at Cincinnati when news emerged that an official was said to have pocketed 1,500 dollars of gate money and fled without trace. There was then talk of discontent in the Anderson camp, with two of her management team under threat of a lawsuit.

The Cincinnati episode contributed towards the general feeling of disapproval towards women's endurance walking that appeared to be deepening all around the globe, not just in America, Britain and its colonies. Critics had by now turned their attention to what they condemned as the 'cruel' nature of this sport, after years of using the well-worn gambling, drinking and Sunday observance arguments. Not long after Ada's Cincinnati disaster came to an end, an issue of the prominent New Zealand journal *Otago Witness* also condemned the sport as "utterly senseless":

"There is, in the spectacle itself, nothing of the slightest interest. In almost all other sports there is some rivalry, some struggle, or an exhibition of the human form brought to a high pitch of muscular perfection. In [women's walking] there is nothing of the kind. A woman walks monotonously around a sawdust track, about which sit a number of stolid spectators, who every now and then break out without rhyme or reason into frantic applause. After walking round a certain number of times she goes off into a room, where she falls asleep. After a certain number of days her feet swell and become painful and later on she begins, it is said, to see visions, and walks round in a sort of dream – can barely stand upright, and has to be forced up to her work. When she finally leaves the track she is in a condition which makes continuous medical attendance a necessity to save her life. Such brutal exhibitions should not be allowed in a civilised community. It is nothing more nor less than a public trial by slow torture, which does not advance athletic sports in the least, for the actual walking done in these sawdust rings is not, as walking, good for anything. It is in fact immeasurably below prizefighting, bullfighting, and a number of other cruel sports, which the police nowadays break up. The curious part of it is that the test lasts so long a time that the 'gate money' taken in reaches a large sum, and a woman may, if she can accomplish the feat, earn a small fortune".

The fact that a select few were apparently earning a good living from completing these strange multi-day walking feats prompted plenty of satire and lampoonery. In New York the splendidly illustrated and groundbreaking journal calling itself *Frank Leslie's Illustrated Newspaper* carried a large pen and ink cartoon they called 'The Decline of Journalism'. This showed the newsroom of a metropolitan paper with an editor proclaiming: "There is more money in legs than there is in brains!". With a junior hired to do all the news reporting, the paper's editorial staff were shown walking laps of their office, attempting to cover 3,000 quarter miles in 3,000 quarter hours in order to boost their incomes!

In June of 1879, the now tainted Madame Anderson Show moved on to Louisville, for an event billed as 1,100 quarter miles in 1,100 quarter hours. It proved another trouble-plagued occasion, and with crowds starting to dwindle things reached a point where the whole thing had to be called off. But Ada was determined to push on with the tour and earn as much as possible before quitting for good, and she was rewarded in July when a visit to Detroit proved very profitable. Here she walked 2,028 quarter miles in as many quarter hours in front of big crowds and – making hay while the sun shone – even took the opportunity to tack on an extra show after the main event was over, this one comprising 300 quarter miles within 300 segments of 12 minutes each. The whole thing ended in mid-August with Ada once again nearly dead on her feet but smiling again.

With precious little time to recover, she headed up to Buffalo (NY), later in August for another session involving quarter miles being walked every 15 minutes – this time reportedly 2,052 of them. Prior to the start, and again during the early stages, she was seriously troubled by problems with her teeth and mouth ulcers. To avoid too much disruption, the decision was taken for her to have two teeth removed during the rest periods early on in the walk. On paper it looks a heroic thing to have attempted, but the public apparently failed to respond positively, some feeling she would be performing at less than capacity and others turned off by the idea of seeing a woman walking while in pain. Whatever their reasons, people stayed away and over the course of the event attendance numbers gradually dwindled.

Perhaps by now the writing was on the wall, with Madame Anderson being seen as a spent force, her popularity and talent no longer the pull it had once (briefly) been. Regardless, the decision was taken to give her career one last push in New York, the scene of her finest hour less than a year earlier. As autumn 1879 turned into early winter, she set off on a mammoth trek at the Tivoli Theatre in downtown Brooklyn, tasked with 4,236 quarter miles to be completed in the same number of quarter hours. However the event was ruined by a gang of so-called "gambling roughs" who interrupted the walk after forcing their way into the theatre. They made their way to trackside and held proceedings up, their aim thought to be laying claim to the 200 dollar reward promised to anyone witnessing Ada missing her start times by three minutes or more. One of the men was reportedly dressed only in undergarments and was claiming the right to perform on the track himself. A scuffle with the police turned into a full-scale brawl, leading to the crowd heading for the exits and everything grinding to a halt. These unedifying scenes – graphically illustrated in a subsequent issue of *The National Police Gazette* – helped the cause of those who wanted women's professional walking banned. Another nail had been hammered into the sport's coffin.

But Ada Anderson was nothing if not determined, and in the run-up to Christmas of 1879, was happy to sign up for a six-day race at the famous venue that had turned her away a year earlier – Gilmore's Garden, now renamed Madison Square Garden. She chalked up a decent tally of 351 miles, but six-day racing had never been her forte and predictably she was beaten by five younger women. It looked like a rather sad ending to the colourful career of a woman with genuine claims to have been the top British pedestrienne of them all.

After her first Brooklyn show, back in January 1879, Ada had hinted at her intention to opt for a quiet life within a year or so, and it seems that is pretty much what happened. In parallel with women's pedestrianism as a whole, she soon faded into obscurity, a development partly helped in January 1880 when the Board of Aldermen in New York City passed a resolution to prevent further endurance efforts taking place. From here onwards there would be just one known comeback effort by Ada – in May 1880 she walked 1,559 quarter miles in consecutive 12-minute periods at Baltimore's Central Theatre. This exhibition was to help launch the new invention of electric light and was staged with the Sunday inactive in order to appease the complainers. At the end Ada took to the stage in typical fashion and made a speech in which she gave thanks to the throng for their support and said she hoped to meet them all again one day. She must have known an era was over.

Interest waned generally over the next decade on both sides of the Atlantic, and by 1890 women doing endurance walking for money was all but finished. Ada Anderson had been a sporting celebrity for just three years, but few women of her ilk made a bigger impact. By the time of her 50th birthday it is thought she had resumed her small-time singing and stage career for a spell. Little is known what subsequently became of her, although records show an English-born woman named Ada L. Paley, wife of William, passed away in Los Angeles a few months before the start of the 1914–18 War, at the age of 72.

FIFTEEN

KNOCKING THEM FOR SIX

Six-day foot racing had emerged as a standard pedestrianism format by the early 1880s – often attracting huge crowds and prestige for the winners – but these 'wobbles', as they became known, were mostly a male pursuit with women walkers rarely getting a look-in.

The six-day race was born from a desire to create a spectacle that was competitive and exciting throughout, yet would last long enough to make good money. The entrants would pile up their mileage during six successive daytimes, recovering with proper sleep each night. To avoid transgressing the sanctity of Sundays the contests tended to start on a Monday and end with a gala night the following Saturday. Depending on the pre-arranged rules, competitors would travel via strict 'heel-and-toe' race walking, or be allowed to run as well as walk in 'go-as-you-please' events.

Major six-day tussles in the USA in the mid-1870s between stylish Edward Payson Weston and Daniel O'Leary had created the initial widespread interest. After this pair put on popular shows in London, Tory MP Sir John Dugdale Astley was inspired to set up a series of six-day races to determine the 'Long-Distance Champion of the World'.

The big names O'Leary and Weston dominated the early part of the series, but Cambridgeshire lad Charles Rowell came good later on to claim the Astley Belt for keeps and make himself a rich man and national hero in the process. One of the first females to try their luck at this type of competition would be a married woman from a remote corner of rural England called Madame Englo.

STORY 20: MADAME ENGLO – FORMIDABLE BUT ERRATIC

A formidable, if sometimes erratic performer who lit up the early 1880s was Madame Englo, a wife and mother in her thirties from Cornwall who had earlier made her living from mantel-making and dressmaking. Englo knew the importance of keeping a crowd entertained and with Madame Anderson having departed for America, worked hard to become the best-known female walker of her day in Britain.

Englo, who stood five feet four inches, was always open to new ideas and tried her luck at a number of different walking formats, including six-day contests. She won a six-day affair at Preston in November 1880, covering 245 miles in fewer than the allotted 72 hours of walking, although the tournament was found afterwards to have been a financial disaster for all concerned. A few weeks later, on a rain-drenched Boxing Day, the prospects of a good payday were considerably brighter in the unlikely setting of the banqueting hall inside London's Alexandra Palace. Englo entered and was regarded as favourite to win this 30-mile contest on the wooden boards of Ally Pally, but did her chances no good by missing her train and arriving late for the start.

Losing 30 minutes of walking time, Englo put in a plucky performance but was beaten by Madame Victor who marched to the finish in 5 hrs 46 mins 27 secs, four miles ahead of Madame Florence and six clear of Englo. Around 20,000 happy punters paid a shilling for the privilege of attending this money-spinning gala, which also included displays by native American tribesmen and women, and a performance of the panto *Puss in Boots*.

Public transport calamities notwithstanding, Englo would prove a tricky opponent and a real star of the sport during the new decade. *Bell's Life* described her as weighing nine stones and in her mid-thirties. In the summer of 1881 she tackled a 300-miles-in-six-days challenge, walking 10 hours per day at the Lord Howick Pleasure Gardens near Charlton Pier, Woolwich. It was a well-attended endeavour which proved a good warm-up for her six-day contest with Kate Brown at Lambeth Baths (covered in detail in the next chapter) which ended in a superb victory. The Baths building, which had recently hosted a 145-hour swim marathon, was where Captain Webb trained for his celebrated Channel swimming exploits. It was sited behind Westminster Bridge Road and well used by the public who could have a swim for sixpence or take a hot bath (with fire) for a shilling.

Madame Englo returned here in February 1882 for an all-female competition involving three-hour walks on six successive nights. She won by totting up 80 miles, two ahead of Mrs McLaren, and six clear of Madame Victor, thus perfect revenge for the Alexandra Palace debacle. The key moment came on the second day, when Victor complained of feeling dizzy and unwell, Englo exploiting this mercilessly, surging past to dominate proceedings from thereon in.

The rivalry was intensifying between the likes of Englo, Victor and Brown and another flashpoint came in early 1882 when Victor publicly demanded to know why Brown was styling herself 'Winner of the Long-Distance Belt'. Victor claimed she had won the only silver belt ever offered for a women's contest three years earlier at Plymouth, and demanded Brown should name the place, date and donor of any belt she possessed. *The Sporting Life*, which regularly published 'challenges' from pedestrians to one another, reported that Madame Flora Lee of Manchester and Madame Florence from North London were also animated over Kate Brown's claims and would be happy to test her right to call herself a long-distance champion.

Throughout this period Madame Englo remained a prominent and colourful character who performed frequently. She looked to be just the woman to shake things up and spark a revival of women's pedestrianism. She was certainly happy to travel wherever necessary to fly the flag for the sport and keep the show on the road. In the autumn of 1883 she found herself around 400 miles from her home territory of Cornwall, which at the time was having to cope with severe flooding caused by abnormally high tides. Englo was instead at the Norfolk port of King's Lynn and well clear of the trouble zones, preparing to take on a daunting 1,500 miles in 1,000 hours. On a very exposed course she was constantly battered by high winds and rain but stuck doggedly to the schedule and success represented a real feather in her cap.

Englo's next major challenges turned out to be the six-day championship in Birmingham in 1884 (covered fully in Chapter 17) followed by a trip to the capital to attempt 1,000 miles in a mere 500 consecutive hours at the popular North Woolwich Gardens venue. These shaped up as potential big earners, and of course huge physical challenges, meaning they dominated her 1884 calendar and would need plenty of preparation and recovery time. Following her disappointing fifth place at Birmingham she would get the best part of four months to recover and then prepare for North Woolwich. Created by entrepreneur William Holland, these pleasure gardens on the northern banks of the Thames (close to the current site of London City Airport) boasted numerous attractions, including the largest dance stage in London, and were a highly popular place of entertainment for the masses, staging swimming races across the river, fancy dress parties and much more.

The unusual nature of Englo's task – covering 1,000 miles twice as quickly as Captain Barclay – ensured substantial public interest. One reporter, who made regular trips to the gardens to monitor her progress, admitted he was favourably impressed by "the genuineness of the manner in which her self-imposed task is being carried out". Also keeping a watchful eye on Englo's progress were well-known pedestrian 'Brummy' Meadows, manager of the grounds Davenport and his team of helpers, and the River Police, who had access to the grounds after dark. This three-week walk kicked off late in the evening of Monday 11th August, and Madame Englo tackled the task of walking two miles within each and every hour with gusto. The track was 110 yards in circumference with sharp corners. The 37-year-old was attired "with great taste" reported *Bell's Life*, having chosen a tight-fitting tunic of plum-coloured velvet, with crimson sash, plus trunks, stockings and high boots. During the first week "she was taken very queer" during the night, according to *The Sporting Life*, but recovered within hours and resumed her earlier pace. Later, when around 800 miles had been completed, she was suffering badly with a head cold but battled on. She was well looked after during these worrying spells by the proprietor's wife Mrs Davenport. The weather didn't help, for it was chilly for August and torrential rain fell during the last few days of the walk. Eventually she completed the job, a remarkable performance considering the problems to overcome. The range of attractions helped boost crowd numbers, particularly in the evenings, with a fireworks display said to have been bigger and better than recent efforts at the Crystal and Alexandra Palaces, an "immense balloon ascent", dancing, a baby show, a soldiers' tug of war, and a Grand Fancy Dress Garden Party.

Madame Englo's family didn't go short at Christmas thanks to one final cash-winning appearance she made in 1884. A five-part contest for female pedestrians was staged on the eastern fringes of London, at the old-established, but recently upgraded Clay Hall Inn grounds in Old Ford Road, Bow. A bumper sum of £100 was on offer for the woman covering the longest distance after four hours walking on each of five evenings. Nine women committed to this walk, which was from Monday to Saturday but featured a rest day on the Thursday (Christmas day). In addition to the cash, the 'neatest' costume was to receive a gold watch. Madame Englo was favourite and started strongest, opening a good lead but had to work hard to maintain it. The weather was bitterly cold but the impressively lit track helped the walkers feel at home and the promoters declared themselves happy with the numbers that turned up to watch in such conditions. Englo won without undue distress, completing just over 87 miles, at least four miles clear of runner-up Miss Read of London, who was highly praised as she was a mere novice at the sport. Miss Evans of London won the vote for neatest costume, but promoter Mr Woods diplomatically assured all the women they would receive a prize for their efforts. Robert Neall's Clay Hall Inn was by now a very popular spot for visitors from different parts of London and Essex, known for its splendid eel pies, cakes, cream, ale and watercress. As well as hosting pedestrianism, the pub grounds housed an interesting feature known as a 'Mill For Grinding Old People Young'. Elderly women visitors were invited to volunteer to be 'ground young again' in the little mill, free of charge, for the amusement of those looking on!

In the summer of 1885 Madame Englo, who had an unhappy knack of attracting bad weather on her walks, attempted a tough challenge against the clock in London and was again battered by bouts of torrential rain. At the Lillie Bridge grounds in West Brompton her solo task was to complete 240 miles over five consecutive days, with 12 hours allotted for walking per day. This required an average of 48 miles each day (four miles per hour), but from the start she fell behind schedule (44 on the first day, 39 on the second) and never really recovered, although battled on in typical style in the rain, finishing with 215 miles to her name. It had been a noble effort but the clock beat her by about half a day.

Englo and the other pedestriennes were by now finding so few opportunities to chase decent prize money in England that in 1886 a number of them decided their prospects would be better served by heading north for a tour of Scotland (see Chapter 16). As we shall see, a good number of events subsequently took place north of the border with the English invaders finding the Scots lasses a very tough nut to crack in their own backyard.

SIXTEEN

MIXED REACTION TO
SIX-DAY RACING

When the novelty of a major six-day walking championship for women was proposed for Birmingham in 1884 there was, inevitably, opposition from some quarters. But it was less hysterical than might have been the case in earlier years, as the venue would be the prominent and respectable Bingley Hall, gambling and Sunday action were both strictly prohibited, there was a magnificent championship belt on offer to the winner and the proceedings were backed by a national daily newspaper who were providing 'qualified' officials.

Most of the active British pedestriennes of the time were unfamiliar with six-day racing and felt more at home with the sedate, albeit highly taxing, 1,000-mile matches. However, their interest in this Bingley Hall extravaganza was boosted by the handsome championship belt on offer. If nothing else, winning this belt would present a potential source of earning power for ever afterwards. And after all, if you could keep walking for 42 days, surely a mere six-day stroll wouldn't pose too many problems?

It had been proved time and again over the previous 60 years that men and women were capable of multi-day treks, but, according to historian Andy Milroy, to make a six-day race a commercial success would require considerable showmanship too. The pedestrian Edward Payson Weston from Connecticut had stepped up to fill that role in the late 1870s. The publicity generated by his exploits inspired many others, the greatest of whom was Irish door-to-door book salesman Daniel O'Leary. Then, in 1876 and 1877, as more British women took to distance walking, Weston and O'Leary came to perform in the UK and boosted public enthusiasm considerably.

America had staged the very first all-female six-day match, a contest in Chicago between Mary Marshall and 18-year-old German-born Bertha Von Hillern in early 1876, won by the former's tally of 234 miles. A rematch took place in New York ten months later and Von Hillern turned the tables with 323.5 miles. Britain's Ada Anderson headed across the Atlantic to join the party in 1878 and the sport became very fashionable for a spell, hitting a peak the following year. Women's cash rewards remained inferior to those available to the men, however, even though major venues and good press coverage was involved.

As it would turn out, women's championship walking in 19th-century Britain never caught on in quite the same way as in the States. The few dozen British women who were proven 'stayers', thanks to all the 1,000-milers, found they rarely got the opportunity to try the six-day format. A rare example had been the match won by 27-year-old Kate Brown of Liverpool in the autumn of 1879 at Sauchiehall Street's Crown Halls in Glasgow. Brown – 5ft 4ins and 10st 2lbs – beat the Scot Janet Day after six successive days walking 'heel and toe' for 12 hours each day. She scooped the stakes of £25 a side, the title of Scottish champion and the Duke of Hamilton's belt and gold medal. The pair had set off at half past noon on Monday 6 October, the ordeal culminating around 10 the following Saturday night. Large crowds attended throughout and it was hailed a success. Both walked impressively on the opening day, covering 44 and 47 miles respectively, but by close of play Tuesday looked exhausted and there was genuine concern the whole thing might end prematurely. The crisis passed however, and before long both were moving well again and at the finish Brown had amassed 185 miles to win by seven miles.

This Glasgow show went well enough, but in the USA that same year a 'go-as-you-please' six-day championship involving numerous women was proposed and the reaction in New York was very mixed. The influential *New York Times* was not in favour:

"The pitiful spectacle of 18 women starting on this six days' walk for money prizes was witnessed by about 1,000 spectators... each wore her number on her breast [and] the prizes for which they are walking are 1,000, 500 and 250 dollars... As soon as the 18 were well under way the fuss began, for the crowd present seemed to regard the affair much in the same farcical light as they would a burlesque entertainment at a theatre. The band played selections from

HMS *Pinafore* and the walkers at once received titles suggested by the music, such as *Buttercup, Hebe, Deadeye*, etc. The dress of most of the walkers is as unsuitable for successful pedestrianism as it can well be made. All the dresses are short, and reach but little below the knee; but instead of being made of flannel and as simple as possible, most of them are heavy garments of velvet and many are covered with embarrassing bows, flounces, and knots of riband. The footwear is various and while some are neatly and sensibly shod with laced boots, others wear low dancing slippers that will quickly fill with sawdust and cause no little trouble to the wearers. The one redeeming feature of this walk is that no smoking is allowed on the floor of the Gilmore Gardens and as the number of spectators is small the atmosphere is comparatively clear. The women are subject to all manner of jesting and insulting remarks from men who hang over the rail surrounding the track and pass comment on each as she passes".

Despite negative coverage of this sort, the show at Gilmore Gardens helped spark what was described as a "mania for pedestrianism" around the USA. One correspondent observed: "Woebegone looking women are [now] tramping around sawdust rings all over Philadelphia clad in fancy costumes, and pitied by a large audience".

So was this just a fad, or would the American surge of interest in women's pedestrianism soon be mirrored in Britain? Some observers were convinced it would, including the *Pall Mall Gazette* who predicted in early 1879 that six-day contests and similar would undoubtedly flourish over here now that the Americans had proved big gate money could be accumulated from women's 'consecutive-period' walking.

The *Gazette*'s prediction proved largely incorrect, despite the efforts of Kate Brown, who enjoyed the six-day format and took up a challenge put up by Madame Englo in late 1881. The pair battled it out at Lambeth Baths Gymnasium in London for £50 a side on a small track of 24 laps to the mile, doing ten-hour stints starting at lunchtime on each of the six days. Brown, slightly taller and stockier than Englo, strode into an early lead on day one (Monday 14th November) but it was short-lived and after roughly three hours of work to keep in touch with her confident-looking opponent, Brown suddenly and dramatically left the track complaining of feeling nauseous. Her attendants fussed over her, and once she felt a little better the contest resumed with Englo more than a mile ahead. Throughout the late afternoon and evening a high number of spectators came and went, many of them women, and the walkers were warmly applauded at the 11pm finish with Englo comfortably leading, 33 miles and 17 laps under her belt.

It was a similar story on the second day of action, Englo increasing the lead enough to treat herself to a slightly late start on the third day, setting off more than 10 minutes after the prompt Brown. By 4pm as Englo passed 77 miles and Brown hit 75, the latter could be seen to be limping heavily although carrying on in plucky fashion. Before long her attendant – the long-distance walker Tom Brown – persuaded her off the track and it was discovered the inner lining of one of her boots had slid down and created a large blister around her heel. After treatment Miss Brown enjoyed a new lease of life and boosted her total impressively. Englo looked strong throughout and soon after passing 100 miles in the final hour of the day noted that she was a good five miles ahead and decided to quit for the night. On reaching 96 miles Brown did likewise.

Day four (Thursday 17th November) saw many spectators pass in and out of the venue's Westminster Road entrance at frequent intervals, but few stayed inside for long, meaning there was never a good crowd in at any one time, leading to a subdued atmosphere. Miss Brown chose a bright pink dress for this day's work but never looked entirely happy and took a long rest around 4pm, allowing Englo to increase her lead to around nine miles. During proceedings a local gentleman presented each walker with a handsome silver locket, but even this gesture couldn't inspire Miss Brown who spent much of the evening moving very slowly and clearly in pain from her right lower leg. By the end of the session Englo had totted up 130 miles over the four days, Brown cutting a sad figure 13 miles or so in arrears.

The penultimate day, the Friday, saw Miss Brown ready to resume and looking in better shape. A much bigger crowd had assembled by the evening as Englo steadily added another 25 miles to her tally, Brown closing the gap a little to end the day around nine miles down. The lead was substantial and final day little more than a formality for Englo, but she didn't relax and put in a ten-hour stint of over 30 miles for the first time since the Wednesday. She finished with a total of 185 miles and 17 laps, more than 20 miles ahead of her younger opponent who ended wearily on 165 miles and five laps. Englo had averaged a shade under 31 miles for each of the six days, her victory never in doubt after the big lead created in the fourth session. An extra attraction as the event drew to its close was the sight of Madame Victor – who had been Englo's assistant over the week – walking against the clock for one hour, and managing to impress the crowd by exceeding five miles in that time. Englo went home with the £100 stake money and Brown received a bouquet of flowers.

It had been a well-organised affair, the venue's manager W. Taylor sparing no expense or effort in caring for the walkers' well-being, plus impressive work put in by referee Bedford, timekeeper Ashbrook and lap-counters Lapham and Attwood. However, the match would not inspire a surge of copycat events in London or elsewhere.

Looking back over the era as a whole, historian Derek Martin pinpoints 1880 as the peak year for British six-day foot racing, with around 40 staged altogether, just over half in Scotland. In her home city of Liverpool Kate Brown staged a return match with Janet Day of Glasgow in the spring of 1880 at the Theatre Royal, while 1881 saw several multi-day races involving Madame Englo. But, says Martin, during 1881 and 1882 numbers dropped off again, with most of the big money enterprises taking place in America.

However, in the spring of 1882 the Sporting Club of Dundee took the plunge, advertising a six-day affair at Cooke's Circus. Even though the advertisements proclaimed it as 'The Great Male and Female Pedestrian Tournament' it seems the venue management didn't initially realise that women were part of the package – and they hastily applied to the local Sheriff's Court to have it stopped. They had never imagined, they said, that such a thing was contemplated as it was contrary to good morals, injurious to their reputation and would attract spectators "of an objectionable kind". Their complaint was either dropped or rejected, for the race went ahead in Dundee anyway.

The women's event took up just 90 minutes a day, compared to nine or ten hours of male walking and saw Madame Englo and Kate Brown going head to head each evening, the men having occupied the track during daytime. The fears about 'objectionable' spectators proved unfounded and there was a good crowd and evidently no trouble. Englo, billed as champion of the world, largely dominated proceedings over the six days, her outfit featuring "a square-cut, blue, sleeved coat, trimmed with gold, blue tights and knickerbockers, low shoes and hair hanging down the back, tied with blue ribbon". Brown, hailed 'Champion of Scotland' also wore plenty of nationalistic blue: "A blue sleeveless tunic, open front ballet, white semet trimmed with scarlet and white gold belt, flesh-coloured tights and blue trunks plus high lace-up boots and wool socks and hair bound with scarlet". Their daily duels proved the highlight of the week for many onlookers, Englo coming out on top to win herself £10 and a gold medal. The event could hardly have gone better, nevertheless six-day racing for women wouldn't reappear in Scotland for another four years or so.

SEVENTEEN

THE WOMEN'S SIX-DAY CHAMPIONSHIP

Birmingham's big 1884 gathering was initially seen as a risky enterprise. It was the brainchild of the Griffiths brothers, Tom and John, who ran the Old Guy Inn with their mother, situated beside the Birmingham Bull Ring market and a short walk from Bingley Hall. Securing use of the famous hall and putting up an expensive championship belt and cash prizes was a very ambitious undertaking by the brothers and when they announced their plans the hypercritical newspaper columnists and letter writers inevitably sprang into action.

Allan Granger, a prominent figure in Midlands' trades union affairs and local government, made no secret of the fact he wanted it banned altogether. Writing to the *Birmingham Daily Post*, he stated: "The hints that some women of recent notoriety would take part suggests the desirability of a peremptory prohibition of the proposed disgraceful exhibition of 'lovely woman' being put a stop to. Have the proprietors of Bingley Hall no sense of the impropriety of such an exhibition?".

The promoters of the event, brothers Tom and John Griffiths, local publicans, were quick to respond. They insisted nothing disgraceful or objectionable would be offered to the public and the competitors would be highly respectable women who would dress appropriately: "Nothing disgraceful to 'lovely women' will be permitted – indeed we must suggest that the evolution of females on bicycles and tricycles is much more open to objection than the entertainment we shall offer".

The brothers were putting a brave face on things, but behind the scenes there was great anxiety as they struggled to attract the best known names to their event. They proposed ten hours of walking on each of the six successive days, with the woman amassing the greatest mileage to take home a championship belt worth 30 guineas and £40 cash from the £100 prize pot. The belt would be retained by the winner for a year and awarded permanently if won twice in succession by the same woman.

Bingley Hall, erected in central Birmingham in 1850, had a roomy interior of well over an acre and was Britain's first purpose-built exhibition centre. It was used for dog, cattle and flower shows, circuses, boxing, political meetings and concerts. It had already staged men's foot racing, but there had never been anything quite like this six-day procession of athletic and colourfully dressed women.

The Sporting Life, which had recently switched to daily publication, backed the event and published a list of nine well-known pedestriennes of the time, reminding them entry to the event was free and urging them to get in touch as soon as possible. The women were requested to contact the promoters via their pub – The Old Guy Liquor Vaults at 57 Digbeth, Birmingham. Of the nine invitees, only two responded to the call to arms and made it to the start line. A third, Madame Angelo, regarded her own walking days as over and sent along her daughter to compete instead. Eventually a further dozen or so women were found and the relieved Griffiths brothers began preparing for the scheduled start on Monday 17 March 1884.

With just hours to go, the 15-strong start list was made public. They would perform from midday until 10pm on the six successive days. It was billed clearly as a walking competition with no mention of a 'go-as-you-please' option that would allow running. Some of the women involved were well known in pedestrian circles, others less so. Most of the married ones billed themselves as 'Madame' instead of plain 'Mrs', while some of the younger ones opted for 'Madameoiselle' instead of 'Miss'. As historian Andy Milroy points out: "There were just four Misses, and the others were Mademoiselles or Madames. The concept that an impression of being an exotic foreigner was good box office had clearly been largely embraced by British female walkers".

The experienced 36-year-old Madame Englo caught most people's eye as the likely favourite. She had been walking successfully at various distances over at least eight years and had emerged as the top British performer over this period, with one of her biggest rivals being Kate Brown, 32, who was also in the Birmingham line-up and expected to do well. Nevertheless, the rarity of six-day racing in the UK meant there was no formbook to go by, and the destination of the new championship belt was surely a wide-open affair.

Admission to the opening day was set at a shilling and, for subsequent days, sixpence after 5pm. To beef up public interest, two bands were booked, comprising 25 musicians in all, plus 'Professor Tattersall' who was billed the 'Strongest Man in the World' and would perform twice each day. The prize list promised £40 for the winner (equivalent to roughly £3,500 in today's terms) plus the championship belt valued at 30 guineas, £20 for the runner-up, £10 for third place and £5 to any others reaching 220 miles over the six days.

As the main backers, *The Sporting Life* was understandably anxious to paint a positive picture of the contest, assuring the sporting world it was a properly organised affair that would be conducted with integrity and good taste. The paper, celebrating 25 years since its founding, announced:

"Of the many contests restricted to females, this one excels in importance and management against anything of the kind previously organised. On no occasion in connection with long-distance events has [Bingley Hall] presented such a tasteful appearance, the flags of all nations being suspended from the ceiling in profusion and the hitherto dull appearance of the whole surroundings is relieved by drapery anything but sombre in appearance. As regards the attire of the ladies, all are dressed with scrupulous neatness".

THE STARTERS:

- Madame Englo from Cornwall ('The Long-distance Champion')
- Miss Kate Brown from Liverpool ('Six-day Champion of Scotland')
- Miss Lucy Richards from Birmingham ('Champion of the Midlands')
- Madame French from USA ('Winner of Bristol six-day tournament')
- Miss Rosina Terry from Wales ('The 8-hours Champion')
- Madameoiselle Letitia Brown from London ('a 1,000-miler')
- Madameoiselle Evans from London ('a 1,000-miler')
- Madame Edwards from Leicester ('a 1,000-miler')
- Madame Violetta from Bristol (the daughter of Madame Angelo)
- Madame Lucelle from Dudley
- Madame Vampiere from Birmingham
- Miss Millar from Leeds
- Madame Norrie from Leeds
- Madame Heeley from Barnsley
- Madame Rollason from Dudley

The Sporting Life announced that the referee and timekeeper would be well-known sports journalist Robert Watson. Such an appointment was not unusual for the time, for Watson had made a name for himself during a period when a reporter would often be called upon to act as referee and stake-money holder in prize contests.

The women's task was relatively simple. They must walk 'heel and toe', lapping the 160-yard track as often as possible for six consecutive days between midday and 10pm. They could stop and start as they wished. The splendid championship belt would go to the woman with the highest mileage completed.

DAY 1, MONDAY 17 MARCH 1884:

The very grand Bingley Hall looked splendid for the occasion, with plenty of fluttering flags and two bands playing on a raised podium in the centre of the rectangular track. The 15 entrants nervously arranged themselves in front of the scoreboard at midday. "They were clad in fancy costumes of the knickerbocker order, or with short skies to the knee", according to one report.

Outside, this imposing landmark building – the first purpose-built exhibition hall of its type in Britain – was basking in unusually warm weather for the time of year, while inside the cavernous arena there was noise aplenty and a good atmosphere being generated. Senior official Watson was backed by Tom West, a well-known one-legged cyclist, who would count the laps and display them on the scoreboard. Watson signalled to everyone and set the women on their way amid raucous cheers.

Madame Heeley at once bustled her way into an early lead, staying there for the first half hour although never opening a significant gap. As one of the lesser-known entrants it seemed this bold Yorkshirewoman was determined to have her moment of glory and let everyone know she was there. Her spell in the spotlight ended when Madame French overtook and completed five miles and two laps as the clock hit 60 minutes. French was by then a lap ahead of Madame Englo, with the next five around 300 yards down, including the well-supported local favourite Miss Lucy Richards. For the best part of the next two hours positions remained unchanged but in mid-afternoon Englo seized the lead from French for a spell and then retired to rest, French quickly following her example. Meanwhile, Richards was rapidly improving and shortly before 4pm went in front to huge cheers, followed eagerly by Madame Vampiere, whose real name was the rather more prosaic 'Mrs Graham'.

Richards was walking efficiently and smoothly and hit 20 miles just before 4.20 with Englo and French working hard behind her again and the former occasionally sped up to keep the lead within reach. Richards left the track for a ten-minute break but to the dismay of the others resumed looking even stronger and soon ground out a commanding lead. Somewhat surprised at all this, Englo endeavoured to lessen her advantage but the youthful Richards stubbornly contested the issue and the pair tussled together for several circuits in splendid style, the younger aspirant receiving loud and prolonged encouragement as she increased her overall advantage. Not highly fancied at the start, Richards was now looking a genuine contender, despite her tender years. There were plenty of miles to go, but this local girl, from the well-known and somewhat notorious Richards pedestrian family, was suddenly being taken very seriously.

During the afternoon the hall was well filled, many of the noisy new arrivals wearing an Irish shamrock and evidently treating their visit as part of their celebrations to mark Saint Patrick's Day. The Irish visitors certainly enjoyed themselves and the two bands taking it in turns to play in the centre of the hall provided further light relief during spells when little of interest was happening on the track.

Miss Richards hit 25 miles at 5.45pm and around this time the walkers all seemed to perk up as they noticed more spectators filing in. Englo responded in particularly spirited fashion by reducing the lead to around a mile and a half. The smaller figure of Richards continued to work relentlessly however, and had no problem battling it out with Englo at close quarters, almost shoulder to shoulder, content in the knowledge she was 15 laps ahead of her rival overall. For a large part of the evening Richards and Englo were walking at the same pace of 11 mins 45 secs per mile but their side-by-side battle came to an end when Englo took a break after reaching 32 miles. This sparked Richards to greater exertion and her lead was duly increased, accompanied by well-deserved hearty cheers for the local girl. Vampiere was in second place with two hours left on the clock and stayed there without a problem until the call of 'time!' at 10pm.

STANDINGS AFTER DAY ONE:

Richards 42 miles and 8 laps; Vampiere 40, 0; Englo 38, 6; Millar 38,6; Keeley 37, 5; Norrie 36, 8; French 36, 5; Evans 35, 2; Rollason 35, 2; L.Brown 33, 5; Lucelle 32, 4; Violetta 31, 2; Edwards 29, 6; K Brown 23, 8; Terry 20, 9.

DAY 2, TUESDAY 18 MARCH:

The attendance was pitifully small at noon when things resumed, the venue only beginning to fill much later in the day. The competitors had a worn and jaded look as they faced the starter, with Evans and Terry absent at this point despite having looked fine when finishing the previous evening. Things would need to liven up if the event was to be kept alive till the weekend.

The missing starters joined the action before too long however, by which time Englo and Vampiere had raced away briskly to the strains of the band. One reporter commented on how little was happening on the track to disturb the quietude of the surroundings in the opening few hours. It was, he wrote, a period "only enlivened by the chirping of the numerous sparrows who flitted about the interior of the building". By 1pm Miss Richards, champion of the Midlands, had forged a good lead with 46 miles, ahead of Vampiere three miles down, Englo third on 41.

Englo was absent for around half an hour but returned to complete a few steady laps and then sped up, keeping good time with the music. French had left the track early on, maybe paying the price for her splendid efforts on day one. Richards hadn't taken long to get into her stride, while Vampiere, who reportedly had prepared specifically for this event, was employing a 'no spurt' policy, and maintained a systematic progression looking strong. Madame Angelo's daughter Violetta, who was better known professionally for performing feats of strength rather than speed (described as 'a lifter of heavy weights and thrower of heavy men using her teeth'), seemed to be struggling but was in no mood to give up.

On hitting the 50-mile mark, Vampiere – 1 mile and 7 laps behind Richards – retired for 17 minutes allowing Norrie to move up to fourth looking very stylish. The chief feature of the afternoon's action was the great form of the consistent Richards and Vampiere. By 6pm, with the factories emptying and the half-price admission now valid, the hall slowly filled up and this led to a visible improvement in performances, the walkers' spirits lifted by the encouraging shouts and by the music from the bands. There was by now "some surprising vitality" on show, according to *The Sporting Life*. As evening advanced the crowd increased and by 9pm the place was packed to the rafters. Every performer was cheered on and it showed in their progress.

Richards and Vampiere looked every inch worthy leaders, the former covering each mile consistently at a few seconds inside 12 minutes. As the clock ticked toward the 10pm finish, Vampiere showed signs of having had enough for the day although the call of 'time!' came as a relief to all of them. Richards and Evans got the biggest cheers for their stylish walking while Vampiere was admired for her stubborn resistance, pleasing the crowd with an uncharacteristic late spurt. Similar ovations were afforded Englo, Norrie and Violetta as they finished with a flourish. The atmosphere at this point could hardly have been more different from 10 hours earlier.

STANDINGS AFTER DAY TWO:

Richards 80 miles and half a lap; Vampiere 76, 2; Norrie 67, 6; Millar 62, 5; L Brown 60, 3; Evans 59, 4; Englo 59, 2; Rollason 56, 1; Heeley 54, 7; French 54, 1; Violetta 52, 4; K Brown 50, 1; Edwards 48, 0; Lucelle 42, 5; Terry 33, 5.

DAY 3, WEDNESDAY 19 MARCH:

The promoters and others behind the scenes had a spring in their step this morning. The scoreboard showed the event had defied the so-called experts who had stated publicly that if 15 women tried to walk for six days, ten hours a day, barely half of them would survive to start the third day. How wrong they were: Wednesday had arrived and not a single walker had quit.

The Sporting Life pointed out how unexpected this state of affairs was, for even in men's multi-day events, the number of contestants was usually well reduced after the end of the second day. Not only were all 15 women still going strong, there had been no real injury scares or signs of distress on the well-worn track so far. It all suggested the female of the species might have a little more stamina and spirit on tap than generally given credit for, as well as a hitherto unacknowledged ability to judge pace and their own capabilities in an organised and non-capricious manner.

After they were sent on their way this morning Englo forged ahead and appeared to have thoroughly recovered her accustomed gait and easy style of walking, while Heeley, Kate Brown and French had shaken off their previous day's lethargy and moved as well as on day one. As regards leaders Richards and Vampiere, both progressed with fixed determination, the applause being cheerfully acknowledged by Vampiere, but not by the inscrutable Richards who continued to preserve a stolid indifference to the entire surroundings. During the first hour the building was as quiet as a church but proceedings became lively when the bands struck up, rousing renewed exertion with Vampiere gaining upon Richards and Englo rapidly improving her position too.

During the afternoon a large and select audience assembled in the hall comprising many of the elite of Birmingham society and several notable faces from theatre and music hall. As Richards neared completion of her 100th mile the excitement built to a crescendo and at 5.30pm loud and prolonged cheering proclaimed the accomplishment of the landmark distance. Vampiere was now four miles behind and Englo, by dint of steely perseverance, gained rapidly just outside the top four. Shortly after 9pm Vampiere for the first time exhibited symptoms of exhaustion and slight lameness, but after traversing a mile slowly, soon regained her old form. Meanwhile Richards continued with little change in speed until the customary acceleration by all over the final couple of minutes.

STANDINGS AFTER DAY THREE:

Richards 115 miles, 8 laps; Vampiere 109, 8; Norrie 92, 10; Millar 92, 5; Englo 86, 9; L Brown 82, 5; Evans 81, 8; French 77, 10; K Brown 76, 10; Rollason 74, 10; Violetta 73, 10; Edwards 65, 9; Heeley 65; Lucelle 60, 6; Terry 44, 5.

DAY 4, THURSDAY 20 MARCH:

All but L.Brown and Evans were on the start line promptly to set off at midday, the missing pair soon joining in and looking particularly smartly attired today. Before 30 minutes had elapsed Millar passed Norrie to go into third, while second-placed Vampiere appeared to be making good ground on Richards. It was impressive at this point that none of the 15 combatants were showing ill effects of three full days of action.

"Vampiere, especially, cheerfully set about her day's work with wonderful alacrity", reported *The Sporting Life*. She was clearly moving faster than Richards and covered 4.75 miles in the first hour, a quarter mile more than the leader. Vampiere even produced an unexpected surge at one point, a reaction to Richards attempting to shrug her off when they found themselves walking in tandem. This tussle may have taken its toll, for Vampiere soon took a brief retirement and when she restarted looked in less impressive shape, while Richards continued to walk at a metronomically consistent pace. It seemed that Englo, who at the outset had been favourite, had by now given up on any realistic chance of winning for she constantly absented herself from the track; she progressed well when visible, but seemed to be needing more rest periods than the others.

The main feature of the afternoon was the superb form of Richards, whose walking looked entirely free of undue exertion and who looked like she could gain a lap on Vampiere whenever she desired. The rest struggled on with gritted teeth, especially Norrie who had since day one coped with various minor difficulties with great courage.

Richards by now looked certain to win, barring unforeseen disasters, having carved a big lead of 11 miles by 6pm. Englo at this point reappeared and did some fine walking to infuse additional interest into proceedings, but looked unlikely to reel in Vampiere who was well clear in second spot. There was a fair-sized crowd during the afternoon and this increased from 5pm onwards to about 8,000. Day four ended amid a fine atmosphere with huge roars of approval as time was called.

STANDINGS AFTER DAY FOUR:
Richards 151 miles, 5 laps; Vampiere 141, 7; Millar 121, 0; Norrie 119, 4; Englo 109, 6; Evans 104, 3; L Brown 104, 2; French 96, 9; K Brown 96, 6; Violetta 95, 9; Rollason 92, 5; Heeley 91, 3; Edwards 86, 5; Lucelle 77, 6; Terry 67, 0.

DAY 5, FRIDAY 21 MARCH:
Richards impressed everyone by maintaining her great form throughout the day, victory beginning to look a formality. Englo was also in determined mood, keen to grab third spot at least, but Vampiere – although accepting she probably wouldn't catch Richards – was pacing herself nicely, while keeping a wary eye on Englo. There was a good crowd throughout the afternoon, much higher numbers than on the previous three days, and they watched intently as Richards reduced her workload, aware of her long lead and the fact Vampiere was starting to have trouble with her feet. Observing all this, Millar seemed keen to try for second place as it was clear Norrie, her superior when fit, was struggling. Vampiere's discomfort got worse as the evening went on and her nearest opponents gained encouragement.

"Good-humoured chaff" enlivened the proceedings as time went on, according to one report, and the competitors – weary though they were – gathered themselves for the latter hours knowing that spurts to entertain the gallery would be required of them now that the much bigger audiences were arriving. Those not in contention for a leading position seemed in good spirits and the entire group impressed onlookers by pushing on courageously, rewarding the support by increasing their pace at various points. Englo and French were responsible for most of these little cameos today, although a number of the others also enjoyed occasionally playing to the gallery when the opportunity arose.

STANDINGS AFTER DAY FIVE:

Richards 181 miles, 6 laps; Vampiere 165, 3; Millar 154, 1; Norrie 141, 6; Englo 136, 4; L Brown 128, 5; Evans 126, 3; K Brown 118, 7; French 118, 6; Violetta 117, 4; Heeley 112, 5; Rollason 112, 1; Edwards 102, 8; Lucelle 100, 7; Terry 92, 1.

DAY 6, SATURDAY 22 MARCH:

Miss Richards knew victory was well within her grasp at the start of the final day. All she had to do was amass a moderate total of at least 10 miles or so and she would surely remain out of reach of Vampiere and the rest. Despite not being widely fancied at the start, her performance over the week had been magnificent – fluent and consistent – and she only had to keep her head, and her feet, and the championship belt would be hers.

Arrangements were made for up to 15,000 spectators on the final day, and the event was being hailed a great success even before Saturday evening's scenes when an estimated 10,000 had packed in for the closing stages. The looming finish and the big crowds inspired the performers, who put in lots of surges and made the racing very entertaining, despite having trouble with the heat and dust kicked up by all the extra activity inside the hall.

At just before 6pm Richards completed her 200th mile looking as fluid as ever. As the evening went on 12 of the 15 walkers continued to the bitter end. Most ended up very foot-sore and some by now looked to be having considerable trouble staying on their feet. Vampiere in particular was seen to be in tears, hobbling around in a very distressed state. She had to lean on the arm of one of her helpers for considerable stretches, but never completely crumbled and claimed second place in valiant fashion, earning respect and admiration from all quarters. She had been well aware Millar and Englo were in better shape physically and making every effort to overhaul her, but stuck to her task.

Richards was relentless and increased her advantage, her stylish walking matched by her neat attire. The two Browns, Norrie and Englo also looked in good shape in the closing stages. A number of bouquets of flowers were thrown on to the track to reward the leaders and all women were cheered loudly at the finish. After a few minutes' rest and time to compose themselves, they were all ridden on a lap of honour through the town in a brake, headed by the band members and followed by a large procession of locals. It signalled the end of a triumphant occasion.

FINAL RESULT:
1. Miss Richards (£40 & Championship Belt) 208 miles, 9 laps.
2. Mme Vampiere (£20) 186 miles.
3. Miss Millar (£10) 174 miles.
4. Mme Norrie 173, 2 laps.
5. Mme Englo 160, 3.
6. Mlle L. Brown 153, 6.
7. Mlle Evans 149, 5.
8. Miss K. Brown 139, 10.
9. Mme French 138, 10.
10. Mme Violetta 137, 8.
11. Mme Heeley 131.
12. Mme Rollason 130.
13. Mme Edwards 123, 7.
14. Mme Lucelle 118, 2.
15. Miss Terry 116, 6.

Naturally, given their involvement, *The Sporting Life* afforded the event plenty of publicity, but, unusually for women's pedestrianism, there was strong coverage elsewhere too. A fine and detailed illustration of the walkers in action was given prominence on the front page of the *Illustrated Police News*, for example. The *IPN* was one of Britain's first tabloids, launched in 1864 and famous for its sensational and melodramatic reports and no-holds-barred illustrations of murders and hangings. For the price of one penny, readers could find out about all manner of horrendous activity that had taken place in the preceding week across the British Isles.

The paper evidently loved the idea of a group of 15 women fighting it out in Bingley Hall for six consecutive days. They described how the competitors wore tights and short skirts, some of them carrying sticks, and pointed out: "But for their dress, onlookers would have thought judging by their style of walking that they belonged to the sterner sex. Some of [these] pedestrians, too, contrasted rather strikingly in point of age and physique with their massive opponents".

Some of the walkers might have had mixed feelings about making front-page news in this particular publication, for *IPN* had blithely dropped them into a boiling cauldron of scandal. Their story was placed alongside detailed descriptions of the bloodied body of a woman murdered by her son at Brixton, a young woman found by a policeman after being strangled, a 13-year-old boy thrown into a canal, a farmer who accidentally shot himself dead in Leicestershire and the tale of a "mad Skye terrier" being attacked by a man with a broom after it had bitten people. This was the fare being served up for the newly literate working classes who were apparently hungry for such entertainment.

There was more strident commentary from *The People*, which reproduced a report they lifted from *Truth* magazine – a crusading periodical founded by diplomat and Liberal politician Henry Labouchere, aiming to expose all kinds of fraud and other controversies. According to this article:

"One of the most ridiculous and disgusting exhibitions to which the epithet of 'sporting' has ever been applied has just concluded at Bingley Hall, Birmingham. What attraction a Female Six Days' Walking competition can possibly have for the public is a matter of mystery; still, about 10,000 people assembled to witness the finish of the race. It is to be hoped that the poorness of the performance will tend to discourage further efforts in the same direction".

Not all the feedback and fall-out was caustic. Some years later the race's referee and timekeeper Robert Watson would publish a book of his memoirs (*A Journalist's Experience of Mixed Society* – Smith Ainslie, 1899) in which he reflected on "the immense success" of the Birmingham six-dayer. He even described it as the only female pedestrian race worthy of the name: "Day and night Bingley Hall was literally packed, people acquainted with the building on political occasions will realise what is meant by the word crowded. Curious to state, I never remember as a referee having less trouble, though a more legitimate race was never presented for public approval".

Interestingly, Watson goes on to suggest that a major reason for the success of the contest was something that had very little to do with the sporting action on the track. Watson reckoned the biggest attraction of all for the paying public had been the "two handsome girls" who had been invited to work as barmaids inside the hall during the week of walking. These were no ordinary working girls, but two local sisters who had recently gained much attention and popularity following a siege at their small rented house not far from Bingley Hall.

Wrote Watson: "These two ladies in the eyes of the public were not only heroines, but known far and near as paragons of virtue. Their names and praises were sung in all circles of society and when the Bingley Hall Racing Syndicate secured their presence [at the race] unparalleled and complete success was assured. A large bar was erected in the centre of the building and thither flocked the elite of the Midland Metropolis as well as the elite of the mire, all anxious to pay homage to the English Joan of Arcs, minus the burning at the stake".

These celebrity barmaids were in fact the Ormond sisters, Fanny and Florence, who had been defying an eviction order from their home in Beaufort Street, Edgbaston, which was rented from a clergyman. The Misses Ormond had gone into lockdown when police and bailiffs attempted to gain entry to their premises and a siege lasted several days immediately prior to the six-day walk starting at Bingley Hall. As word spread around Birmingham of the excitement, big crowds would gather outside the house to watch the fun, with the two young women providing great entertainment as they appeared at the windows and had lively exchanges with the police and bailiffs outside. Food would be sent in by sympathetic members of the public who had taken the unmarried pair to their hearts. It seems the sisters happily agreed to appear at Bingley Hall as by now they were evidently enjoying their new-found status as working-class heroines. Local and national paper coverage had helped spread their fame far and wide and the idea of inviting the pair to Bingley Hall proved to be a stroke of marketing genius.

On the surface, at least, the championship race had been a success and it was anticipated a repeat would follow in subsequent years. Sadly, however, instead of sparking an outbreak of copycat events, it would go the way of so many other pedestrian events, its aftermath littered with outbreaks of discontent, recrimination, claim and counter-claim.

Despite the good-sized crowds, it appears the Griffiths brothers didn't make as much money as they'd hoped over the six days. Miss Richards, whose family were no strangers to court actions in the past, found herself seeking compensation for being short-changed over prize money and without an opportunity to defend her title. The ill-feeling dragged on for several years and it was not until May 1890 that Miss Richards, and her father John Henry Richards of Moseley Street – listed as professional athletes – were able to bring a court action against John Griffiths, then of the Star Tavern in Summer Lane, and Thomas Griffiths of the Old Guy Inn.

Miss Richards sought to recover the balance of the prize money she claimed she was owed from the 1884 six-day event, and also demanded delivery of the championship belt itself or payment equivalent to its value. The Richards' legal representative, Mr. Dorsett, told the presiding judge the Griffiths brothers had refused to pay more than £16.10s in prize money back in 1884, well short of the advertised sum of £40 she was entitled to and, in addition, they never provided her the opportunity to claim the belt as her own for they didn't stage any repeat events as expected. Judge Chalmers ruled that Miss Richards was not entitled to claim the belt, but did recognise she was treated badly by the brothers and ordered them to pay her the missing £23.10s.

EIGHTEEN

A SCOTTISH RENAISSANCE

Despite stated intentions to the contrary, the battle in Birmingham for the championship belt would never be repeated, but two years later a brief renaissance of women's six-day racing did take place in Scotland. It came in 1886 at a point when men had largely abandoned multi-day events, the resurgence almost entirely driven by the women.

There would be no fewer than seven female-only tournaments that year, four in Aberdeen, two in Dundee and one in Glasgow, featuring 60 starters in all. Around half a dozen leading professionals came up from England to join the action. In February 1886 Aberdeen offered a bumper £60 in prize money, with a 16-hour walking contest over six days, involving two or three hours of action per night at the Bon Accord Recreation Hall. The organisers recruited "five London ladies" who arrived looking the worse for wear after suffering sea sickness on the 36-hour journey by boat up the North Sea coast. Around 5,000 people, including many women, packed around the Recreation Hall's 195-yard wooden track defying earlier suggestions that such a spectacle would "shock the propriety of an Aberdeen audience". The partisan home crowd enjoyed the sight of local women Lizzie Reith and 'Miss Lorimer' (married name Margaret McPhee) keeping the four experienced southerners at bay. Leith pipped Lorimer by a matter of inches in a rip-roaring finish that thrilled the noisy onlookers.

News travelled fast of the success of this contest and three weeks later Dundee – which was soon to be created Scotland's first official city – hosted an event on very similar lines. They used the tiny 42-yards-per-lap Newsome's Circus track and Miss Lorimer picked up the £20 first prize ahead of Madame Lucelle of Wimbledon. Another five women's races followed in quick succession: a week later the group of women from south of the border moved to Glasgow's Albion Hall for a six-day, 16-hour event, where they shared £50 in prizes as no local opposition was found for them. Returning to Aberdeen for a 14-hour event in May, the tourists were again up against locals Miss Lorimer and Miss Reith. Kate Brown and Madame Englo also took part, but it was Aberdeen walkers who enjoyed an extraordinary triumph, scooping all the £60 prize money between them, led by Miss Jeffrey (83 miles).

The pattern was similar in the three other races of 1886, the impressive Aberdonian lassie Miss Jeffrey winning them all, beating Englo at Dundee in June and a month later repeating the trick in an outdoor event at Aberdeen that lasted 14 hours spread over the six days. The last race of the year started in Aberdeen at the end of December, and saw three southerners – Lucelle, Leslie and the seasoned Englo – make a final bid for some Scottish pound notes. However the £15 prize was trousered by Miss Jeffrey, in red hot form, amassing 100 miles in a 16-hour event played out over eight days.

These indoor events were not for the squeamish, as historian Derek Martin points out: "In the big venues, such as the Agricultural Hall in London or Madison Square Garden in New York, there were laps of 250 to 290 yards – six or seven to the mile – and a bark or sawdust track, but at the provincial venues the best you could hope for was a reasonably spacious hall. Concert halls, recreation halls, meeting halls, drill halls or even town halls were used or maybe a gymnasium or a warehouse. You might have a wooden track and sharp corners. But a circus ring could be worse. Cooke's and Newsome's circuses in Dundee, Aberdeen and Glasgow were used for at least a dozen of the Scottish races and were probably semi-permanent wooden structures".

Martin points out that tracks were sometimes painfully short – often only around 40 yards, meaning around 45 laps would be needed to complete a single mile – and also narrow, which could lead to friction between exhausted performers. At the Drill Hall in Perth, for example, on a tiny 41-yard track, tempers became frayed and at least three male performers came to blows and were disqualified. Martin believes Scotland's final multi-day indoor race for male professionals was the 21-hour contest over seven days in Aberdeen in 1886 with a field of 26 chasing a £20 first prize. For the women the Aberdeen race over the New Year 1887 period was the last to offer worthwhile prize money.

One of the top performers at the series of Scottish races had been the Aberdonian Mrs Margaret McPhee, who walked under the name 'Miss Lorimer'. Like many other pedestriennes before her, Margaret was married with young children, and in her case involvement in the sport reportedly caused much strife at home. In early 1886 her husband would be arrested for allegedly attacking her after they argued about how her walking took precedence over her domestic responsibilities. The *Aberdeen Weekly Journal* called this episode a warning to any women thinking of giving pedestrianism a try.

The McPhees appeared in court at Aberdeen in March 1886, the magistrates told that William McPhee was a scavenger (street cleaner) who had attacked his wife Margaret at their Seamount Place home. She was described as a former fishwife who had found fame as a female pedestrian, but her husband had become angry as it meant she now neglected domestic duties. She was in bed exhausted when the row began, shortly after she returned from a notable victory in a 16-hour walking tournament in Dundee. William had met her at the station and shortly after they arrived home neighbours raised the alarm on hearing loud screaming from the couple's children. The court was told Margaret had gone straight to bed, when her husband began to forcibly make his point. When she dismissed his views and said she was too tired to do housework or even argue with him, he knelt on her chest and grabbed her by the throat saying he would ensure she never became tired again and threatened to kill her there and then. The children began to scream and the police were called and took him away.

William pleaded not guilty and told the magistrates he had been annoyed his wife was away so often due to her walks. He not only had to work long hours himself, but her walking meant he also had to care for the children, do the cooking and the housework. He said things had not improved even though his wife was bringing in extra money since becoming smitten by her sport. Resentment had built up between them and that night it boiled over into harsh words and violence. He was found guilty of assault and fined 10s 6d with the alternative of five days in prison.

Coincidentally this was not the only occasion in early 1886 that violence broke out involving a well-known Aberdeen pedestrian. At a slaughterhouse in West Hutcheon Street, a drunken row ended with well-known walker Joe Leith, 29, being fatally stabbed in the heart with a butcher's knife.

Those women who had competed diligently over the Christmas and New Year period of 1886–7 set an impressive example that was evidently not followed by fellow Scot Edward Duffy, an Army reservist from Stirling. Duffy had announced his intention to spend January walking from Stirling to Dover, then to France by ferry and returning home, all within 40 days. He spent an evening wandering around Stirling's pubs with a subscription sheet in an attempt to collect enough money to finance his adventure. Sadly the cash he accumulated proved too tempting and he spent most of it on drink, ending up in a police cell after becoming blind drunk and causing a breach of the peace! He appeared before magistrates claiming the disturbance had not been due to his behaviour, but out of people's curiosity over his proposed walk. He said he was out of work and needed the 40-day walk to earn a living, but the bench was not impressed and ordered him to pay a ten shillings fine or serve 14 days in prison. A crestfallen Duffy had no funds so settled for the latter, and said his big walk would have to be cancelled.

Other bizarre long-distance walks met with varying degrees of success over the same period. Bricklayer John Welsh, in his late forties, planned a fundraising walk from Newcastle to London and back, carrying four bricks on a small plank of wood balanced on his head. He said he had been driven to this by poverty and hunger. Welsh was no doubt inspired in part by the 'wheelbarrow craze' that briefly hit Scotland and parts of Northern England during the winter of 1886–7, having apparently originated in the USA. Dundee's James Gordon and John Cochrane, David Drummond from Stirling and Francis Clifford of Coatbridge, were four examples of destitute Scotsmen who had recently set off separately for London pushing wheelbarrows, in a desperate bid to earn money. A few days later a Mrs Adams attempted the same thing, also aiming for the English capital, a mere 450 miles from her home in Crieff. She was followed by mother-of-four Mrs McGowan from Perth, whose husband was out of work, who decided to push a pram to London containing her eight-month-old baby. These were clearly desperate people, but the press was largely unsympathetic: "It is high time this sort of thing was ended", said the *Dundee Courier*. The *Kirkintiloch Express* also tut-tutted at all the "excesses and absurditites of professional pedestrianism".

Other Victorian six-day endurance events, such as swimming and cycle racing, were also emerging around now and the success of the biking version in particular helped ensure the heyday of six-day foot races (or 'wobbles') would ultimately prove quite short-lived.

"The long-distance professionals put on a few challenge matches, but public interest was not enough to sustain another bout of professional pedestrianism", says Derek Martin. "By the end of the 1880s the six-day era in Britain and America was played out. After a dozen years when it had been a popular and lucrative sport it had reached the end of the track. The non-specialist audience were thought to be losing interest in the gigantism of these events. Other sports had experimented with the six-day format, swimming, cycling and even roller skating, but could not stand against the [new] Saturday afternoon sports of football and rugby. For the competitors, amateur athletics was still available as a sport and in Scotland in particular professional pedestrianism lived on for the sprinters, but this was not an option for the women".

NINETEEN

THE LAST OF THE PEDESTRIENNES

The absence of the better-known English walkers during their Scottish sojourn of 1886 left the field wide open for any newly emerging pedestriennes to make a name for themselves south of the border. The only woman to step up and fill the breach was an unmarried farmer's daughter from the Merseyside region. She proved to be quite a talent and was able to eke out a living for herself as a walker for at least four years. As things turned out she would be able to lay claim to being 'the last of the pedestriennes'.

STORY 21: MADAME DOUGLAS ELVEN – THE LONE RANGER

Madame Douglas Elven was single, highly resourceful and something of a free spirit. She loved to go on solo tours of regions of Britain to perform her walks, apparently undaunted by the potential hazards of being a woman alone in a strange place. Her events went off with a minimum of fuss, staged on public roads and without helpers. She made a real success of being a loner and continued her walks into the early 1890s, putting her among the very last of a dying breed.

This admirable woman's start in the sport came on Monday April 19th 1886 on what had become known across Britain as 'Primrose Day'. Large numbers of the population wore a primrose on their clothing, to mark the anniversary of the death of former Prime Minister Benjamin Disraeli on this day in 1881.

Elven immediately came across as an articulate, intelligent woman who would chat happily about her walking, although she told at least one reporter her policy was not to disclose personal information. Before long, however, she let slip she was unmarried, a farmer's daughter from the north of England and was in her late thirties.

Over the next three years or so the popular Elven would become a well-travelled and consistent performer, opting mostly for solo feats against the clock of 50 miles in 12 hours. Many of her walks took place in small-to-medium-sized market towns, some of them rural and remote where the locals lapped up free entertainment and turned up in very good numbers. Elven's early efforts were mainly confined to locations south of the Thames – Kent, Surrey and Sussex – which she no doubt judged to be best for potential rich pickings, being near the capital and in a region where well-off 'toffs' might live. She made a number of ambitious tilts at covering 1,000 miles in 500 hours, including an outing on a tiny track at St James' Hall in Brighton and a dizzying 25-laps-to-the-mile circuit at the Kite's Nest ground in St Helens Road, Hastings. She went for 1,000 in 1,000 hours at the Sportsman Inn Grounds, Dover, in the autumn of 1886.

Towards the end of that first year she walked three miles an hour for six successive 24-hour periods at Faversham in Kent, and took on a similar task around Christmas 1886 at Sittingbourne. Here she bravely overcame difficult weather, including rain, snow and a slippery frost-bitten track. Good crowds attended these solo outings despite the conditions and Madame Elven was encouraged to press on with her new-found career. Before long she shifted her focus to the north of London and East Anglian locations in particular. There was, it turned out, good earning potential in these more rural settings. She is recorded as performing in Essex towns such as Chelmsford, Romford, Braintree and Colchester, in Suffolk at Bury St Edmunds, Newmarket and Stowmarket, with excursions further afield into Diss, Norwich, Ely, Wisbech and Cambridge among others.

News of Madame Elven's exploits would reach the editorial department of the *New York Herald*, who wrote in glowing terms about her: "A female pedestrian with a vengeance. She thinks nothing of a 50-mile walk and may almost be said to emulate the nimble Puck, such reliance does she place in Shanks's pony... she can cover 50 miles in less than 12 hours, but thinks that until Lord Lytton's new race is born, and people are endowed with the almighty 'vril' her present performance is sufficiently exacting... Madame Elven makes a very decent living out of her walking, but it is a curious method nevertheless". [*Note: the term 'vril' used by the Herald was a reference to the proto-*

science-fiction novel The Coming Race *by Lord Edward Bulwer-Lytton, who created a subterranean world occupied by advanced beings using the mysterious 'vril' as an energy source.]*

At the start of 1887 Madame Elven discovered, at dangerously close quarters, that pedestrianism often threw up some unexpected and nasty occupational hazards. During a well-attended six-day walk at Sheerness, she suddenly found herself dodging a firework that a young sailor had thrown as she went past. Edward Carter – an 'engine room artificer' in the Royal Navy – duly appeared before Sheerness Police Court charged with throwing fireworks in public streets. The prosecution was brought by the local Board of Health, and Carter pleaded guilty. The court heard a large number of people had gathered in the streets of Sheerness on January 29, following in the wake of Madame Elven who was just about to complete her feat of walking three miles per hour for six days and six nights. The defendant threw a lighted 'squib' among them which exploded. Police Constable Packman said when he saw this he seized the arm of Carter, who at this point dropped a bundle of unlit squibs on the ground. Carter claimed he committed the offence through thoughtlessness and the firework had exploded harmlessly in the air. The officer disagreed and said it went off in the midst of the crowd. The magistrate imposed a £10 fine plus costs.

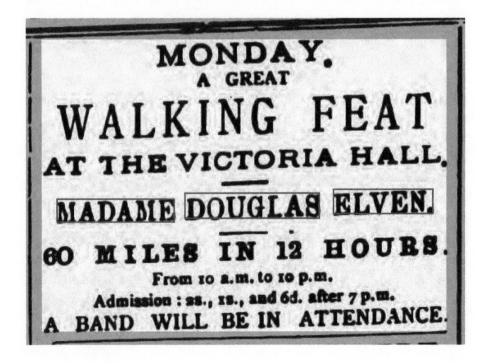

Through 1887 Madame Elven took her tally of walks in Kentish towns to a dozen, performing three miles per hour over six consecutive days and nights in Whitstable in March. Her chosen course was between the Two Brewers Inn on the Canterbury Road and the Harbour Gates. She performed to big crowds dressed in a brown velveteen tunic and knickerbockers, with cap to match and carrying a riding whip. Reports marvelled at how she untied her long hair and allowed it to hang down her back, a bold move that was seen as verging on the seductive. In the summer she performed for the people of Bromley, walking two miles within every hour for a week, accompanied at all times by a 'referee' and again pulled in good crowds. The *Nuneaton Advertiser* columnist was even inspired to quote the 18th-century poet Edward Young, when he wrote: "At the conclusion of her journey I should think she would be in the humour to woo 'tired nature's sweet restorer, balmy sleep'".

In the autumn she crossed the border into Surrey to perform a similar feat at Epsom. The *Croydon Advertiser* praised her for choosing "a very sensibly devised costume" and for moving "with an easy grace and a fair heel and toe stride". Then followed performances for the people of Kingston-upon-Thames and Hampton Wick, at the latter walking two miles an hour for five consecutive full days, thus covering 240 miles in all. The plan had originally been to do six days but unfavourable weather intervened. Her HQ was the Old Kings Head at Hampton Wick and she did large laps which involved all the local main streets and crossing the Thames twice.

One reporter wrote glowingly of her as a pleasant, cheerful and courteous conversationalist, proud of her athletic achievements "but with none of the boasting so often heard among professional athletes". Her appetite and health were always good, she told him, and she rarely felt seriously fatigued. She declined to reveal full details of her diet while walking, but admitted the feats had not been accomplished without alcohol. Across the week her Kingston walk had attracted increased interest by the day and for much of the time she was followed by large groups of playful young boys – hence the occasional need for the riding whip!

Most of Elven's 1887 outings generated good public interest, but normally nowhere near the huge numbers who flooded the streets of Woolwich to see her in late January and early February of 1888. One local paper suggested the crowds watching her Saturday night finale in particular were unparalleled in that region of London. A police spokesman even admitted: "There has been no previous occasion – including General Elections, public processions or Royal visits – where so many people have been out on the streets of Woolwich as there was last Saturday between 9 and 11." The early signs had not been good, reported the *Kentish Independent*, with Madame Elven greeted initially by "apathy, mingled with ridicule and annoyance", but she pressed on and turned the whole thing around by bringing out the crowds and ultimately creating "the liveliest sensation on record". It was reported that even "the roughs and gamins of the streets" who were at first disposed to jeer and molest her, simply because they did not understand her, did an about-turn and became her most vigorous supporters.

The stir she created was felt throughout the area and shopkeepers in particular benefitted, doing the best Saturday business in living memory. Several of the local taverns also reported their day's takings were up to £20 above the norm. Some of the grateful traders rewarded Elven by presenting her with gifts and bouquets of flowers, which she carried and waved during her last few miles. One jeweller sent over a gold watch and chain, to add to the umbrellas and travelling bags she'd already been given. The streets were so packed in the latter stages of the walk that she needed a quartet of police officers to escort and protect her at close quarters, and the help of an 'advance guard' of youngsters to force a gap for her to pass through. This in addition to nearly 50 policemen marshalling the crowds.

At some of the windows that the procession passed there were fine displays of 'coloured fire' (a type of pyrotechnic/firework) and the general atmosphere resembled a carnival or pageant. After one of her final miles was completed Elven had to sacrifice her rest period, having been invited to mount the platform at the Royal Assembly Rooms where a concert was taking place, to say a few words to the audience. The walk was officially declared over by 11.30 on the Saturday evening. Although Woolwich had been brought to a grinding halt by the crowds, there was very little disorder and no arrests. The police and other local authorities evidently took a tolerant view and didn't attempt to curtail this 'unofficial' event or disperse the crowds. Had they done so, Madame Elven would no doubt have claimed immunity from prosecution having not pre-advertised the walk by posting bills or encouraging people out, and had merely exercised her right to walk on public streets as a law-abiding citizen. As it transpired she was very grateful for the close attention of the police, for there was little doubt the whole affair could never have been completed without their help amid all the congestion.

Such was the interest created that the *Kentish Independent* took the unusual step of sending a reporter to meet Madame Elven a few days after the dust had settled. In the recent past the pedestriennes had been seen as shameless hussies who ought to know better than walk the streets for money, and few editors would allow them much coverage, let alone a lengthy one-to-one interview piece. But the *KI* appreciated that here was a woman who was bright, articulate, honest and with an interesting story to tell. The paper commented:

"The result of the conversation was an impression left upon [our reporter] strongly favourable to the lady, whose pleasant demeanour, ready explanations and evident candour, combined with an easy command of language and a good intellect, all served to prepossess a stranger in her behalf. She was dressed plainly in black, her costume being of the usual feminine cut, and being of no resemblance to the professional garments in which she has appeared on her public parades".

REPORTER: I CONGRATULATE YOU MADAME ELVEN ON THE SUCCESS OF YOUR EXPLOIT, AND HOPE YOU SUFFER NO ILL-EFFECTS?

Elven: No, I was never better in my life and my health is always good. The general impression is that I must be weak because I am thin, but I have a splendid constitution as my work proves!

HOW LONG HAVE YOU BEEN ENGAGED IN PEDESTRIANISM?

Less than two years, and all the time in Kent except in the three Surrey towns of Croydon, Epsom and Kingston-upon-Thames.

ARE YOU A KENTISH WOMAN?

No, I was born in the north of England where my father is a farmer. I would rather not mention the place for obvious reasons, but I may say that my life on the farm probably hardened me for my present occupation. Although called Madame by courtesy, I have never married. Always from a child I had an idea I could walk and endure fatigue and when I read of [Edward] Weston and the rest I thought I should like to try. I have done this feat a good many times now and have never thought of failure. My plan is always the same as it had been at Woolwich. I began, as you know, on Sunday night, or rather half past 12 on Monday morning, and walked two miles in every hour until 12 on Saturday night. I never announce myself or my purpose, but leave the performance to advertise itself, which it always does. I never set foot in Woolwich until the

Tuesday before I began and I took no means whatever to let anyone know anything about me. The first who noticed me were the police. One or two constables got into conversation with me during the night and I told them my objective, and the police have been kind to me throughout for which I thank Inspector Clark and all of them.

HAVE YOU EVER BEEN STOPPED [FROM WALKING] BY THE POLICE?

Quite the contrary, they have assisted me everywhere. At Bromley about 30 of them escorted me and a band played me through the town, but I would not consent to a band here as the streets were so full.

THE ROUTE THROUGH THE CROWDED STREETS MUST HAVE GIVEN YOU EXTRA FATIGUE?

The crowd was not so bad as the route. I like to walk in the road but the roads just now are either out of repair or being put into repair and I had to take the footpaths which compelled me to get up and down the kerbstones. That one rainy night was very trying.

EXCUSE THE QUESTION, BUT HOW DO THE PUBLIC KNOW THAT YOU KEEP AT YOUR WORK ALL NIGHT?

That is a question for the public! They know my pretensions and can watch if they like. But in point of fact people are about every hour and see me do it. The taverns do not close till half past 12 and folks loiter about till two or later, and at three the men begin going to their employment, and the police of course see me all night.

DO YOU PREFER WALKING BY NIGHT OR DAY?

I like the day best, but the quiet of the night seems to refresh me.

DO YOU FIND YOURSELF MORE DISTRESSED AS THE TIME GOES ON?

No, Tuesday was my worst day last week and I felt very tired on the Friday and wanted very much to sleep. Practically, you see, I get no sleep worth the name. I make a rule of walking my two miles every hour and then resting, if ever so little, before I begin again, but sometimes I take two spells close together and get nearly an hour to change my clothing.

DO YOU TRAIN FOR YOUR EXERCISES?

Never! I do not need it for I am always in training.

BUT YOU DIET, I SUPPOSE?

Not at all – I eat just that which I fancy and when I want it.

ARE YOU AN ABSTAINER?

No, but I do not believe in stimulants. I attribute my constitution to good sound food and exercise when I was at home and really all that I do is a good week's work without rest.

YOU ALWAYS SELECT LARGE TOWNS FOR YOUR APPEARANCES?

Not always one so populous as Woolwich, but the result is nearly always the same for the people come in from the villages to see me. My first walk last year was at Sheerness which is not a very large place, but there were 10,000 people following me there! The Queensborough Fife and Drum Band escorted me and the inhabitants gave a ball in my honour which was attended by 400. At Canterbury, Faversham and wherever I have been, the report is always the same – more people and more excitement than ever was known before!

YOU MUST FEEL LIKE A CONQUERING HEROINE?

Yes! [laughing] It is enough to make a creature vain.

I BELIEVE YOUR PRACTICE IS TO MAKE A COLLECTION FOR THE PURPOSE OF MEETING YOUR EXPENSES?

Yes. I have not been round yet but from the number of presents which have been sent to me I have no doubt that it shall be well supported.

I HAVE HEARD SOMETHING SAID ABOUT YOUR MAKING CONTRIBUTIONS TO CHARITABLE OBJECTIVES?

Pray do not mention the subject. It is one within my own breast. You may like to know that a Friendly Society held at the Lord Whitworth is having a special medal prepared for me. And here is a silver star which I have had sent to me today inscribed: 'To Madame Douglas Elven, in token of admiration for her splendid prowess'.

HAVE YOU DECIDED WHICH TOWN IS NEXT?

No, I shall rest awhile and shall suddenly make up my mind and start upon another week's work – but I like Kent, which has been my friend!

*

Despite her penchant for performing in bucolic Kent, the so-called Garden of England, Madame Elven completed her commitments at Woolwich and set off westwards the following month to perform twice in Devon. Some money was made here from collections, but she may have regretted the decision to travel so far as both events ended in relative failure. The first, in March 1888 saw her tackle a challenge of completing 60 miles in 12 hours at the Victoria Hall in Exeter, a cavernous building in Queen Street that hosted circuses and trades union rallies, but she quit after more than nine hours of walking, explaining that she had injured her hand on a protruding nail. By that point the target was out of reach as it would have required another 17 miles to be covered in 2.5 hours, an almost impossible task having already trudged 43 miles. During the afternoon session, when it became clear she was moving slower than the required pace, a railway guard accompanied her for nine laps before retiring, followed shortly afterwards by a porter joining her for several laps. With the majority of paying customers expected after 7pm the band played on and Elven bravely continued, but finally called it a day around 9.30pm.

A week or so later her plans were revised and she ventured a few miles out of Exeter to the small town of Crediton, her task to cover 150 miles in four days, walking for 12 hours per day. It involved walking up and down a stretch of the busy High Street and the only reward would be from the collection taken afterwards among townsfolk. She set off at 10 on the morning of Wednesday 21 March, her route taking her from the Ship Hotel via the High Street to a spot at the end of the railings in Union Terrace and back to the Ship again. Her style of walking was seen as perfectly fair with steps that were somewhat short and jerky, strongly reminding one writer of Edward Weston's well-known gait. During the first day the weather was fine and the road in good condition and she clocked up 34 miles. On the second and third days rain set in and her progress suffered badly, the bad state of the road forcing her to use a seriously uneven footpath for the most part. It was clear she would be forced to stop early and that 150 miles was out of the question in such conditions, but farmers' daughters don't give in easily and she pressed on doggedly into the fourth and final day. A long way behind schedule, she finally came to a miserable halt around 8pm, the final straw being when the rain was replaced by falling snow. Sympathetic Devonians who witnessed the sad scene were able to compensate when the collection box came around.

Around now Madame Elven decided one-day walking should be the order of the day and set her sights on more unconquered territory in the south of England. After completing 50 miles in 12 consecutive hours in Maidenhead in the summer of 1888, she headed into Slough to repeat the trick in early September. The weather was favourable and she again preferred not to advertise the event in any formal way in the preceding days, but an hour before the scheduled 9.30 start did use a town crier to announce the walk to townsfolk who were out and about that morning. Enough curiosity was aroused to inspire a good crowd to gather for the start opposite the Crown Inn in High Street. She had two separate one-mile routes measured out, allowing her a little variety to allay the monotony of the day's business. These rather twisty routes covered a number of different streets in the town centre and allowed her to take a brief refreshment rest when required, as they both passed her HQ, the Queen of England Inn. A straight mile up and down the High Street might have made her a little more visible, but would have meant missing out on the treats needed for sustenance; these included mugs of beef tea, grapes and a pear or two.

Interest grew as the day wore on and by the final stages a large crowd was pressing in on her, occasionally impeding progress, and she occasionally needed to brandish her small riding whip to clear a path. She was a small woman and in danger of disappearing in the melee until help arrived in the shape of pub landlords Frank Fortescue (Queen of England) and Ben Heath (North Star) who walked alongside and repelled any overenthusiasm as the crush increased. One report noted that by now she was looking fatigued and had removed her hat and let loose her long hair.

Typically she stuck to her task in plucky fashion and finished just after 9.10pm with nearly 20 minutes to spare. Completing her 50th and final mile at the Crown, she walked on to the North Star where she received a big ovation and soon afterwards returned to the Queen of England and was looked after by Messrs. Fortescue and Heath. Her mile times had been consistent, ranging from 13 to 16 minutes and in the proper 'heel and toe' style. No doubt the occasional private wager would be laid in connection with her reaching her target in these type of events, but according to Elven herself, the only income she personally derived would depend on the generosity or otherwise of the public. Encouraged by the numbers who watched her at Slough, she announced her next venture would be in nearby Staines.

Performing one-day walks in small and medium-sized towns in the southern half of England – places that rarely witnessed pedestrianism events on their streets – was proving relatively successful. Sometimes, especially if the post-walk collection in the main streets failed to yield a good reward, Elven would spend the following morning knocking on doors to add to her earnings before heading out of town. Her pleasant manner must have helped enormously in this respect.

It seems by now very few women across the country were attempting to make a living from pedestrianism, but Elven had hit on a formula that worked for her, and saw no reason to quit yet. Being unmarried and with no family to care for, she had a distinct advantage over many other pedestriennes as she really was footloose and fancy free. And, of course, as a farmer's daughter would have known only too well the need to make hay while the sun shone!

During the summer of 1889 Elven may well have noted and approved of news that women's rights campaigner Emmeline Pankhurst had founded the Women's Franchise League. Pankhurst's aim was to press for women to have the right to vote in local elections and this led to the rise of the suffragette movement.

Over the course of this landmark year Elven decided it was time to head for new territory and give the wide open spaces of the East Anglian region a try. Most of her performances were in the middle of busy market towns in areas dominated by farming, where the population at large would lap up the sheer novelty of a woman attempting a solo sporting feat on their streets and thus providing several hours of entertainment free of charge.

In mid-April Madame Elven pitched up at Colchester, Britain's oldest recorded town, the place where another brave female invader – Queen Boudicca – had wreaked havoc a few centuries earlier. Unlike her predecessor, Elven came in peace, her sole intention to ply her unusual trade and earn a few pounds and the odd sparkly gift along the way. Colchester welcomed her with open arms, the townsfolk going about their business on Tuesday 16 April 1889 fascinated to see her and generous with their applause and good-natured banter. The feat of walking 50 miles in 12 consecutive hours commenced at 9.15 in the morning from the High Street outside the Town Hall, next door to her rooms at the Angel Hotel. She set off briskly and spent the day describing an almost perfect one-mile square around the busy town centre, via Headgate, St Botolph's Corner, Queen Street and High Street. Interest grew towards the evening and by the time the sun went down most of the route was packed as they cheered her home, having completed the task inside the allotted time.

Colchester provided an almost perfect route for Elven's 12-hour stint, but later that year in Diss, on the Norfolk-Suffolk border, she would encounter what she called the most difficult terrain of her entire career. Although she was again attempting 50 miles on the main streets in the centre of town, this time heavy rainfall saw the surfaces become muddy, uneven and stamina-sapping in the extreme. It may have been a Friday market day in July's high summer, but this was no cakewalk in the sun. Despite the rain there was considerable interest in the town, the locals agog having apparently never seen anything quite like it before. The *Diss Express* described Elven's efforts in very positive terms, calling her "a marvellous walker" and praised the way she coped with shocking weather throughout the second half of the walk.

Large numbers thronged the streets to encourage her and the final hour saw great excitement drummed up as she acknowledged a huge ovation when approaching the Crown Hotel for the final time to finish. Afterwards she told the *Diss Express* reporter for the past three years she had performed 50 miles in 12 hours at least once every week, and her total mileage had come to nearly 8,000 miles in that time. As was now her post-race custom, she proudly sported on her bodice two handsome silver medals presented by the Ancient Order of Druids to mark the occasion she covered 288 miles in six days in Woolwich in early 1888. Asked how she came to embark on such a way of life, she said that it was from hearing and reading about others doing similar. She added that in all her walks she had never encountered more difficult ground than these streets in Diss; coming down the fairly steep Pump Hill had proved particularly tricky in the mud. Buoyed by the great reception from this small and rural community, a week or two later Elven moved on to another small town, Ely, hoping for a repeat performance but in better weather and easier conditions.

In the shadow of Ely Cathedral she set off from John Newstead's popular Dolphin Tavern in the Market Place on the morning of Thursday 1st August. It was another 50-miler in 12 hours, her circuit including Market Hill, Fore Hill and Broad Street, each lap measuring around 1.2 miles. The vast majority of laps were timed at around 17 minutes, apart from the odd occasion she popped into the Dolphin for a quick wash and a glass of port wine containing a beaten egg. With roughly an hour left she performed her by now customary gesture of disposing of her headwear – a jockey-style cap – allowing her hair to hang loose behind. Her progress in the evening attracted large crowds who lined both sides of Ely's main streets to cheer her on.

Then came Wisbech – where the local paper seemed a little uncomfortable that Madame Elven's brown velveteen skirt was "very short". Here she found it necessary to use her riding whip a good number of times to deal with packs of excited youngsters who congregated around her from time to time, unwittingly blocking progress. She commenced at 9.30am from the New Inn in Union Street, through High Street to the Swan Inn, Old Market, returning via High Street, Timber Market, crossing the road opposite the Ferryboat Inn, through Church Terrace, Market Place, and Union Street and back to the New Inn – a lap of exactly a mile. She walked at a strong, uniform pace for the entire 12 hours, each mile taking well under 13 minutes and her only rest was seen to be two refreshment breaks of around 20 minutes each.

At one point Elven slipped and crashed heavily to the ground near the Royal Hotel, but the only serious damage was to her dignity and she was able to quickly resume. As the crowds grew considerably later in the day she again had to deal with well-wishers impeding her and temporarily disrupting her even pace. But these issues proved harmless as her timekeeper Mr Richer briskly announced at 9.22pm that she could stop now as she had covered more than 51 miles with eight minutes to spare. This East Anglian tour of 1889 was going well and she happily remained in the region for a few more weeks, making plans to perform in Bury St Edmunds and Stowmarket.

After the 1889 Christmas period was done and dusted, Elven single-handedly dragged female pedestrianism into a new decade with a series of further walks in Kent and Sussex during the early weeks of 1890. She walked 25 miles in under six hours at Sevenoaks, creating a good deal of interest as she went back and forth from the Parish Church to Smith's Brewery in the first week of January.

A week or so later news filtered out of Brighton that a mystery pedestrienne calling herself 'Madame Palestrina' had been entertaining locals. The format of her walk and the confirmation she had performed over 1,000 miles in Brighton several years earlier, gave credence to the idea that this was Madame Elven having fun with a new 'persona'. Quite a crowd gathered to watch proceedings despite some miserable weather. 'Palestrina', who had apparently named herself after a small town in Italy, set off on a Wednesday lunchtime aiming to cover 25 miles in six hours. She was attired in brown velvet knickerbockers that reached to the knee, with a short skirt covering them, all topped by a jockey's cap. A noisy band of young boys followed her from the start outside the Jireh Chapel in Malling Street, Lewes, to the main town clock and back. She finished with 20 minutes to spare and took refreshment at the Rainbow Tavern, where she was said to have reaped a rich harvest of coppers after passing a hat around. Without fully revealing her identity, she did let slip that 48 hours earlier she had performed a similar walk at Tunbridge Wells and her collection there yielded around £50, most of which she had given to charity.

Later in January she pitched up in Eastbourne where she found the streets very muddy and tricky to negotiate, but put up a good show and the Sussex Agricultural Express reported that "the appearance of this female Weston excited the greatest amusement". In mid-February 1890 there were further reports that an unnamed pedestrienne, almost certainly Elven again, had walked from Ashford to Ramsgate, where she then undertook a task of walking 40 miles in ten hours. Starting early on a sunny Friday morning at the bottom end of Chatham Street, she marched via the town centre to the Ramsgate Brewery and back again for ten hours, taking four short breaks in that time. Once again no wagers were involved, merely collections at the end and the following morning.

Travelling around solo and doing walks that required very few (if any) helpers, and no complicated advance arrangements, worked very well for Madame Elven. It was a *modus operandi* apparently unique among the established pedestriennes. By continuing to make a living from this way of life for nearly four years, she helped keep women's pedestrianism alive up to 1890, even though the sporting world was changing fast and there was little room for maverick and unregulated pursuits such as multi-day walks.

The writing was on the wall. The Amateur Athletic Association was up and running and establishing a formal set of rules and ethos for all forms of foot racing, meaning pedestrianism was being shunted into the margins. The pedestriennes were fast disappearing into obscurity.

EPILOGUE

WHAT HAPPENED NEXT?

Even though the pedestriennes kicked aside many of the barriers impeding the growth of women's sport, the positive effect was not immediately obvious. It would take several decades after the women walkers' heyday before female athletics in general began picking up the pace again.

So although the pedestriennes paved the way for more women to take up the sport, what caused the sudden decline in women's pedestrianism seen around the turn of the 20th century? Sociologist Dahn Shaulis's academic paper in the *(North American) Journal of Sport History* of Spring 1999 provides some answers:

"Organised social pressure by temperance officials, religious conservatives and doctors against women's sporting entertainment appears to be a major factor in its marginalization. Government actions ranging from arrests to legislation against the events are also factors. Managers and theatre owners who exploited women performers and created a dangerous atmosphere also contributed to discouraging spectators. Apparently it was not simply public disapproval of the women's morality, but also efforts to protect women that led to a reduction in vigorous sporting efforts. As events were represented as cruel torture against women, it would have been difficult for suffragists or doctors to continue supporting the performances. Bloody sports such as cockfighting and dogfighting had already been reduced because of their cruelty to animals. Certainly women deserved at least the same protection. The impression that such events were abusive towards women, as well as immoral, seemed to tip the scales toward greater marginalization. It should be noted that men's professional events also fell into disrepute for their excesses and abuses as amateur sports became more legitimate and newsworthy".

The woman labelled the best female foot racer on the planet – the American Amy Howard – died in childbirth in October 1885, and the scant coverage this received in the US press seemed to confirm women's pedestrianism was dying in the USA too. Howard's six-day record of 409 miles (achieved aged 16 in May 1880) would remain unbeaten for more than 100 years. Perhaps fed up with the lack of challenges for pedestriennes, a Spanish immigrant called Zoe Gayton made headlines in 1890 when she decided to cross the USA on foot by following 3,400 miles of railroad. She set off from California accompanied by a pair of poodles, one of which died after a confrontation with a train.

According to folklore, another 'unofficial' sporting adventure saw Greek mother-of-seven Stamata Revithi complete the Olympic marathon route (then 40 kilometres) in March 1896. Stamata was a poor 35-year-old from the island of Syros, but an unusually strong and active character, determined to improve her lot in life. She was convinced running the marathon route would make her famous and help her large poverty-stricken family. So she made her way to Athens, carrying her 17-month-old baby, only to be told she had missed the race entry deadline. She was told she might be able to run shortly after the official Olympic marathon had taken place, alongside a group of American women, but this sideshow failed to take place and Stamata ended up running solo the following weekend. She set off from the village of Marathon at breakfast time and arrived in Athens five and a half hours later covered in dust. She scurried around for signatures on a time sheet to prove her achievement and told journalists she would have been even quicker but for several stops to obtain oranges.

After the turn of the century and Queen Victoria's death in 1902 there remained scant evidence of women's sport getting a foothold in Britain. Occasionally new heights of novelty were attained – such as the 1903 foot race for waitresses staged from the London Stock Exchange to Hyde Park. It proved a Whitsuntide Bank Holiday treat for 100,000 spectators, who cheered 167 girls over a 4.5-mile course. That year Australia followed suit: the waitresses of Adelaide walking in high temperatures to Glenelg, where dozens of them were said to have fainted at the finish line. "The cabmen did good business taking home busted competitors", noted one report.

Also in 1903, the city of Paris witnessed a huge 'midinettes' walking race, with nearly 4,000 young women trekking the 7.5 miles from Place de la Concorde to Nanterre. Midinettes were the girls employed in dressmaking trades, so called because at midday they scamper out of the workshops in their thousands to eat their 'dinette', or hasty snack. For the 18-year-old winner Jeanne Cosminee there was a suite of bedroom furniture plus the equivalent of £14 in cash, plus prizes for the first brunette home with blue eyes and the first blonde to finish. Hundreds of thousands of spectators filled the Champs-Elysées, police and military powerless to keep the roads clear. The crowds were much smaller in August 1905 when a large group of young women from Honolulu took up the challenge of walking hundreds of miles around a large part of the island of Hawaii for more than a month with overnight stops. The majority were members of the Punahou College faculty, who completed the event in short army cloth skirts, shirts and army felt hats, and carried blankets and canteens.

Things were beginning to change in Britain, where the sporting horizons of our women had by now been widened further thanks partly to a process that gradually seeped down the social scale. Upper-class women were the first beneficiaries, but the sports of the masses, including darts, cycling and swimming, were embraced. By the year 1907 women's athletics events had started taking place on an unofficial basis under the auspices of the Amateur Athletic Association (AAA) and finally, in 1922, a separate Women's AAA would be born. Thanks, at least in part, to institutional male chauvinism, this new organisation had to go its own way for at least 10 years before a working agreement was reached with the main AAA.

In 1908 Miss Ida Browne struck a blow for female foot racers by being the only woman to take on a field of 17 men in the Minehead 'Marathon' (actually just under 10 miles). She injured her foot in training beforehand but still placed well among the 18 starters and was given a special prize as the only female competitor. She proudly told reporters she was of Scottish extraction and related to the exiled Doones who had inspired the novel *Lorna Doone*.

Long-distance hiking slowly gained new disciples around Europe as time went on, and in 1913 a notable event was staged in the heart of the Austro-Hungarian empire to promote the feminist movement. The hiking habit had spread to the young women of Vienna where a 300-strong club organised the trek, not this time to establish women's right to vote, but to promote the idea that women should have a much bigger say in matters such as health and education.

Although women's football became surprisingly prominent in Britain during World War One, athletics and most other sporting pursuits largely came to a grinding halt. Britain's best runners, serving on foreign fields, did see plenty of action as foot messengers though, wearing special red armbands as they delivered critical pieces of information from one command unit to another. At the tail end of the war in September 1918, the Tour de Paris Marathon took place and photographic evidence confirms a woman found her way in among the male runners, race number 171 proudly pinned to her bodice. The course was said to have been about 500 metres longer than the 26.2 miles established as the official distance at the 1908 London Olympics. The 'interloper' was 23-year-old Marie-Louise Ledru who finished in 5 hrs 40 mins in 38th place, thus becoming the first female to complete a race over the classic marathon distance.

Women walkers made very few headlines for years, but that briefly changed when the headline "Man-hater wins Brighton Walk" appeared in more than one publication in May 1923. The plain-speaking Miss Doris Grasty didn't hold back when speaking to reporters after coming home first in the 52-mile London to Brighton walk for Ministry of Pensions clerks. The South Londoner strode all the way from Westminster to the Brighton aquarium in 12 hours and 2 minutes to win the gold medal and then revealed her intense dislike of the arrogant men who had inspired the win: "Men are so conceited. I have no use for them at all, except to prove them wrong. Beat the men was my idea right through, I shall never marry."

A big cheer greeted Miss Grasty's arrival on the seafront and she was described as "a fragile-looking girl with bobbed fair hair and wearing a blue and white Tam o'Shanter, a white sweater and a tangerine skirt". Around 40 office workers took part, the 13 women competitors benefitting from a two-and-a-half-hour start. Despite stopping for a massage in Redhill, Miss Grasty came in well ahead of fastest man H. V. Henry. Unluckiest competitor was probably Miss LeGrand, who led for most of the race but fainted with exhaustion at the roadside not far from the finish.

In the autumn of 1926 came a real red-letter day when another feisty Londoner, Violet Piercy, ran the Polytechnic Marathon course from Windsor to London in a time of 3 hours and 40 minutes and 22 seconds, setting what would be regarded as the first 'world best' by a woman at the distance. The Women's AAA praised her effort as unprecedented, but confirmed it was a personal endeavour and not run under their auspices. Two cars occupied by friends accompanied her when she set off at 4.20pm from Windsor, finishing outside Battersea Town Hall well after 8pm after encountering traffic congestion in the latter stages. Violet appeared to enjoy her new-found fame, and especially the potential to earn from it, and would go on to complete several more marathons. Her picture was on the front of the *Daily Mirror* among others, and she appeared on BBC radio and Pathe News in subsequent days. She said her motivation had been to prove USA women were not the only high-achieving sporting females, clearly a reference to Americans Gertrude Ederle and Millie Corson having recently become the first women to swim the English Channel.

But Violet's efforts failed to spark British women into action on the roads, and by the start of the 1939–45 War she had faded into obscurity. Only recently has new research been carried out on her pioneering exploits. Remarkably her 'world best' marathon time would stand for more than 37 years, finally beaten in December 1963 by Merry Lepper of the USA.

The view in Europe that women were too fragile for long-distance athletics endured well into the 1950s. The Belgian Medical Society for Physical and Sporting Education carried out a study and concluded women should not take part in competitive sport: "Women are restricted in their training and sporting efforts because of their glandular structure, they are overvulnerable to emotional factors and they are extremely liable to organic upsets". The AAA field events coach and former long jumper George Pallett, president of Herne Hill Harriers, was unimpressed by this and said it seemed the fears of these medical men were based on their knowledge of female anatomy and physiology and not founded on practical experience. Pallett added: "Parents can set their minds at rest, and women can enjoy sport without apprehension – as long as they use their common sense".

Britain's place at the top of the women's marathon charts was regained in 1964 when Dale Greig from Paisley in Scotland ran 3:27:45 at the hilly Isle of Wight Marathon a week after her 30th birthday. Special arrangements were made on Greig's behalf – including an ambulance following her throughout – but she rewarded the anxious organisers by becoming the first woman in the world to go under 3 hrs 30 mins. Remarkably, within a few weeks New Zealander Millie Sampson beat this mark by more than 10 minutes, although Greig did remain Britain's fastest female marathoner for 11 long years.

The so-called Swinging Sixties liberated British women in a variety of ways, and towards the end of the decade there was even a new magazine introduced specifically for female athletes – *Women's Athletics,* edited by Cliff Temple. It was widely welcomed at the time, but failed to go the distance in commercial terms. It lasted less than two years and only 12 issues before being absorbed as a section within the already well-established *Athletics Weekly.*

It had taken around 100 years since the pedestrienne glory days, but finally the 1970s in Britain witnessed a significant increase in women taking to the roads and tracks. A good number of them were probably inspired by Kathrine Switzer and Roberta Gibb's infamous infiltrations of the men-only Boston Marathon of 1966 and 1967. By the end of the seventies women's races had become an official part of the marathon scene and North Londoner Joyce Smith had taken the British best time down to a remarkable 2:36:27. Within a few more years she had sped under the magical 2.30 barrier at the age of 44, statistics that shocked the male old guard who were still largely controlling the sport.

By the 1980s colourful and talented British female athletes were proliferating. Women like Scots-born physiotherapist Leslie Watson, whose remarkable staying power saw her star in more than 150 different marathons and ultras. Other ultra-distance specialists like Eleanor Robinson (formerly Adams), Hilary Walker and Sandra Brown chalked up record after record.

However, women's participation in foot races at the Olympic Games advanced even slower than for the marathon. As recently as Moscow 1980 the longest race for women was the 1,500 metres – the so-called metric mile – which had only been included itself as late as 1972. Women were first allowed to compete from 1928 onwards, and even then problems occurred: in the longest race that year (800 metres) many competitors were apparently poorly prepared, several collapsing with exhaustion. This led Olympic officials to agree the two-lap race was simply too strenuous for women and wouldn't allow its reappearance until 1960.

Slowly, change did come, particularly after the citizen running boom of the early 1980s. The International Amateur Athletics Federation (IAAF) president Adrian Paulen was so impressed by what he saw at an international marathon in Tokyo that he announced his full backing for 5,000 metres, 10,000 metres and marathons for women within the Olympic Games. Although his announcement was somewhat lost in all the headlines about the end of amateurism at the Olympics, his thumbs-up signal was a major breakthrough, even if achieved much later than necessary. Women began to close the gap on men very quickly, notably when Britain's Paula Radcliffe ran the 2003 London

Marathon in 2:15:25, a time so good it has eluded many of the nation's best male club runners ever since.

The type of multi-day event put on by the Victorian pedestriennes have long been extinct of course. However, in the modern era multi-record-breaking Brits Sandra Brown, Sharon Gayter and Eleanor Adams-Robinson have achieved world bests at 1,000 miles. In 1998 Adams-Robinson covered the distance more than twice as quickly as Ada Anderson had at King's Lynn's Athenaeum 120 years earlier.

Back then an exhausted Anderson had ended that vintage walk in Norfolk by clambering up on stage to make an impassioned plea to all women to follow her example and take up walking and other sporting pursuits. She ignored the crippling tiredness she must have felt at that moment, desperate to encourage other 'ordinary' women to throw off their shackles and enjoy the benefits of simple exercise. Her words may not have had huge immediate impact, but we can be sure this 19th-century 'pioneer in bloomers' would have thoroughly approved of the many extraordinary ultra-distance women who have emerged since the 1980s. Had Ada known what the likes of Eleanor Adams-Robinson and Sandra Brown would accomplish, her pride and delight would have been off the scale.

ACKNOWLEDGEMENTS

My thanks for their kind assistance go to the following people and organisations: Andy Milroy, Peter Lovesey, Sandra Brown, Derek Martin, Kathy Nicol, Gina Bridgeland, Kay Lyons, Peter Radford, Hamish Thomson, Alan Mead, Ron Carlton, Katherine Prior, Paul Marshall, Roger Robinson, The British Library, The British Newspaper Archive, Essex Record Office, the office of the New Zealand Prime Minister Jacinda Ardern. All illustrations sourced from private collections or property of the author.

BIBLIOGRAPHY

Amusing the Victorians – Pamela Horn (Amberley, 2014)

A Short History of Slavery – James Walvin (Penguin, 2017)

British Athletics 1866–1880 – Peter Lovesey & Keith Morbey (NUTS, 2016)

British Sport: A Social History – Dennis Brailsford (Lutterworth, 1992)

Classic Guide to Athletics – Montague Shearman (Amberley, 2015)

Consuming Passions: Leisure and Pleasure in Victorian Britain – Judith Flanders (Harper Press, 2006)

Deerfoot: Athletics' First Superstar – Rob Hadgraft (Desert Island, 2007)

Front Runners – Warren Roe (Book Guild, 2002)

Gendering Walter Scott – C. M. Jackson-Houlston (Routledge, 2017)

Grace, Beauty and Banjos – Michael Kilgarriff, (Oberon, 1998)

History of Women's Boxing – Malissa Smith (Rowman & Littlefield, 2014)

How to be a Victorian – Ruth Goodman (Penguin, 2003)

Indian Running: Native American History and Tradition – Peter Nabokov (Ancient City Press, 1981)

Laisterdyke Lives – Gina Bridgeland (ed), Laisterdyke LHG, 2001)

Marathon Medicine – ed: D. Tunstall-Pedoe (RS Medicine Press, 2001)

Pedestrianism – Matthew Algeo (Chicago Review Press, 2014)

Pedestrianism – Walter Thom (Pinetree, 2010)

Pleasures and Pastimes in Victorian Britain – Pamela Horn (Amberley, 2011)

Running Over 40, 50, 60, 70 – Bruce and Sue Tulloh (Tulloh, 2015)

Running Through the Ages – Edward S. Sears (McFarland, 2001)

Sport and the British – Richard Holt (Oxford Univ. 1990)

The Celebrated Captain Barclay – Peter Radford (Headline, 2001)

The Great American Sports Book – George Gipe (Doubleday, 1978)

The Long Distance Record Book – Andy Milroy (RRC, 1988)

The Men Who Stare at Hens: Great Irish Eccentrics – Simon Leyland (THP Ireland, 2019)

The Pedestriennes: America's Forgotten Superstars – Harry Hall (Dog Ear, 2014)

The Victorians – A. N. Wilson (Arrow, 2002)

Ultra-Marathoning: The Next Challenge – Tom Osler & Ed Dodd (WPI, California, 1979)

Wearing the Trousers – Don Chapman (Amberley, 2017)

Wobble to Death – Peter Lovesey (Arrow, 1981)

RESEARCH PAPERS

Peter Radford (Women's Foot Races in the 18th & 19th Centuries, 1993)
Dahn Shaulis (N.American Journal of Sport History, Volumes 18 & 26, 1991 & 1999)
Dave Terry (Women's Athletics in Britain & Ireland From its Earliest Days, 2008)
Samantha-Jayne Oldfield (George Martin: Wizard of Pedestrianism, 2011)
Derek Martin (Various pedestrianism papers, BSSH/MMU, 2014–20)
David Pendleton (The Pub and Pedestrianism in Victorian Bradford, 2014)
Archie Jenkins (19th Century Foot-Racing: The Tyneside Connection, 2014)

NEWSPAPERS & PERIODICALS

The Era, Bell's Life in London & Sporting Chronicle, The Sporting Life, The Stage, Illustrated Sporting & Dramatic News, Track Stats, The Referee, Illustrated Police News, Huddersfield Chronicle, Boston Guardian, Stamford Mercury, Edinburgh Evening News, Nottingham Journal, Dundee Evening Telegraph, Burnley Express, Irish Sportsman, The Graphic, Kirkintilloch Herald, Kerry Evening Post, Bury & Norwich Post, Sunday Illustrated, The Sketch, New Sporting Magazine, Norwood News, Athletics World, Leeds Intelligencer, Leeds Times, Danbury Guardian, Leamington Spa Courier, Bolton Chronicle, Essex Herald, Wilts Independent, Monmouthshire Beacon, Norfolk Chronicle, Devizes and Wilts Gazette, Leicester Journal, Banner of Ulster, Leeds Mercury, Liverpool Standard, Illustrated London News, Yorkshire Gazette, Eddowes Journal, Star (London), Belfast Commercial Chronicle, Tyne Mercury, Lancaster Gazette, Westmorland Gazette, Sun (London), Newcastle Courant, Cheltenham Journal, Windsor & Eton Express, Globe, Morning Advertiser, Dublin Evening Packet, Durham County Advertiser, Kentish Weekly Post, Saunders's Newsletter, Oxford Journal, Carlisle Patriot, London Courier & Evening Gazette, Public Ledger, National Register, Morning Advertiser, The Times (London), John O'Groats Journal, Elgin Courier, Manchester Courier, Notts Guardian, Bolton Chronicle, Edinburgh Evening Courant, Nottingham Review, Shipping & Mercantile Gazette, Canterbury Journal, Bristol Times, Lady's Own Paper, Newcastle Guardian, Lincs Chronicle, The Atlas, Hereford Journal, Halifax Courier, Cambridge Chronicle, Express (London), Eskdale & Liddesdale Advertiser, The Advocate, Freeman's Journal, Northern Whig, Suffolk Chronicle, Burnley Gazette, Bury Times, Cheshire Observer, Ashton Weekly Reporter, Shields Daily News, Buchan Observer, Liverpool Mercury, Bradford Telegraph & Argus, Staffs Sentinel, Todmorden Advertiser, Western Mail, Falkirk Herald, The Scotsman, Greenock Telegraph, Airdrie & Coatbridge Advertiser, Wishaw Press, Shields Daily Gazette, Birmingham Daily Gazette, Western Morning News, Eastern Daily Press, Brighton Guardian, Portsmouth Evening News, Heywood Advertiser, Rochdale Observer, Wigan Observer, Todmorden District News, Merthyr Express, York Herald, Ulster Examiner, County Express (Brierley Hill, etc) Lowestoft Journal, Lloyd's Weekly, Woolwich Gazette, Hampshire Advertiser, Hampshire Telegraph, South London Chronicle, Daily Telegraph, Pall Mall Gazette, Taunton Courier, Oxford Times, Hastings & St Leonard's Observer, Cambridge Independent Press, Bury Free Press, Aberdeen Evening Press, Dundee Courier, Dundee Advertiser, Northampton Mercury, Birmingham Daily Post, Totnes Weekly Times, Middlesbrough Daily Gazette, Birmingham Mail, Manchester Evening News, Monmouthshire Merlin, Gloucester Citizen, Cambs Times, Essex Standard, Windsor & Eton Express, Western Times, Wisbech Standard, Gravesend Reporter, Kentish Independent, Star of Gwent, The Field, Plainfield Daily Press, Sussex Agricultural Express, London & Provincial Entr'acte.

For writing and publishing news, or
recommendations of new titles to read,
sign up to the Book Guild newsletter: